Cambridge New Architecture

Nicholas Taylor
Philip Booth

Leonard Hill
London
1970

Third Edition 1970, published by
Leonard Hill Books, a division of
International Textbook Co. Ltd,
158 Buckingham Palace Road,
London, S.W.1.

© Nicholas Taylor and Philip Booth, 1970

Limp edition   ISBN   0 249 38880 4
Hard back   ISBN   0 249 44081 4

First published 1964. Second Edition 1965.

Printed in Great Britain by
W. S. Cowell Ltd, at the Butter Market, Ipswich

Contents

Photographs

Except where specifically credited, all the photographs were specially taken for this book.

James Austin, page 25

Cambridge News, page 99

City of Cambridge, page 123

Alfred Cracknell, page 168

John Donat, page 193

Brecht-Einzig, pages 21, 111

Richard Einzig, page 111

Richard Hardwick, pages 59, 83, 90, 97, 175

Edward Leigh, pages 22, 148, 154, 156, 195

Grant Lewison, pages 42, 76–9, 84, 87–8, 96–7, 167, 185

Sydney W. Newbery, pages 18, 47

Park Studios, page 183

John Rawson, page 44

John Rodger-Brown, pages 29, 38, 40, 46, 49, 61, 67, 75, 80, 85, 93, 101, 106, 115, 124, 142, 142, 147, 163, 176, 181, 194

Andrew Schumann, pages 35–6, 56, 84, 107, 109, 120–1, 129–30, 151, 153, 157, 159, 187

Henk Snoek, pages 92, 196, 199

Harry Sowden, page 54

General Map

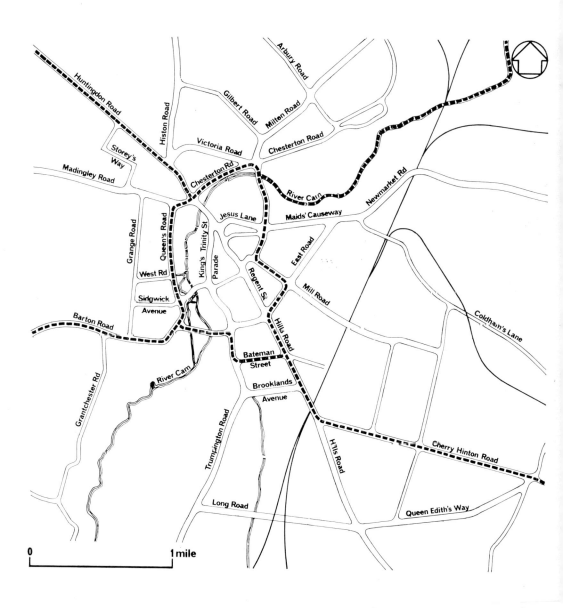

Foreword

by Professor Nikolaus Pevsner

In 1950 I gave a course of sixteen Slade lectures which was called The Young Person's Guide to Cambridge Architecture. The last lecture dealt with recent buildings entirely, and as my remarks on such additions to the Cambridge heritage as Garden Hostel of King's and Sir Albert Richardson's at Christ's were outspoken and challenging, I had reserved question time at the end. But no-one asked questions, no-one felt insulted, no-one defended the anaemic character of the buildings and the timidity of the colleges. No-one outdid me in insults either; no-one in fact was interested. In 1954 the Cambridgeshire volume of my 'Buildings of England' came out. My comments on the same buildings were the same, though expressed a little less outrageously. But I had hardly anything to set against them as examples of how collegiate building in the mid-twentieth century ought to be handled instead. The only collegiate buildings in the twentieth-century style were Hughes & Bicknell's plucky little job for Peterhouse and Murray Easton's staid and urban one for Caius. I complained bitterly about the conventional and reactionary attitude of the university, though I could just add a long stop-press footnote on Sir Hugh Casson's and Neville Conder's Sidgwick Avenue group praising its brilliant handling of townscape or rather of universityscape.

Since then all has changed, and we are in the middle of a tremendous activity which no-one can call reactionary, nor indeed conventional. My wishes have been fulfilled to an alarming degree and, in many of the fulfilments, hit back at me. For most of what is going up points in a direction quite different from what I expected or pleaded for. The rational so-called International Modern of the Thirties abortively presented to Cambridge by Walter Gropius in his designs for Christ's never gained an *entrée*. Instead it is a much more recent irrational international Modern that spreads. The result is a number of buildings with plenty of character, no timidity whatsoever and a last-minute up-to-dateness which is certainly a novel element in the history of Cambridge architecture. The emotional pitch is so high that one wonders that 'Zuleika at Cambridge' could ever have been written.

The following chapters are impressive both for volume and scale of building. They are also impressive for the way in which the buildings are presented. The author and editors are former, only-just-former undergraduates. The writing nowhere lacks gusto. But though 'incomparably ugly', 'decidedly unpleasant' and such pithy phrases appear when the savagery of youth finds them appropriate, the text is throughout serious criticism, positive as well as negative, and the balance between technical information and comment is as professional as can be found in any architectural periodical. Cambridge can be proud of this result of her education in the arts and in architecture. I do not always agree in detail—that goes without saying—but I do agree in principle. Bradwell's Court for instance I might have treated more kindly, and Robert Hurd's funny at Emmanuel will one day be loved by undergraduates in an indulgent way, which is more than one will ever be able to say of the Prudential opposite.

My main concern as a historian with the last few and the next few years of Cambridge building is this. The best architecture of the International Modern of the Thirties started from an analysis of functions and proceeded to work on how best to provide for them. What is visible in the elevations expresses them, and the rationalism inherent in this procedure expresses itself in a crisp, clear, carefully detailed, neutral style. Is this style dead now, as Cambridge seems to indicate? Has it been wholly replaced by a free-for-all, or architecture-for-architecture's sake? Not wholly, as the pages of this book show occasionally. But by and large the major new buildings want to be masters rather than servants of the life acted in them. Can something so personal last—something that may be aped, a motif here, a motif there, but cannot establish itself as a school? On the strength of my experience as a historian I would say not. Georgian could, the Gothick follies could not, Art Nouveau stayed creative for hardly ten years, Expressionism about 1920 for hardly five. On the other hand, the one building in Cambridge which in violence of challenge and in demonstrative originality vies with some of the most recent buildings, Waterhouse's range of Caius facing down King's Parade, represents an attitude that was prevalent for twenty years and more. Has it benefited Cambridge? It has added a richness which had been absent for long, though it has destroyed much of the unity of scale and character which Cambridge had possessed until then. The new areas west of the backs, that is the west fringe of that new campus whose east fringe runs from Magdalene and John's down to Queens', have richness certainly and utter diversity of character certainly too.

My attachment to Cambridge is the outcome of six years of staying a day and a night a week but never being in full residence, and of weekly visits in the following, that is the last nine, years. This is just the right proportion of presence and absence. It keeps the flame of enthusiasm burning. What is the enthusiasm for? In spite of King's Chapel, Trinity Library and the Squire Law Library, it is not for the individual buildings but for the townscape. Most of the individual buildings are in fact on the conventional side and a little short of vitality. Take the Brick Building at Emmanuel of 1633, or Burrough's Palladian work of 1740 at Peterhouse, or most of Wilkins's Gothic work of the 1820s. But whatever the quality of the single units, it is the way they make up into courts, large and small, and colleges and groups of colleges and ultimately architecture and landscape, that matters. Sir Hugh Casson and Neville Conder understood that when they planned the Arts Precinct. Nearly all the others are deeply or superficially concerned with individual expression by single buildings. In the western area, it might be said, there is enough space for that, though I doubt it. In the centre it must not happen. The small building of King's at the corner of the Market Place shows, in my opinion, how it can be avoided without any stylistic compromise.

But perhaps I am too susceptible to the old. Perhaps the new stretch of contrasts is too strong for me. Perhaps those who can work while two transistors in rooms adjoining left and right communicate two different programmes, can take what I can't take. So it is for the young to speak in the rest of this admirable book.

What in 1964 I wrote to accompany the first edition of this admirable book can stand. Some of the buildings being erected now or having just been completed, in fact bear out what I then put forward, the concrete savagery of the Zoology Laboratories and the anti-architecture of the Faculty of History, but there are a few others now which use this forceful and assertive style of today with mastery and without brandishing cudgels. Cripps Building is among the most perfect of the last quinquennium anywhere in England, the University Centre, though it operates with the motifs at the moment in fashion—excessive canting and chamfering, and raw concrete—does so with full maturity, the Chapel of Churchill College has a serenity inside not before aimed at by its architect, and the intricate interaction of Cats and Kings only reaching the surface in two places, is a test of what can be done on a squeezed site in a collegiate manner.

These are judgements, and they don't always coincide with those to follow in the pages of this book. So once again, a user may find it more profitable to listen to the young than to the old. They are, as they analyse building after building, well worth listening to, and in the preparation of the second edition of my own Cambridgeshire in 'The Buildings of England', I had to lean heavily on their descriptions.

Acknowledgements

First and foremost we must thank the triumvirate of editors who organized and published the first edition: Grant Lewison, Nicholas Hughes and Tom Wesley. They were joined by Malcolm Rowe for the second, and Stephen Prickett for the preparation of the third edition. Without them this book would never have appeared at all, let alone sold 9,000 copies from Trinity Hall. Jane Holmes and Stephen Kowalski drew many new plans for this edition, and the typing of an unusually difficult manuscript was done by Mrs. Jolly and her assistants. Finally, we look forward to thanking all those who bring errors to our attention, so that the fourth edition can be even more reliable.

NT/PB London/Cambridge 1970

Introduction

Not since the early sixteenth century has Cambridge had the attention of the country's leading architects to the extent that it has in the last ten years. The output of new buildings has been prodigious and their designers have invariably been men of national repute: Spence, Casson, Martin, Matthew and Johnson-Marshall, Llewelyn-Davies, Lasdun, Chamberlin, Sheppard, Dowson, Stirling. On the surface the climate of opinion among bursars and councillors has changed remarkably since J. M. Richards's depressing survey for 'The Architectural Review' in 1951 and Nikolaus Pevsner's Penguin guide fourteen years ago. One thing, however, has not changed: the planning row which has raged continuously between county, city and university since the publication of Professor Holford's report in January 1950. A detailed account of this by Lionel March can be found in 'Cambridge Opinion 30', June 1962.

The city council's best architecture of the late fifties was the direct result of the Holford Plan: David Roberts's East Road flats, built on a layout superior to that envisaged by Holford himself. Other buildings, large and small—Highsett, St. Bede's School, the Perse, the Swimming Pool—began to show that modern architecture of quality could exist in quantity outside the university. The two largest non-university works, however, were a bitter disappointment; the new Addenbrooke's Hospital to the south and the large Arbury Estate to the north. Discontent with Arbury was a principal reason for the foundation of the Cambridge Civic Society (1961), and for the city's decision of 1962 to appoint a city architect and planning officer (Gordon Logie), the only non-county borough in the country to do so. He has been responsible for a number of interesting projects started under the borough surveyor, and King's Hedges, next to Arbury, is gradually being transformed from a by-law suburb into a coherent 'environmental area'.

The county's power in Cambridge has been largely indirect, because of the delegation of most planning powers to the city. W. L. Waide, the county planning officer 1948–67, was a formidable proponent of Holford's ideas. His study of shopping habits in the U.S.A. led to plans for four or five out-of-town shopping centres, which have now been shelved. His policy of 'containing' Cambridge by decentralizing people and industry to the villages has been helped by their proximity to London (closer than the L.C.C. expanded towns of Haverhill, Huntingdon and Thetford); and development has been as rapid as it has been undistinguished. (See Appendix A for the exceptions.) The most promising fruit of Waide's work is the building, since 1965, of a complete new village between Lolworth and Dry Drayton to a compact and well-detailed design by Covell, Matthews & Partners, Cubitt's the building firm being the developer. Disappointingly, the county's own official architecture has displayed little of the pioneering spirit seen before the war in Gropius's Impington village college and in works by the then county architect, S. E. Urwin.

The university, as distinct from the colleges, has produced surprisingly little of merit. The Chemistry and Engineering laboratories on confined sites, cast a bulky utilitarian shadow over the southern end of the centre. The Arts Faculties in Sidgwick Avenue are gradually rising to picturesque designs by Casson, Conder & Partners, repeatedly held up by lack of money; to them James Stirling's History Faculty is a brilliant, if over-antagonistic, addition. Physics, Mathematics, Metallurgy and Zoology still occupy the extraordinary slums of the New Museums site, and Denys Lasdun was commissioned to replace these fast-growing faculties on the same cramped space; published in 1961, his excessively bulky designs have been skilful, but revised twice after opposition from the planning authorities. The low-rise part for Zoology is now at last taking shape under Philip Dowson, of Arup Associates. University

Library extensions, first proposed in 1951, are still barely off the drawing board (this time of Gollins, Melvin, Ward & Partners).

Yet, by contrast, the ancient colleges have erected a great variety of sumptuously expensive buildings by leading architects; and there are three entirely new colleges of the old kind. There are also two graduate colleges under construction, and a third planned. Churchill College, housing 600 of the university's 9,000 undergraduates, had an original 'target cost' of £1.1 million, yet it will finally cost some £2.75 million, more than the vast Chemistry laboratory, which cost £2.25 million. This remarkable disparity between college and university expenditure is the symptom of a growing imbalance. The colleges are autonomous and some of them are exceedingly wealthy. King's, Trinity, St. John's and Caius control over half the total unearned income of the 21 colleges. Yet the university, apart from certain benefactors (Wolfson's for a university centre, for example), is almost solely dependent for its new buildings on the University Grants Committee—like any other university.

Until Peter Chamberlin was appointed in 1962, the university had never tried to prepare a comprehensive plan for its future buildings. Even so, Mr. Chamberlin was only concerned with the central science sites, not with the new academic area beyond the Backs, to which the science faculties were reluctant to move, in spite of the flexibility of expansion on green fields. After Lasdun's New Museums scheme was drastically reduced and rephased, the Deer Report in 1965 recommended at long last that Physics should move out, only the smaller faculties being left in New Museums site and in the forthcoming redevelopment of the old Addenbrooke's site for which Arup Associates have prepared an excellent development plan. A master plan for the West Cambridge science site was then prepared by Robert Matthew, Johnson-Marshall & Partners; though the future of the western area as a whole still remains deplorably vague. The university has a chief architect, Alec Crook, but he is concerned only with restoration work and minor buildings. The colleges gallantly responded to Robbins by 15 per cent, thereby increasing their own income, but the university has no power to assess the financial priorities of residential and academic accommodation. Planning advice is given to the university by its own Estate Management Advisory Service, but this seems to be concerned more with telling the county how to plan the city than telling the university how to plan beyond the Backs.

In spite of the pressing need for speed, economy and flexibility, the university has only just started making some use of the new industrialized methods of building construction (in the King's–St. Catharine's scheme, page 31). Only Great Eastern House, the Queen Edith's Way Grammar School and the Manor Schools illustrate system building in Cambridge. It is surprising that Professor Sir Leslie Martin, the former architect to the L.C.C., who has been so prominent since 1956 both in revitalizing the School of Architecture and in the planning arguments concerning the city, should have failed to exert his influence in this direction. Sir Leslie's buildings for Caius and Peterhouse, massive and sculpturally exciting, in fact epitomize the wayward luxury of recent collegiate architecture. Cambridge has passed without a break from the irrationalism of the olde worlde to the irrationalism of the New World (neo-Yamasaki at Fitzwilliam, neo-Kahn in Lasdun's rejected Cavendish towers, neo-Johnson at New Hall). A still more potent influence has been the massive brickwork and heavy concrete of Le Corbusier's later works, such as the Maisons Jaoul. Clients have been guided more by traditional collegiate ideas of grandeur than by functional logic, and in spite of the money lavished on the buildings, still far too little seems to be known about students' needs. Another aspect of snobbery is the concentration on fashionable London architects. East Anglian architects such as Peter Barefoot, Johns, Slater & Haward and Feilden & Mawson have found commissions outside the university only; while Tayler & Green, having spent considerable time on preparing schemes for Southacre and Madingley, had them nonplaced by Regent House. Of the college buildings that have been built, Diana Rowntree has said: 'That they are a gimmicky lot is not surprising, for these are gimmicky times.' However, these are also the times of Sheffield and Cumbernauld and CLASP (a whole CLASP university is rising at York). Admittedly, the craftsmanship in Cambridge's new buildings is exceedingly good (mainly by the 'big four' of local builders: Rattee & Kett, Sindall's, Kerridge, Johnson & Bailey). Small details are often sophisticated, for example the lettering cut by Eric Gill's pupil, David Kindersley, who lives at Barton. Restoration work on old buildings has been carefully done. However, in spite of (or perhaps, because of)

Planning

all this luxury building work, many students still live in 'digs'.

The real trouble with Cambridge is that the genuine picturesque quality of its old buildings breeds an artificial picturesqueness in those who add to them. The best criticism of Cambridge's new architecture was given in 1851 by 'The Ecclesiologist', the organ founded by the Cambridge Camden Society. Describing a church in Tasmania by Street, in which a triangular site had been cleverly exploited, 'The Ecclesiologist' admired the expertise but added: We are more and more convinced that the true picturesque follows upon the sternest utility.' This is perhaps the theme of this book; so often we admire the expertise, but doubt the utility.

Professor W. G. Holford & Professor Myles Wright's report in 1950 to the county planning authority stated clearly that Cambridge must remain 'predominantly a university city' and not go the way of Oxford. Therefore the population should be levelled off at 100,000, with a corresponding increase in the local village population. Holford had diagnosed two main sources of traffic congestion: through traffic along the Backs and local traffic along the Hills Road–Bridge Street 'spine'. He proposed to re-route both immediately east of the historic centre, on a new 'spine relief road'. This would run from Histon Road, across the river at Jesus Lock, to Jesus Lane and then across Christ's Pieces. Through traffic would continue out of Cambridge past Parker's Place, but local traffic would go down Emmanuel Street into the new Lion Yard shopping centre. Multi-storey car parks were to be provided in the Lion Yard and in King Street and Park Street.

It comes as a shock to find that Holford's Lion Yard shopping centre was not to be a pedestrian precinct. A broad dual carriageway (Guildhall Street) was to run from the Guildhall, parallel to Corn Exchange Street (with a multi-storey park for 400 cars between them) and was to join New Emmanuel Street at a monumental road island opposite the entrance to the Downing site, where six roads were to meet. Holford's proposals were broadly accepted by the Minister in 1954 as part of the county development plan. By now it was definitely intended to have a pedestrian precinct in Lion Yard. In 1958 the city council invited schemes from property companies and selected the plans of Edger Investments Ltd., designed by Stone, Toms & Partners (authors of many London office blocks, including the Earls Court skyscraper). It was proposed to rebuild the entire area, with an underground park for 730 cars and a new four-storey frontage for Petty Cury. A three-storey pedestrian precinct, roughly following Holford's Guildhall Street and opening into Petty

Cury, was to be dominated by two twelve-storey slab office blocks. Part of the accommodation was to be offered to the university. On the island between New Emmanuel Street and Downing Street were to be a semi-circular central library and a twelve-storey hotel. After a public enquiry, the Minister (Henry Brooke) rejected the scheme, on the advice of his inspector, J. Burkitt, as 'basically unsound', on the grounds that offices, shops and car parks would all tend to cause still more congestion. All the other designs considered by the city, even that prepared by Frederick Gibberd, had the same drawbacks. Yet both county and city had accepted the Edger scheme in principle.

The way was now open for a third set of proposals, from the university, formulated principally by J. F. Q. Switzer and R. Stafford-Smith of the Department of Estate Management (divided in 1962 into the Estate Management Advisory Service and the Department of Land Economy). Ever since its objection of May 1952, the university had consistently recommended the alternative expansion of shopping on the other side of Christ's Pieces in the Fitzroy Street/City Road area. It was opposed to the spine relief road's division of the historic centre from the residential areas on a line across Christ's Pieces, which is geographically the modern centre of the town. Detailed plans, which were prepared by a team under Switzer and Sir Leslie Martin, and were published in 1962 in time for the quinquennial review of the development plan, advocated a new ring road enclosing the nineteenth century housing areas. From Brooklands Avenue and the station, it would follow Gwydir Street, then cross the river by the new Chesterton bridge (also part of the Holford plan) and then follow the line of Victoria Road. Between it and the centre the inner areas would be developed at 70–100 persons per acre, with special higher density housing in the Lion Yard (to pump life back into the centre). The rest of Lion Yard would be used as a civic centre, with a multi-purpose hall, library, exhibition gallery and arts centre, hotels and restaurants. New shopping would be concentrated within the 60 acres of the Fitzroy Street area, forming a major regional centre with adequate access and parking facilities for 7,000 to 10,000 cars.

The principal disagreement between county and university is whether such a regional centre is necessary or desirable. Curiously, it is the county which wishes to keep the city's population down and preserve university character, while accommodating new shopping in the Lion Yard. Increasing regional needs, the county has said, could be satisfied by out-of-town shopping centres on the American pattern, such as that at one time proposed for Trumpington. The county plans to turn most of the historic centre into a pedestrian precinct, in which only service vehicles will be permitted. It will be ringed by the new car parks, of which that at Park Street has already been built (see page 66). The university replies convincingly that 'university predominance' is a myth when for the most part Cambridge is much like any other town coming within the orbit of Greater London. With greater affluence and mobility it will require more shops in the centre than the Lion Yard can hold. The great weakness of the university scheme is its uncertain phasing and doubtful ability to entice the multiple stores to a new site. Nevertheless, two other planners have confirmed its basic analysis. Peter Smithson, for the Civic Society, and Ralph Erskine, the Swedish architect, for a technical group headed by Leslie Bilsby of Span and R. Stafford-Smith of the university's estate management advisory service, both prepared sketchy 'plans' in 1962 in which a new shopping centre east of Christ's Pieces was advocated. Smithson laid particular emphasis on the extension of Cambridge's already far-reaching system of pedestrian paths and alleyways, together with a balanced system of suburban car parks and central public transport.

The most recent plan[1] for Cambridge has been produced by Gordon Logie, the city architect and planning officer. Published in March 1966, it embodies many of the ideas of the Switzer and Martin plan, including the inner by-pass. From this are to radiate service roads to garages around the edge of the centre which would leave the centre completely traffic-free; in that, it resembles the county's plan. There are many attractive features in the scheme, including the closing of two major roads: Queens' Road along the Backs, from which traffic crossing Silver Street Bridge would be diverted along West Road and back down Grange Road, which would also be closed to through traffic; and Fen Causeway, which would be replaced by another bridge, first suggested by Holford, crossing to join the by-pass at Chaucer Road and Brooklands Avenue. On the other hand, the western by-pass has been retained—which Martin regarded as unnecessary—in order to link Barton and Huntingdon Roads; Robert Matthew, Johnson-Marshall & Partners in their plan for the

1. 'The Future Shape of Cambridge.'

scientific departments in West Cambridge considered it an important traffic route. The routing of the inner by-pass, too, from the Northampton Street –Castle Street Corner along the river bank to Jesus Lock is surely questionable in environmental terms: would it not have been better to take it along the line of Victoria Road instead? Realistically, Logie has rejected the county's policy of 'containment'; he recognizes that Cambridge must and will grow, and suggests that the best way is to organize growth positively in linear 'tongues' along existing main roads. These would extend beyond the urban area to join up with the villages which the county has expanded. In effect, these tongues are an equally realistic consolidation of the prewar (and postwar) ribbon development that already exists—southwards to Stapleford, eastwards to Fulbourn, and northwards to Girton and Heston. But what of the villages not on these routes? Considerable suburban growth has already occurred, and many villages have inevitably lost their old form: can this trend be halted anywhere?

'The Future Shape of Cambridge' was proposed by Logie with full acceptance both of the need to redevelop Lion Yard and of the need for a new regional centre east of Parker's Piece. Indeed, the report had been preceded by two attempts by Logie to draw up a plan for Lion Yard. The first, in 1963, proposed a large underground service road with car parks. It would run from Emmanuel Road under Lion Yard, Market Hill and Green Street to emerge at Jesus Lane. The scheme was a compromise solution in that it avoided the need for a spine relief road and provided sufficient regional shopping in the centre itself; it also permitted far larger areas of shopping space and pedestrian streets. But the technical and financial estimates proved crippling, and there was justifiable doubt whether even this extension of shopping facilities would avoid congestion and eventual chaos.

The Minister's long-delayed decision on the county's proposals at the quinquennial review was finally published in September 1964. It was in general a victory for the university. 30,000 sq ft of extra shopping space is to be allowed in Lion Yard, instead of 90,000 for which city and county had asked. The second of Logie's proposals for Lion Yard, this time following the lines of the Minister's decision, was published in June 1965 and is described in more detail on page 67. This scheme was one of those for which the Minister promised Government support in 1967 and presumably work will now go ahead on the basis of this plan.

In the 1964 review the Minister also called for an immediate study of the Fitzroy Street–City Road area, and to that end the university generously donated £20,000 to the city. The following year the economic consultants Gerald Eve & Co. submitted a report in which it was estimated a net addition of 150,000 sq ft for shopping was needed including Lion Yard. In the report, however, they urged the paramount need for unity in the city's shopping centre; so on the strength of this Logie proceeded to compare six alternative schemes for the development of a 'link' between Lion Yard and City Road, continuing the existing pedestrian precinct of Bradwell's Court (see page 71). The decision reached (and fiercely attacked by many who misunderstood its purpose) was to develop the southern end of Christ's Pieces and to provide car parking on the opposite side of Emmanuel Road. Additional open space, as compensation, would be provided by opening out Christ's Pieces towards Jesus Lane. Llewelyn-Davies, Weeks & Partners are now preparing a detailed scheme on those lines, but whether it will be accepted remains to be seen. Its advantages would be the close link with the old centre via Bradwell's Court and relatively easy access to the already developed Fitzroy Street–Burleigh Street area. Moreover the land would be immediately available. Because of its proximity to the old centre, there is much more possibility that this scheme will draw off the multiples from the centre and act as an alternative path to Lion Yard than a scheme which started farther east. The Minister of Housing, however, still supports at least the northern half, from Histon Road to Jesus Lane, of the hopelessly outdated spine relief road; and the Minister of Transport has offered the grant for it only on condition that the rest of the road is built too. If built, it will cause immense damage by dividing off the new centre from the old. The irony is that the Minister has bit by bit rejected all the parts of Holford's plan to which the road was relevant.

Meanwhile, congestion grows worse in Cambridge and the university and city alike are being strangled by the ever-increasing traffic. Certain projects, such as the long-awaited Chesterton Bridge, could be undertaken swiftly. The latest plans for Cambridge present it, for the first time, with a viable alternative to chaos: but unless action is taken quickly, there will be no further reprieve.

Gropius's project: Hobson Street frontage

patio behind Stevenson's building.

The three floors of undergraduate rooms above the shops were to be identical, each with two staircases and 17 undergraduates' sets opening off the central corridors. Each set contained an entrance lobby with gyproom, a living-room with much built-in furniture, a bedroom and, for those facing the garden, a balcony. Above the long block, at fourth floor level, were to be two fellows' sets. The structure was to be a steel frame, faced with stone, with steel balconies and windows.

At the southern end of the long block was to be the Senior Tutor's house, a three-storey building with a walled garden. Its facing in brick instead of stone exaggerated its clumsy relationship to the rest of the scheme, physically connected but functionally almost wholly detached.

In spite of Gropius's village college at Impington, Cambridge still has hardly any buildings designed from abroad (but see Keelson, page 86, and Clare Hall, page 144). The argument that such 'alien' work would not be in scale or proportion with Cambridge was effectively killed at birth by the Christ's design, in essence a reinterpretation of the traditional open-sided court. Cambridge is in any case a European university.

Chancellor's Building and Memorial Building

Date. 1948–50: 1952–3

Architects. Professor Sir Albert Richardson and Eric Houfe

Contractor. Rattee & Kett Ltd.

Cost. £170,000

Requirement. Rooms for 90 undergraduates.

Description. The two ranges form the college's Third Court, together with the Stevenson building (1889, west portion 1905).[1] Although almost identically planned and detailed, they are not parallel with each other, nor with the rest of the college. Chancellor's Building lies between Stevenson and the Fellows' Building of 1640. Memorial Building shuts off the new three-sided court from the service entrance and backyard next to Hobson Street. The two ranges are of 13½ in brick cross-walls, faced with Ketton stone, with floors and stairs of concrete.

1. Richardson and Houfe also added a sprightly lantern to the west pavilion of the Stevenson's building.

There is a recessed attic storey containing storage space and service rooms. The four floors of undergraduate bed-sitters open off central corridors, with a staircase at each end lit by a tall vertical window at its rear, running through three floors and projecting from the rest of the façade. Each room has a panelled bed recess, with a strip window of reeded glass giving 'borrowed' light to the corridor. The court has a circular sunken lawn with a low parapet.

Comment. Although the neo-Georgian style is not yet dead in England, Professor Richardson was probably the last architect to use it with integrity and finesse. He undoubtedly relished the fact that the steel shortage in 1948 made a frame structure impossible. His buildings are orderly, simple and beautifully made. Their scale towards the court is rather muddled, but the vertical staircase windows at the rear have a justifiable monumentality in the style of Cockerell. However, in contrast to the expensive stone facings, the rooms within are small, cheaply finished and filled with dowdy furniture, and the corridor and staircases are poorly lit and detailed. In overall planning, too, despite the convincing shape of Third Court, it fails to relate adequately either to the medieval First Court or to Hobson Street.

Clare College   n

343 undergraduates, 105 postgraduates, 48 fellows.

Clare has an enviable tradition of far-sighted planning and sensitive architecture. The cultured Ivy League atmosphere of Sir Giles Gilbert Scott's Memorial Court of 1924–35, the first major structure beyond the Backs, was admittedly marred by Sir Giles's own addition in 1953–5 of Thirkhill Court. Its staid neo-Georgian details were partially redeemed, however, when in 1961 the college placed Henry Moore's violently kinetic 'Falling Warrior' on a central pedestal in the court. This was one of the first major examples in Cambridge of 'public' patronage of the arts by the colleges. The building of David Roberts's successful Swedish-modern suburban hostel on Castle Hill (1957–8) has been followed by the appointment in 1964 of the famous English-born Swedish architect, Ralph Erskine, to design the new graduate community of Clare Hall (see page 144).
Since 1960 the fabric of Old Court has been externally restored and internally remodelled by W. F. Haslop (of Rattee & Kett) and David Roberts respectively. Mr. Haslop's cleaning and partial refacing of the seventeenth century Ketton stone has been done with great tact and sensibility by the 'dry' method (scraping), which preserves some of the inherited patina, in contrast to the violent treatment by the 'wet' method (washing) of the Old Schools nearby.[1] The S.C.R. has been refurnished by Sir Gordon Russell (1960) and the Master's Lodge remodelled internally by David Roberts (1961–2). In 1965, Lyster & Grillet contrived 18 undergraduate rooms within the roof space of Memorial Court. David Croghan has recently completed (1967) the renovation of the Small Hall and also the screens passage to the S.C.R.

Corpus Christi College   r

195 undergraduates, 84 postgraduates, 50 fellows.

Corpus Christi's kitchens were remodelled in 1947–8, by Ernst Freud, the psychologist's son. He did a skilful job, keeping intact the medieval exterior, that of the original hall, by inserting an independent steel frame structure within it (engineer, H. Hajnal-Konyi). Old Court was restored in 1951–3 and New Court in 1952, both by Donovan Purcell. New Court's unfortunate attic, however, dates from 1920. The Hall was amusingly decorated in 1959–60 with a ceiling pattern derived by Dr. M. A. Burgess vaguely out of William Morris. In 1962 the Master's Lodge was remodelled internally by Lyster & Grillet.
More recently, Corpus has taken the lead in providing new graduate accommodation with Arup Associates' excellent extensions to Leckhampton House, on the other side of the Backs (see page 146). The college's next (and surely final) central building is likely to go on the other side of Bene't Street, behind King's Parade.

---

1. Carried out in 1960–3 by the university's chief architect, Alec Crook, with interiors redecorated by David Roberts. The Senate House nearby was admirably restored by Sir Albert Richardson (1956–8).

Downing College   c

306 undergraduates, 46 postgraduates, 38 fellows.

William Wilkins's 1804 plan for Downing, the first 'campus' plan in the world, was never finished. By 1821 only parts of the west and east ranges had been built. These were enlarged by E. M. Barry in 1873; and in 1929 Sir Herbert Baker built L-shaped ranges in the north-east and north-west. This involved a change of plan, for Wilkins's central range with chapel and library was originally intended to be at the Lensfield Road end, facing northwards down the court to a propylaeum, beyond which open parkland stretched into the city centre. However, the park was sold to the university in 1906 to become the Downing Site and Baker's desire to screen the subsequent mess of laboratories with his post-war connecting range of Graystone Buildings is understandable. But he did it in a compromise of style more subtly destructive of Wilkins's severe geometry than the most bigoted 'modernism' would have been. After a 1953 scheme to spend £50,000 on a new grand gateway to Regent Street had been abandoned, the same half-Bakered clichés were perpetrated as late as 1959–62 in Kenny Court near the back entrance in Tennis Court Road.

Sensibly, the college has now turned to its open end beyond Wilkins's hall to provide better common rooms and kitchens, and to a younger generation of architects in Howell, Killick, Partridge & Amis. Their very promising scheme, described below, will tidy up the back entrance in Tennis Court Road. Now that Chemistry's bulk oppresses it, the southern side of the campus could also be screened with advantage; so it is disappointing that for his second residential phase Howell does not attempt to prolong the college in this direction. Instead he proposes an isolated block on the same Tennis Court Road site. To the north a slightly projecting wing will enable it to form a symmetrical response to Kenny Court across the entrance drive. On the south side it will help to enclose West Lodge garden as another three-sided court, and through the building, connecting its two staircase towers, will run an access path from Tennis Court Road to the new kitchen service court on the other side of the garden.

Graystone Buildings and Kenny Court

Date.   1951–3, 1959–62

Architect.   Alex T. Scott of Sir Herbert Baker & Scott

Contractor.   Rattee & Kett Ltd.

Requirement. Graystone Buildings, chapel and rooms for 36 undergraduates and two fellows. Kenny Court, rooms for 39 more undergraduates.

Description and Comment. Graystone Buildings would have been acceptable either in Wilkins's style or in the international modern manner. Sir Herbert Baker and his successor Alex T. Scott, while superficially harmonizing in Ketton stone, chose neither. Baker's 1929 ranges are in a fussy late seventeenth century style, Scott's Graystone Buildings are Palladian. Both were doomed to failure in their attempt to combine the classical grand manner with the low ceiling heights of today. Baker and Scott have fitted in three storeys in place of Wilkins's two; hence the underscaled, cramp proportions. The structure is loadbearing brick faced with Ketton stone. The residential accommodation is arranged round staircases with short lengths of corridor.

Behind Scott's central hexastyle Ionic portico is the chapel, a vaguely Byzantine tunnel-vaulted room, its whitewashed apse framed in a wide stone arch without capitals. The 'stripped Georgian' stalls were made by Laurence Turner, and the altar cross and candlesticks designed by Prof. R. Y. Goodden and made by Leslie Durbin. Lively expressionist glass by L. C. Evetts was inserted in 1963 into the five apse windows. Their style is strongly influenced by French designers such as Max Ingrand, the semi-abstract forms in red, grey and blue representing the Lamb of God and the Four Horsemen of the Apocalypse.

Two three-storeyed blocks, also in loadbearing brick faced with Ketton stone, form the three-sided Kenny Court with Baker's north-west range. They are connected by walls with archways, and face the entrance drive from Tennis Court Road. Scott continued to pursue the classical image—the donor is said to have required this—though by now his detail was so diluted as to disappear almost completely in the vestigial mouldings and mini-balconies of iron.

Downing College new dining hall, with Wilkins' range to the right: model

Kitchen and S.C.R.

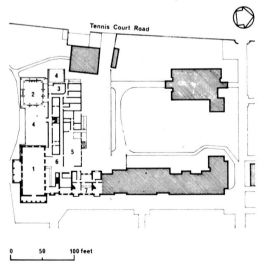

Tennis Court Road

0   50   100 feet

1 Hall 2 Combination room 3 Parlour 4 Terraces
5 Kitchen 6 Servery 7 Undergraduates' bar

Designed. 1966

Architects. Howell, Killick, Partridge & Amis

Requirement. Enlargement of existing hall; new kitchen, service rooms and offices; new senior combination room and parlour.

Description and Comment. The dining hall is the pivotal room of Downing, not just socially but because its small size and unsophisticated kitchens at present preclude any increase in the college's numbers. Convincingly Elysian externally in its Ionic harmony with the Master's Lodge across the grass, the hall in fact only occupies two-thirds of a messily sub-divided block. Howell proposes to enlarge it to take up the whole area, purifying the drab décor (mostly E. M. Barry, 1873) and giving much-needed natural light through windows opening on to a new paved terrace to the west. The new S.C.R. stands forward into the Master's Garden as an isolated single-storey pavilion, and faces the hall across this terrace. There is a formal corridor linking the two rooms, which externally forms a massive two-storey 'backdrop' of Ketton stone to the terrace, blind except for a vertical door slot. To the north of the S.C.R. will be a second room, the parlour, overlooking a subsidiary terrace towards Tennis Court Lane, next to the existing squash court. Behind and parallel to the formal corridor is a tightly planned block consisting of the buttery and plate room (artificially lit and ventilated) with first-floor college offices, then a long service corridor, and finally a new single-storey kitchen, with larders and staff rooms, entered from the service court off Tennis Court Road. Within the main Wilkins block will be wash-up space, servery, screens and undergraduates' bar.

This is an exceedingly elegant solution. The load-bearing brick kitchen block has buff facings which Howell hopes will help to unify Wilkins's white brick backs with his Ketton stone façades. The service court and the kitchen itself, with its massive walling and trabeated clerestory, is clearly distinguished from the alternating square windows and tall doors of the offices which open on to a roof terrace above it. Howell admittedly has hidden his brickwork on the campus side behind the Ketton stone veneer of the Great Wall, but only the most literal-minded functionalists will fail to appreciate the value of this, both for 'rounding off' visually Wilkins's façades on this exposed corner and also for its symbolic value as a formal link between hall and S.C.R.—a screen to the corridor in wet weather and a backcloth to the sheltered terrace in fine weather. The pavilion form, carried out in post-tensioned concrete framing with an oak and lead roof and Ketton stone infill panels, is consciously influenced by recent Japanese work; the danger is that over-elaboration in detail may outweigh the cool harmony with Wilkins's pediments and porticos shown on the architects' model.

Emmanuel College   d

368 undergraduates, 81 postgraduates, 45 fellows.

Emmanuel is the only college whose new buildings have aroused a public demonstration of protest (by the Anti-Uglies). Its first three post-war developments were typical of many colleges: a mediocre out-of-town hostel by Bird & Tyler (see page 90), new kitchens and an overflow hall, and restoration of the college's ancient fabric. The late Robert Hurd, a well-known Edinburgh architect and Emma man, was responsible for the second hall and kitchens, described below, and also for the restoration of the old hall and the other stone-faced buildings in Front Court (1959–62). Renewal has generally been clean and competent, but Brick Building in 1962–3 lost attractive texture, as well as decayed stucco. The lawn of New Court has been transmogrified into a herb-garden with beds in acute-angled triangles and unpleasantly fussy paving in flint and red tile patterns. Since 1963 Tom Hancock, a prolific London architect of the younger generation, has added to Emma two gratifyingly undemonstrative buildings, both described below: a new Master's Lodge as an isolated pavilion in the college garden, and a new irregular court forming a complicated sequence of townscape between Chapman's Garden and the new Janus House offices in St. Andrew's Street (see page 70). For this court designs were first made by Gollins, Melvin, Ward & Partners.

Further shopping developments are bound to threaten the college, which stands on the crucial isthmus between Lion Yard (see page 67) and City Road (page 12). Leonard Stokes's North Court is about to lose its porter's lodge for road widening; further piecemeal erosion, particularly of this Edwardian masterpiece, should be firmly resisted. Emma needs a planning consultant to advise it comprehensively on future policy. Perhaps it could 'do a deal' over the unimpressive late Victorian hostels by Pearson and Fawcett at the back of the garden; if their Parker Street frontage were sacrificed to the city's need for a strong commercial link between City Road and the historic centre, the college could ask in return that undergraduate rooms be built overhead. Such collaboration between Town and Gown, achieved by Caius in Market Hill as early as 1934, could positively extend the virtues of a 'university town'; otherwise the new shopping centre will be just shops.

Second Hall and kitchens

Date. 1957–9

Architect. Robert Hurd

Contractor. Rattee & Kett Ltd.

Cost. £87,000

Requirement. New kitchens and rooms for kitchen staff: a secondary dining hall, the Robert Gardner Room, seating 120.

Description. The site, at the corner of St. Andrew's and Emmanuel Streets, was previously occupied by 'obsolete Victorian premises'. It provides new kitchens at ground level and above them, connected by service lifts, is the new overflow dining hall, as well as six rooms for kitchen staff. Towards New Court there are only a few small windows at first floor level, set in a large rough stone wall from the Elizabethan kitchen; to preserve this, the natural lighting of the hall has been concentrated in three new gabled dormers facing west. Artificial lighting is partly concealed and partly by glass pendants between these tall windows. The asymmetrically hung ceiling is lined with ash boarding. The structure is a concrete frame, concealed externally by various facings intended to harmonize with the adjoining buildings: Ketton stone for the St. Andrew's Street façade, with rendered plaster for the gable end and the garden wall.

Comment. There are certainly worse new buildings in Cambridge than this little Scottish cottage, exotic in its very dourness. But the intended picturesque asymmetry is completely lacking in positive character and the quaintness of the 'harling' (Scottish for rendering) has already gone shabby, including rust marks from a trellis. The gabled windows may be of Lowland vernacular precedent, but such nostalgic eclecticism does not mean much on one of the best sites in Cambridge. The Essex façade and Arthur Brown's stucco-Tudor block are unimposing neighbours; the college's decision to 'harmonize' the new building with them, rather than to strike out afresh, was basically misguided. The internal layout is said to be inconvenient; and the Robert Gardner Room is one of the most depressing post-war eating places in Cambridge, its prettily

slatted ceiling clashing with the blue-painted acoustic tiles on the end wall.

Master's Lodge

Date. 1963–4

Architect. Tom Hancock

Contractor. Kerridge Ltd.

Cost. £34,000

Description. The isolated site lies in the garden to the east of New Court and to the north of Wren's chapel, Blomfield's lodge having been demolished in 1963. Towards the college is a raised podium with two flights of steps and portico leading to three double-height rooms, secretary's room, drawing room and master's study. The main windows to the south open towards Wren's chapel across a spacious raised grass terrace. Contrasting with this is a three-storey block of private rooms, with the kitchen and other services extending in a north wing at right-angles. A lean-to copper roof against this wing shelters the paved way to the garage. Because of the raising of the reception rooms, there is a split-level formation around the central staircase. The structure is of loadbearing cross-walls with handmade red brick facings; the concrete floor slabs and roof and also the portico are faced with reconstructed stone. Windows are of timber painted white, with spandrel louvres of aluminium.

Comment. It is a relief to find, in place of Blomfield's 'uncommonly ugly brick villa' of 1873–4, a serious attempt at rethinking the ceremonial residence in modern terms. By a skilful use of split-level planning, on a raised garden terrace compacted from Blomfield's débris, the public entertaining required of a college head has been clearly distinguished from his private life. The blocky three-storey tower and the curved grass terrace have the right kind of quiet hauteur, and the brick facing is neatly channelled to express formally the cross-wall rhythm. But somehow the house fails to add up to much. Clumsy external jointing between the two halves, confused scale in the pointlessly tall secretary's office, indecisive veneering in reconstructed stone (which has weathered badly on the porch) and an

Emmanuel College, Master's Lodge from the Wren cloister

afterthought of a chimney-stack—none of these were apparent in the nice elevational drawing which illustrated the house in our first edition. As so often, a two-dimensional design has failed in the mass. Yet, without resorting to eclecticism of any kind, Hancock has succeeded in meeting Wren's chapel and the Old Library on level terms—and that is no small achievement.

South Court

Date.   1965–6

Architect.   Tom Hancock

Contractor.   Johnson & Bailey Ltd.

Cost.   £245,000

Requirement.   Study–bedrooms for 70 undergraduates, four fellows' sets, two guest rooms, new J.C.R. and service rooms.

Description.   This H-shaped court (or courts) has two residential wings with the J.C.R. as the cross-bar, and occupies the rear half of the former New Theatre site. It is reached from First Court via the Westmoreland Building; a winding paved pathway leads through Chapman's Garden, with the seventeenth-century Brick Building on the left, to a raised plateau of brown tiles, on which sit the three-storey butt ends of the two new wings. Between them at a slightly lower level is the fully glazed single-storey J.C.R., which is entered through sliding doors from the terrace. The tapered concrete ribs of the J.C.R. roof converge on a single column in front and are supported on the brick walls of service rooms, games room and bar at the rear.
The alternative approach is by a narrow alleyway from St. Andrew's Street, between Janus House and No. 55, a fine Regency house owned by Emmanuel, which has had its projecting right half set back and rebuilt. The 6 ft wide alley leads to the new western wing at the point where the ground floor shops of Janus House project forwards to face the lower eastern wing across the large service court,

New South Court, from the west

paved in brown tiles; this gives access also to the communal bathroom, laundry and plant room at the back of the J.C.R.

The two residential wings each have a loadbearing brick spine of artificially lit and ventilated service rooms, and a series of semi-circular concrete staircases with five bed-sitters on each landing. The concrete floors are carried externally on columns which on the court side form ground floor cloisters faced with Clipsham stone. The upper walls faced in pink handmade bricks, are cantilevered 2 ft outwards to contain window seats, ducts and perimeter heating. Rooms are divided by non-structural 9 in brick partition walls. On the court sides are 40 bed-sitters, and on the outer sides 30 larger rooms, which have a folding partition to an intermediate column so that the bed space can be shut off. At the Chapman's Garden ends are the guest rooms and the three-room fellows' sets, which can alternatively provide a two-room research fellow's set and a non-resident fellow's study. Windows, double-glazed throughout, are flanked on either side by bronze-faced 'shutter' panels, which can be opened out at the top only or entirely. Furniture is of oak, with a special wall unit incorporating clothes storage, book shelves, light fittings and an electric heater (supplementing radiators); the bed can be slid back as a divan against the upholstered doors. Window walls have capstone seats with hessian clad softboard

above; other walls are plastered, with oak-veneered panelling.

Comment. A complicated piece of urban renewal has here been turned into a dry and reticent sequence of collegiate residences. The Janus House approach provides the rare case in a bylaw-ridden post-war city of a really narrow and intimate alleyway, snaking in medievally from behind the street fronts to the broad brown-paved spaces of court and cloisters. An oddity of the layout is that the main inner space overlooked by rooms is merely a service area, however beautifully paved; whereas there are subtle relationships outwardly to Chapman's Garden and to the main college garden. Ninety-nine other architects would merely have closed in Chapman's Garden by a straight east–west range; Hancock by contrast has prolonged its space southwards by placing the two wings not only at right-angles to it, but very slightly askew. As a result this is one of the few recent college extensions which actively encourages future growth and change.

The horizontal lines, which symbolize such growth and incidentally harmonize with those of Brick Building, are formed by continuous drip mouldings —an all-too-rare case of their reintroduction into modern architecture to promote good weathering. In particular they keep rain off the bronze-faced shutters—another unfashionable feature which, by letting in some fresh air and outer space, humanizes the artificial climate of double-glazing. In other details, however, these buildings carry corniness beyond a virtue. The Clipsham stone facings thicken up the reinforced concrete columns so as to lose almost entirely the flow of space in the cloisters; and the shutters themselves, while giving vitality to the façades in their irregular opening, are excessively heavy, clashing in scale with the modest pink brickwork on the artfully modelled first floor slab. The staircases, although attractively luminous in their white-painted boarded concrete finish, bring an intruding convex shape into the bed spaces of the larger rooms. The furnishings are sensibly designed, particularly the use in the larger rooms of a folding partition to shut off the bed space (cf. St. John's).

Gonville & Caius College   m

395 undergraduates, 92 postgraduates, 66 fellows.

Caius has the most difficult college site in Cambridge, entirely hemmed in by other colleges and by shops. St. Michael's Court of 1901 (Webb) and 1934 (Easton), though competently designed, meant the destruction of much valuable town property. The college has now taken the sensible decision to move across the Backs with the brilliant and controversial Harvey Court by Sir Leslie Martin & Colin St. J. Wilson (see page 155).
Caius has also looked after its old buildings well. Waterhouse's Tree Court was one of the first Victorian masterpieces to be properly cleaned and cared for. Since then the Gate of Honour has been carefully, if rather excessively, restored (1958–9) by Mr. Topper (master mason), Mr. Whitaker (carver) and Mr. Whitmore (mason), and Salvin's kitchens and hall have been painstakingly remodelled (1962–6) under the direction of Alec Crook. He has left the whitewashed hall devoid of atmosphere; but the rebuilding beneath it is undeniably ingenious, with a cast iron spiral escape stair connecting screens and kitchen. In 1960 an excellent silver cross and candlesticks by Gerald Benney (the designer of the communion plate for Coventry Cathedral) were added to the chapel. The cross is made in the form of a V-section obelisk, 3 ft high, with a textured front panel; the upswept tapering crossbars are fixed close to the top. The candlesticks are similar, with upswept wax pans.

Jesus College   g

368 undergraduates, 77 postgraduates, 43 fellows.

Jesus is still the ex-urban monastery it was in the Middle Ages, and its spacious courts have altered little since the war. Marshall Sisson furnished the War Memorial Library in a neo-Georgian manner (1952) and remodelled the inside of the Carpenter building in Chapel Court (1953).
In the late fifties the Chapel interior, with its Morris ceilings, was carefully cleaned, and in 1961–2 considerable remodelling under David Roberts was carried out around the original sixteenth-century Hall, which is at first floor level on the opposite side of Cloister Court. The kitchens beneath it have been completely re-arranged; the Hall staircase annexe added by Waterhouse as a projection into Outer Court has been demolished, and three deeply splayed brick lancets built into the blocked up opening of its door into the screens passage; and the original main staircase, restored to its former dignity, has been carried up a further two flights to gallery level. There, behind the famous oriel 'spy' window, a suite of rooms has been cleverly combined into an overflow hall, the removal of the partitions revealing a substantial Tudor roof covering the whole space. Apart from the beefy woodwork of the servery screen, Roberts has restricted his decoration here to simple whitewashing, so as to play up the accretion of centuries in the curious fenestration. Though post-war portraits are not generally part of this book, the three examples in the second hall of Jesus must be made an exception, for the sake of comedy: Eric Kennington's 'hard-boiled Holbein' of Dr. Tillyard (the Elizabethan World Picture in person), Sir William Coldstream's Expressionist blood-bath of Prof. Page in full regalia, and the ineffable Boys' Own Paper rendering of Steve Fairbairn, the famous oarsman.
The same architect was commissioned for Jesus's first major post-war building, the new North Court of 1963–5 beyond Waterhouse's *schloss* in Outer Court. As might be expected in the college where Sir Leslie Martin is a fellow, the new building, described in detail below, is placed skilfully so as to enhance the open-sided extendibility of the older courts.
Most recently (1966–7) David Roberts & Geoffrey Clarke have designed an unusually successful garage compound to the south-east of the chapel, which

courageously tackles the problem of storing away cars in an historic setting. Behind the existing white brick wall to Jesus Lane are hidden eight new lock-up garages (brown brick piers and black painted timber lintel), then a trussed Finnish-type mono-pitch roof shelter to six reserved parking spaces, and finally, at right-angles to these, the new brown brick bicycle shed. This has an all-timber interior on an aisled cruciform plan, like a miniature cathedral, the 'crossing' being rooflit; and between its back wall and that of the Master's Garden is a new formal entrance to the college from the Lane. The curved brick wall and patterned brick paving here are perhaps a little too neo-Martin and will 'date', if pleasantly; the gate would have been better as an all-iron infill, instead of having brick side-pieces.

North Court

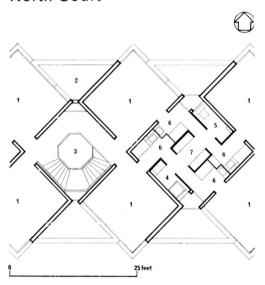

Part plan
1 Undergraduate's room 2 Terrace 3 Staircase
4 Shower 5 W.C. 6 Washroom 7 Kitchen

Date.	1963–5
Architect.	David Roberts
Contractor.	Rattee & Kett Ltd.
Cost.	£200,000

Requirement. Study–bedrooms for 70 under-graduates, three two-room sets for graduates, two three-room sets for fellows, sick bay, changing room for adjoining games field, stores.

Description. Built in two continuous phases, this two-and-a-half-sided court extends north and west from the Outer Court building by Waterhouse, whose isolated North House (for tutors) was demolished as soon as the first part was ready. There are playing fields and mature trees to north and west, and relandscaped gardens towards the college.

Roberts's bed-sitters are placed diagonally for natural light and privacy, each with its own triangular balcony entered through a window wall which terminates in a projecting oriel. They are double-banked around diamond-shaped cores containing stairs and service rooms alternately (see plan). Each staircase, octagonal in form, serves four rooms on each of the three residential floors, except at the south-west end, where the building rises to four-and-a-half storeys. Each of the service cores, artificially lit and ventilated (apart from two slit windows), includes a dressing room (with basin) for each resident, shower room, lavatory and kitchen; these are all entered from living rooms, not staircases, so that each resident meets people from the next staircase as well as from his own. The larger sets are placed on the north-west and north-east outer corners, with service rooms placed on the court side and clerestory lit to prevent overlooking. The half-sunk basement contains entrance halls, a changing room for the playing fields, communal baths, boiler house, stores and cleaners' rooms.

The structure is of loadbearing brick cross-walls with concrete floors and stairs (pre-cast treads) and timber roofs. Facings are of Himley handmade bricks, pale pinkish-brown in colour. Windows are framed in aluminium, with copings of slate to all parapets and balcony walls. Walls inside are plastered and painted white. Woodwork is sealed Columbian pine, with specially designed built-in cupboards and book-shelves; heating is by panel radiators.

Comment. At a time when new college buildings tend to superimpose aesthetic fisticuffs on relatively ordinary plans, Roberts has here gone unfashionably to the opposite extreme. To say that 'everything at North Court is good except the architecture' would be a dangerous half-truth, as strategic planning is the primary job for an architect in build-

Jesus College, New North Court

ing up a community; and North Court is brilliant as a two-dimensional diagram (see plan). Having proved at Castle Hill hostel (see page 114) the advantages for natural lighting of placing rooms diagonally in echelon to catch the sun, Roberts here fills in the serrated gaps on the plan with secluded balconies large enough to form outside rooms, not just flower boxes. They flexibly extend the inevitably minimal space within. Furthermore, he has reconciled Cambridge's traditional dichotomy between private-but-isolated staircases and communal-but-exposed corridors by linking men from adjoining staircases in shared service cores, which have rooms double-banked round them. By receiving by-law permission for artificial lighting and ventilation to these cores, Roberts has set an example in compactness, socially and economically, which has since been followed at Emmanuel (see page 21) and Sidney Sussex (page 47).

It is the working out of such complexity in three dimensions that seems ultimately to have defeated the architect. The horizontal pull of the balconies, broken by the projecting oriels, prolongs convincingly the rhythm of the old college buildings when seen from the Gatehouse approach at a distance. But from close at hand the inexplicably massive brickwork of these mere screen walls (that is all that

balcony fronts are) confuses irreparably the diagonal build-up of the real structure of staircases and service cores behind. Such deception would perhaps have been justifiable (or at least explicable) in terms of fashionable Mannerist paradox, as at New Hall (page 161), but Roberts has rejected artful detailing. Only at one point—at the tall south-west corner where the building is chopped off halfway through a service core—does he begin to establish in the stacks of lavatories and kitchens the kind of logical hierarchy of structure and services which architects have learnt from Louis Kahn (who has recently employed a very similar diagrid plan for dormitories at Bryn Mawr College, Pennsylvania). The plinth of half-sunk basement rooms, clerestory lit, also has a promising scale, but this is destroyed immediately above by the collision between Roberts's balconies and his flimsy aluminium oriels, with their floor-to-ceiling glass; the balcony brickwork is vainly chamfered back a little, in order to minimize casualties. Ultimate disintegration takes place in the fracturing of the cross-wall structure at different widths in alternate bays, so as to let a little natural light into the staircases and into half the dressing rooms. This is the stuff of compromise, and it incidentally forces the staircases into a cramped octagon when they could easily have just been toplit.

King's College

292 undergraduates, 152 postgraduates, 73 fellows.

Ever since Hawksmoor's day, King's has been champion at the Cambridge game of rejecting designs from eminent architects. Increasing numbers of students, particularly postgraduates, have recently made the enlargement of the college imperative, and thanks to the inter-war bursarship of John Maynard Keynes, it has been rich enough to do so. In 1948–50, Geddes Hyslop's weakly post-Bloomsbury Garden Hostel (see page 160) seemed to presage westward growth across the Backs; but then the college switched back to its land in the city behind King's Parade, for a proposed new court by Sir Leslie Martin, described below. Although this design was discarded and its ideas developed elsewhere for Caius (Harvey Court, page 155), part of the Market Court site was eventually used for the Market Hostel by Architects' Co-Partnership (1960–2), also described below. In spite of its intrinsic excellence, the hostel must be deplored as yet another effort to cram more undergraduates into the old town centre, involving as it did the destruction of a fine Georgian house, the Central Hotel.

Within the main precinct of King's, one major site, however, has been overdue for renewal—the backyards towards St. Catharine's College around the bleak building known as King's Drain. Keynes suffered in the Drain as an undergraduate and left the residue of his personal estate to rebuild it. Feasibility studies of this and other sites in the town centre and beyond the Backs were carried out (1961) by Chamberlin, Powell & Bon and other architects. Fello Atkinson of James Cubitt & Partners was commissioned for the actual job, when the money became available on Lady Keynes's death. However questionable some of the detailing may be, as described below, the new courts gain immeasurably from having been carried out (1965–7) as a joint piece of urban renewal with St. Catharine's; such lessons of inter-collegiate co-operation urgently need to be learnt by those building beyond the Backs. The next project of King's (for postgraduates) will surely be in that direction, either joining Garden Hostel in the Fellows' Garden or using some of the playing fields of the college's Choir School, to which Robert Matthew, Johnson-Marshall & Partners have recently made a distinguished addition (see page 185). Further west, off Barton Road, the

King's–Clare sports pavilion (see page 188) was designed in his spare-time (1959–60) by the chief architect to the Ministry of Health, W. E. Tatton Brown.

Meanwhile, back in Chapel Court, the wealth of King's has financed continuous fun. The hall was thoroughly restored in 1950, Gilbert Scott's lanterns (replacing Wilkins's) being themselves replaced with suitably frivolous pseudo-Regency ones designed by W. F. Haslop of Rattee & Kett; and in 1967 its interior has been re-arranged by Fello Atkinson and redecorated by John Fowler as part of the 'King's–Cat's' development (with which it is described below). Chapel Court was repaved in 1951 by Prof. W. G. Holford (as he then was) and Prof. H. Myles Wright, in a sensitive layout of slabs and cobbles. In 1955 Lord Holford (as William Holford & Partners) designed an extension of staff flats to Bodley's Building down by the river; the concrete frame of this is disguised by extremely diluted Tudor detail, which is more damaging to Bodley's convinced medievalism than any modern contrast would have been (cf. Holford's fan vault of concrete to the chapel of the sister college at Eton). More recent alterations include the heightening by David Roberts (1958) of the stone-faced Webb's Building, with a row of dormers and a clumsy red brick gable; the recobbling of the King's Parade forecourt (1962), with Wilkins's lamp posts unfortunately set back from the pavement; and the admirable conversion of rooms in the old Provost's Lodge into a music library and reading room by Lyster & Grillet (1964), furnished in light wood and dark blue leather. The same architects have since carried out (1967) a £12,000 remodelling of the 'new' Provost's Lodge (1926–9, by Kennedy & Nightingale), which sports neo-Georgian fronts in plum-coloured brick to Webb's Court and honey-coloured stone to the garden; to the latter a polygonal-ended copper-roofed study for the Provost had already been added in 1955–6 by Bird & Tyler. The new work consists of a private entrance from Queens' Lane for the Provost's family, overlooked by a small dining-kitchen; the brick-paved steps and raked brick walls, blue-black in colour, are pleasantly modish. The two big rooms facing the garden are being refurnished for ceremonial use. Kennedy's brick slits on the Webb's Court front have been pointlessly blocked up. Lyster & Grillet also designed the interior of Michael Jaffé's flat beneath the pediment of Fellows' Building (1964). As an international expert on Rubens, Mr. Jaffé has been closely involved with the most important and controversial of all the college's post-war projects; the incorporation of the superb 'Adoration of the Magi' into the Chapel as its new High Altarpiece.

In 1960–1 Robert Maguire & Keith Murray had prepared an excellent scheme for a liturgical renewal of the east end; but the arrival of the Madonna led ultimately to their replacement as architects by Sir Martyn Beckett. His eclectic décor, superimposed on the main elements of Maguire's scheme, has been carried out as part of a complete internal restoration in the winter of 1967–8 and is described below—as also is the dignified sales counter of 1965–6, designed by Bernard Holdaway with Sir Hugh Casson as consultant. Whether the chapel will end by looking more like an art gallery than a place of worship remains to be seen.

King's College Chapel Restoration

Date. 1967–8

Architect. Sir Martyn Beckett, based partly on project by Robert Maguire & Keith Murray (1960).

Contractor. Rattee & Kett

Cost. £110,000

Description and Comment. When in May 1961 Major A. E. Allnatt gave to King's his £275,000 purchase of 'The Adoration of the Magi', it was naturally assumed that the painting would return to its original function as a High Altarpiece—as it was in the Carmelite convent at Louvain, for which Rubens painted it in 1634. Such is the distinctive character of King's Chapel, however, and of the liturgy performed within it that the transfer could not be as simple as at first it appeared to be. Robert Maguire & Keith Murray had been appointed more than a year earlier to re-establish the High Altar visually and liturgically as the focal point of the Chapel, and had already, for these reasons, condemned Professor John Skeaping's statues of 'mummified Madonnas' (Dr. Plommer's description) and the sonorous Edwardian reredos by Detmar Blow in which they were set. (Blow in turn had replaced James Essex's reredos

of 1770, and Essex had filled the gap left by the Elizabethan removal of the original High Altar.) Maguire & Murray proposed to remove all the panelling—Blow's and also Cornelius Austin's of 1662–3 —back to the choir stalls, puritanically revealing the original ashlar stone facings of the side walls. Against this serene grey backdrop—a contrast to the answering three-sided elaboration of the choir stalls, the altar was to be the sacrificial centrepiece, brought a bay and a half nearer the congregation, so that Holy Communion could be celebrated with the priest in the 'westward facing' position.

The introduction of the Rubens Madonna, however beautiful in itself, inevitably disrupted the purity of Maguire's design, establishing a non-liturgical focus of wholly different proportions from altar and sanctuary. The painting is 10 ft $9\frac{1}{4}$ in high by 8 ft $1\frac{1}{4}$ in broad, not counting its frame. Maguire and Murray showed that, even eliminating all the sanctuary steps and setting the Rubens back against the east wall as a separate object, it would still rise above the lower sill-line of the east window which is part of a unifying string course with fleurons round the sanctuary; more important it would almost cut into Galyon Hone's stained glass of 1526—itself a major work of Flemish art and totally different in tone-colour and texture. They therefore suggested placing the painting instead in the antechapel, in a position in front of the west door or forward from the choir screen, which respected the donor's insistence that it should be on the main east–west axis. The disadvantage is that this would reduce the amount of seating space available for special services. The best solution of all perhaps would have been to have negotiated with the donor an alternative site on the chapel's only cross-axis, immediately opposite the main south door; this is now occupied by the excellent new literature stall (or tables of the money-changers), designed by Bernard Holdaway with Sir Hugh Casson as consultant (1965–6). This has ebony-stained display cases in four movable units; the brightly coloured goods are picked out by vertical strip lighting, set in black stove-enamelled metal turrets which echo the lines of the Perpendicular without irritating its details.

The final solution of the east end of the chapel will have been carried out in December 1967–April 1968. In place of Maguire, whose aesthetic honesty was evidently regarded as obstructive, the college appointed Sir Martyn Beckett, Bt., an aristocratic architect who has restored a number of country houses for the National Trust. Mock-ups of his design have been on show since 1964. He follows Maguire closely in eliminating all existing panelling, furnishings and steps, but he sets the High Altar as well as the Madonna fairly close to the east wall. The altar will be handsomely wide, with an abstract frontal in green and gold. The Rubens in its new 11-in black and gold Antwerp frame, remains out of proportion with the east window (both of them too tall and too narrow) and an attempt has been made to counteract this in the later mock-ups by making it the centre of a rather phoney triptych, with blank side panels painted green. For normal purposes a 'demountable altar' will be placed in front— a confession of failure to reconcile Rubens and the liturgy. Fortunately the idea in the first mock-up of concealing floodlights behind two free-standing pseudo-Baroque 'candelabra' (bulgy obelisks imitated from a church in Prague), has been discarded; and Sir Martyn has instead tried his hand at imitating 1960 in four 'sconces' attached symmetrically to the side walls. These consist of two bunches of metal sticks with a rough surface, the inner circle of 14 painted black and concealing electric bulbs, the other circle of 16 gilded and holding candles. George Gilbert Scott Jn's splendid Renaissance standard candlesticks of 1882, retained by Maguire, have unfortunately been discarded.

The opportunity is being taken (making the total cost £110,000) to clean the entire interior of the chapel and to lay underfloor heating, replacing the radiators; and the marble paving at the east end will be relaid to the 1702 design of stepped diamonds which had survived only between the choir stalls. There was a complete cleaning as recently as 1947 but the radiators had quickly carried dust and candle-smoke up to the vault, making the creamy stonework seem hard and wiry, as well as dark. This time the decisive break with tradition has been made of installing electric light throughout, though candles will continue to be the most prominent lighting for services. Perhaps an intelligent re-ordering of some of the side chapels for practical Christianity could help to prevent this place of worship from becoming an embalmed art gallery.

Market Court project

Proposed. 1957

Architects. Sir Leslie Martin & Colin St. J. Wilson

This was the second of Sir Leslie Martin's studies in courtyard planning with a repetitive cross-wall structure[1]—studies culminating in his recent Whitehall Plan and in the establishment of the Cambridge Centre for Land Use and Built Form Studies. The site was an irregular quadrilateral, bounded by St. Mary's Passage, Peas Hill, St. Edward's Passage and a new alleyway roughly on the line of David's bookshop. Rooms for about 50 undergraduates were to be on two levels over ten ground floor shops and an open cloister giving access to the court, where the off-centre space allowed for open terraces stepping back on the north and east. This was the germ of the 'hanging gardens' in Sir Leslie's third scheme, Harvey Court of Caius College (see page 155). Long internal corridors, widening in places to catch patches of natural light, connected rooms to two semi-circular staircases in the new alleyway. The terraces, joined also by outside steps (an improvement on the rigid separation of Harvey Court's levels), could have provided seating spaces for theatrical happenings in the court—an ingenious idea. Against Market Court's case was its destruction of some attractive town property—though St. Mary's Chambers would have been no loss. In its favour (by too narrow a majority of the dons for the college to proceed with it) was Martin's superb use of different levels on a central urban site. His rigorous discipline of brick and timber was here applied to an 'urban grain' far more appropriate than the isolated Harvey Court.

---

1. The first was Knighton Hostel, Leicester—in a suburban garden.

Market Hostel   A

Peas Hill

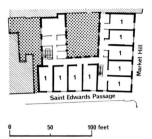

First floor plan
1 Undergraduates' rooms
Dotted areas indicate enclosed open spaces
Shaded area indicates existing buildings

Date.	1960–2
Architects.	Architects' Co-Partnership. Kenneth Capon, partner-in-charge
Contractor.	Kerridge Ltd.
Cost.	£125,000

Requirement. Study–bedrooms for 21 under-graduates with bank premises below; remodelling of adjoining hostel rooms.

Description. On a site previously occupied by the early eighteenth-century Central Hotel and by a smaller house on the corner of St. Edward's Passage, Market Hostel's main eastern frontage to Peas Hill is four-storeyed. There are five bed-sitters on each of the three upper levels, with rear corridor access, cantilevered forward on 'mushroom' columns of reinforced concrete over the fully glazed ground floor, which, with the basement, is let to the Midland Bank, who commissioned Whinney, Son & Austen Hall to design the interior of the banking hall. A side wing to St. Edward's Passage has two floors of three rooms each over the windowless flank wall of the bank; beyond it a narrow passage leads through to the entrance stairs in a low west wing, which completes the enclosure of an upper level courtyard (or light well) over the bank. The corridors round this lead through to St. Mary's Chambers, another King's hostel, via some remodel-

King's Market Hostel and St. Edward's Passage

led rooms over the bank's Early Victorian annexe in Peas Hill.

The brick cross-wall structure of the upper floors is faced with panels of cream-white bricks of special density and regularity, imported from Venlo in the Netherlands. The floors themselves (of concrete), the mushroom columns and second floor spandrel panels are faced with blue-grey Welsh slate. The asymmetrically pitched roof, clad in copper, stops short to allow the third floor rooms a continuous balcony, with alternate parapets of slate-faced brick and iron railings. Furnishings in beech designed by the architects include cupboards, shelves and a special divan bed beneath which a foldaway table can be stored.

Comment. The excellence of Market Hostel lies in the scaling of its parts, precise and formal while mercifully free from tricks of style or personality cult. The two façades nicely blend with, yet do not imitate, the buildings on either side, the differences in gabling and fenestration being closely tied to what actually happens within. The white plaster and beech joinery give a luminous and

29

spacious feeling to the interior, while the cast-iron fire escape provides an amusing diversion on the court side.

But the building remains slightly uneasy, besides (and perhaps because of) being over-expensive. The Venlo bricks, glittering gaily in strong sunlight, tend on a dull day to look ostentatious compared with the cheap whitewashed Cambridgeshire stocks of David's bookshop next door. A hostel is only a simple lodging house; yet for the bank beneath, where marble might have given appropriate airs, the slate substitute seems rather bald, particularly as the colonnade is glazed anti-socially to exclude passers-by. The blank wall to St. Edward's Passage firmly maintains the alleyway's enclosure; yet a clerestory window could have mitigated the Stygian gloom of the bank inside, with the depressing neo-Georgian furnishings by its own architects. In the bed-sitters, double glazing to the street would have kept out traffic noise better than double doors to the light well; and the light well itself could have been made a habitable outdoor terrace, as at the nearby Arts Restaurant.

King's Lane Courts   **B**

for King's and St. Catharine's.
Between Trumpington Street and Queens' Lane

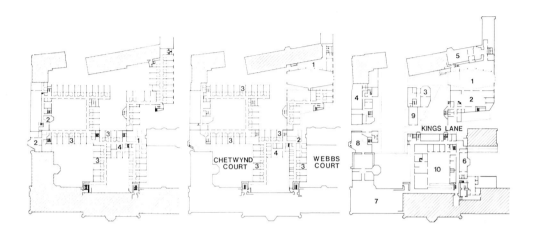

Ground floor (left)

1 St. Catharine's Hall **2** St. Catharine's kitchens
3 Store rooms **4** Offices **5** St. Catharine's Senior
Combination Room **6** Private dining room **7** King's bar
and common room **8** King's concert hall **9** King's
Muniment Room **10** King's kitchen

First floor (centre)

1 St. Catharine's Hall—upper gallery **2** King's research
centre **3** Study-bedrooms **4** King's staff common room

Second floor (right)

1 King's research centre **2** Fellows' sets
3 Study-bedrooms **4** Guest rooms

Date.	1965–8
Architects.	James Cubitt & Partners. Fello Atkinson, partner-in-charge
Contractor.	Bovis Ltd.
Cost	£1,250,000

Requirement. For King's, 65,750 sq ft—rooms for 80 undergraduates; new kitchen, buttery, staff rooms and offices; S.C.R. extension and private dining room; music room, muniment room, workshop and store; basement cycle sheds, laundry and entertainment room.
For St. Catharine's, 65,600 sq ft—rooms for 85 undergraduates and sets for seven fellows; new dining hall, graduate parlour, kitchen and offices; conversion of present hall to S.C.R. and reading room.

Description. These five new courts are a praiseworthy, if belated, beginning in Cambridge of collaboration in building between two separate colleges. The site of 1·8 acres lies between Chapel Court of King's and Principal Court of St. Catharine's. It is crossed by the service road of King's Lane which previously twisted from the northern end of Queens' Lane (formerly Milne Street, truncated by Henry VI) past a motley collection of outhouses: on the right, the kitchen, garages and service rooms of St. Catharine's; on the left, the kitchens of King's and Fawcett's lecture room wing of Chetwynd Court; on the right again, a gloomy detached wing of King's (reached from Chetwynd Court through a lavatory-tiled tunnel) known as 'The Drain'—it was to redeem his suffering here as an undergraduate that Lord Keynes left the residue of his estate for its rebuilding, money which eventually became available on

Lady Keynes's death in 1962. All these buildings have been demolished.

The whole area is divided up in an almost regular grid, axial to King's Chapel Court, making four more or less square enclosed courts, with a large irregular open court where the grid stops short of St. Catharine's Chapel and Hobson's Building, which are on a slightly different alignment. The roofline throughout is uniform at four storeys, except for the recessed fifth storeys of the Bull Hotel and of the new research institute wing between the existing Webb's Court of King's and the college's new Kitchen Court.

On the Trumpington Street front Scott's Chetwynd Building (1870) has been preserved. Its ground floor has been remodelled as television and reading rooms, bar and mail room, with a large ante-room to the new two-storey music room, with a gallery which projects southward across the old line of King's Lane. Its strongly modelled bay window, echoing the adjoining street façades, is clad in roach bed Portland stone. Next to it on the south is another old façade, that of the plain and solemn stone-faced Bull Hotel (1828, James Walters), penetrated on one side by the realigned King's Lane (at this end for pedestrians only); its ground floor front is being converted for lettable offices, with the existing Rushmore Room and bed-sitters of St. Catharine's above. The back of the Bull has been torn down and rebuilt entirely in brick, with a fifth storey set back; on each upper floor it provides a bed-sitter and a fellow's set, the latter with a polygonal bay window for its living room and with its bedroom spanning the new King's Lane.

Behind these Trumpington Street frontages lie the five new courts. Occupying two-thirds of the area of the new courts lies a 34,000 sq ft basement area abutting only on those of the existing buildings which already have basements, so as to avoid underpinning. It contains (to satisfy the planning authorities) 50 car spaces for St. Catharine's, entered by a ramp from Queens' Lane, parking space for cycles, boiler rooms and ventilation plant rooms for both colleges, and various workshops and stores.

The two courts immediately behind Scott and the Bull, Chetwynd Court and King's Lane Court, are connected by open cloisters or *pilotis* at ground level to form a continuous space parallel to Trumpington Street, the southward view being prolonged into Principal Court of St. Catharine's between the Chapel and Hobson's (between which a screen wall has been removed). The floor of the two courts, mainly cobbled, will be landscaped down the centre in a formal pattern of paving, enclosing large trees and rectangular pools of water with fountains.

The *in situ* reinforced concrete frame of the basement and ground floor supports a completely repetitive industrialized system of precast concrete crosswalls and floors for the rooms. The two colleges sensibly decided on a standard bed-sitter size within which the furniture could be arranged flexibly on a modular basis; and certainly the rooms are large by Cambridge standards and also well furnished: three low tables as well as a desk and the usual divan and chairs. There are two peculiarities which together intimately affect external appearances. Between each room and its corridor, besides a lobby with generous hanging space and shelves, there is an individual bathroom, an unheard-of luxury for Oxbridge and explained by the college's commercial as well as intellectual necessity of attracting the custom of summer conferences during the Long Vacation (stout Welsh miners have been known to blanch before the communal sanitary appliances of most colleges which are a great deal inferior to pithead baths). These bathrooms were made up off-site and hoisted in as 'heart' units. Secondly, and partly because of the extra width of each block resulting from the bathrooms, rooms are only single-banked (instead of the double-banking usual in luxury hotels): that is to say, in the three courts immediately next to Trumpington Street, whereas Chetwynd Court and the irregular St. Catharine's Court are overlooked by the long strips of wall-to-wall bed-sitter windows, King's Lane Court is entirely overlooked (except on the Bull side) by the thin triangular oriel windows, which give patches of light to the corridors. These upper floors are faced with precast concrete panels veneered with roach bed Portland stone—the same stone from the rougher Portland beds, gnarled with the built-in weathering of primeval worm-casts, that the Smithsons used on the 'Economist' building in London. The top floor panels form a slightly 'embattled' skyline, with roof flashings of copper. Windows are of stove-enamelled steel.

The first 'band' of courts is flanked at ground level by certain special rooms expressed as loadbearing infill structures in dark purple brick with some Ketton stone dressings. Next to Chetwynd Court is the new kitchen of King's, surrounded on the ground floor by three ranges of buttery, staff dining room, stores and larders. Above are three ranges, forming a new Kitchen Court overlooking the kitchen roof, repetitive bed-sitters on the Chetwynd east side, a first-floor staff dining room with some staff flats on the south, and the King's research institute on the west. These upper ranges are connected to the old buildings only by two staircases, one to Chetwynd Buildings and the other to the screens passage, so as to avoid taking light from the hall windows. The institute range is five-storeyed and its rooms are double-banked, overlooking Webb's Court as well. The private dining room on the west side has a broad bay window; over it, besides bed-sitters, are a series of academic and staff offices. At right-angles to the dining room, forming a single-storey projection into Webb's Court on the site of the former kitchen (and of Mr. Saltmarsh's roof-top 'pulpit'), is an extension to the college's S.C.R. with various small ancillary rooms.

The fourth court (as yet unnamed) is divided between the two colleges, like King's Lane Court, from which it is separated on the ground floor by a muniment room, a workshop and some stores; it is not completely enclosed by rooms, its southern range being cut off abruptly to make an opening through to the irregular St. Catharine's court. On the west side of the two latter courts is the kitchen and hall range of St. Catharine's which faces Queens' Lane. Unlike the rest of the buildings, its Queens' Lane façade is clad entirely in the same dark purple brick, that is used sparingly elsewhere, with Ketton stone dressings. A double height hall, in plan an irregular hexagon, runs the full width of this range, expressed by an oriel window on the Queens' Lane side and a deep single-height bay at the other side, which accommodates the high table. Running the full length of the hall, on its southern side, is a gallery seating 50, the concrete parapet of which is adorned by a gilt Catherine wheel. North of the hall are the kitchens and servery; above these are staff rooms on the first floor. South of the hall are various college ancillary rooms, including the pantry and buttery. Here there is access through to the S.C.R. now in the lower half of the old hall (the upper half is the library reading room). On the top two floors are more undergraduate rooms; the top floor is an aluminium sheathed mansard. Webb's Court of King's is being re-landscaped: in front of the private dining-room a broad terrace extends into the court, protected by a wall from the lower level of the existing court. To reach the upper level there is a ramp which is to spiral around a tree.

Comment. The fact that this is the first time two colleges have collaborated on a new building is undoubtedly the most significant feature of the enterprise. Partly, of course, it was sheer necessity that forced this co-operation, since neither college could otherwise have successfully exploited the land which so urgently needed redevelopment; and partly it was a question of finance. It is perhaps a shame, then, that the colleges could not see their way to sharing kitchens and boiler rooms, thus liberating even more land for use. It is also encouraging that a largely industrialized method of building has been employed. The design itself has proved something of a mixed blessing. The site is extremely awkward and basically the problem of exacting greatest possible use from it has been well solved, while not resorting to tower blocks. Potentially, the regular grid of courts provides attractive and usable external spaces with a layout of rooms which fosters a sense of community. But, apart from Chetwynd Court, the courts are bleak and unexciting, in spite of the vista from Chetwynd Court through to St. Catharine's Court—although even this may prove to be too wind-swept for comfort or use. Nor does the internal layout of the rooms seem to bear much relationship to the pattern, or provide any breaking down into smaller groups. Instead, there is a maze of long soulless corridors, unfortunately faced in a dreary, heavy-duty vinyl. This has been brought about by the single banking of rooms, in its turn a reflection of the colleges' desire for individual bathrooms. In any case, the whole concept of individual 'hotel-type' rooms must surely be suspect in a design for student accommodation. The public rooms, on the contrary, are more successful. On the whole, there has been a careful separation of functions providing considerable clarity of layout: certainly the use of brick on the ground floors, both externally and internally achieves this well. The most successful room is the King's bar (actually a conversion of the ground floor of the Wilkins building east of the hall) with its deliberately garish colours and its skilful use of two levels to create an interlocking pattern of fixed benching. The private dining-room, which has dark stained slatting on a dark background should prove popular, with its large bay. Less successful is the St. Catharine's Hall which has a barn-like quality: and the irrationality of a large oriel at one end, with the high table pushed under a lower ceiling at the opposite end.

The detailing of the buildings is far from satisfactory.

The basic aesthetic approach is contained in the long, banded windows and the band of stone-faced slabs below. The top storey, however, entirely upsets this pattern with its recessed windows and battlement effect, implying a solid masonry building, and not a thin veneer, as the lower storeys (correctly) suggest. This *volte-face* is a typically English wilfulness: a failure to comprehend the significance of any one form in relation to any other, and here the change was simply a vague, picturesque fancy, since the top floor rooms do not differ for the most part from those below, Whether the use of roach bed Portland stone was right in any case is highly dubious. A textured surface implies, surely, a solid mass and not a thin membrane: it is not surprising that pioneers of the thirties who first introduced the motif of banded windows should have sought the smoothest of possible finishes, white-painted rendering.

Such picturesque details proliferate. It is perhaps unfair to take the architects to task over the Queens' Lane building with its half-heartedly seventeenth-century oriel, since this was as much as anything the will of St. Catharine's. The bricks do not exactly match the existing buildings, and the difference is an irritation. It deadens, not only St. Catharine's seventeenth-century range, with its delicate details, but the whole of Queens' Lane, which remains a draughty corridor. The music room with its bay is more the architects' responsibility. They aimed for a bold form for the Trumpington Street façade (unrelated to anything that occurs behind), but were they right in the circumstances? The result is in open conflict with Scott's heavily modelled façade, and in particular, the corner tourelle. Surely the aim should have been to create some sense of unity in the continuous street front it has created. Then, too, there is the back of the Bull Hotel, also in brick, another disparate element to be added to the list, another poor attempt at harmonizing with the old. And so this basically sound scheme falls apart little by little, until the totality can be seen as indefensibly mediocre, built upon a whole series of missed opportunities and poor briefing. It is sad that this should be the outcome of years of waiting for a new Drain.

Magdalene College   h

258 undergraduates, 63 postgraduates, 26 fellows.

Magdalene's post-war development has been generally most imaginative, apart from the neo-Georgian panelled dining room in Bright's Building by Louis de Soissons (1949). The main work has been on the other side of Magdalene Street. Here there were already Redfern's quaint remodelling of a former vinegar factory, known as Mallory Court (1925); tho one completed wing of Lutyens's grandiose Benson Court (1931–2); and an attractive jumble of cottages of many periods which Lutyens had intended to sweep away. In 1952 David Roberts, now a fellow of the college, was commissioned to prepare a 15–20 year plan for the area. The first phase of 1953–8, described below, is a classic example of self-effacing urban renewal, completing Benson and Mallory Courts with a mixture of converted cottages and new buildings. The second phase, the creation of Buckingham Court on the site of the college's present car park behind Mallory Court, consists of a major new building by David Roberts & Geoffrey Clarke, also described in detail below, together with another series of conversions.

Back on the other side of Magdalene Street (across which the college might do well to build an actual bridge), First Court has been completely restored (1959–66) by Stephen Dykes Bower. There seems no reason why the scraping and replacing of the brickwork should have been so uniformly fierce. A masterpiece might have stood such treatment, but Magdalene's quiet Tudor, until climbing plants regain control, will tend to look like a training college of just the kind that Dykes Bower himself might have designed. Fortunately, there are excellent details by others to admire: the War Memorial lettering in the chapel cut by Will Carter; the small abstract sculpture by Henry Moore loaned to the Fellows' Garden by Mr. Ede; the admirably converted J.C.R. in First Court with its two tripartite screens of columns and its elegant aluminium light fittings, by David Roberts (1964). Best of all is the remodelling of the Porter's Lodge in the main entrance by David Roberts & Geoffrey Clarke (1965–6). Suddenly adopting a James Stirling manner, they have clothed the floor, the three-sided counter and a window-seat with an overall covering of bright red tiles. Even the post shelf is a massive red-tiled box, with an inner frame of black-painted wood. The next major improvement planned is the remodelling of the kitchens.

Meanwhile a new Master's Lodge has been built (1966–7) on the site of Buckler's gaunt villa of 1835. This is one of the several buildings in which David Roberts & Geoffrey Clarke—once again the architects—have used a rationalized brick structure, and here it has become almost neo-classical in appearance.

Magdalene, Benson Court: cottage conversions

Benson and Mallory Courts

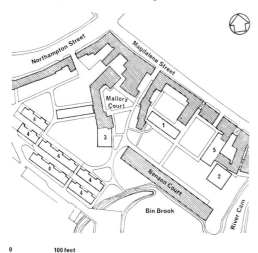

1 New building 2 River building 3 Conversion
4 Buckingham Court 5 Bicycle shed
Shaded areas denote existing buildings

Date.   1952–8

Architect.   David Roberts

Contractor.   A. J. Nunn & Son (stage 1 and later conversions). Coulson & Son (new building and conversions). Kidman & Son (river building)

Requirement.   Accommodation in sets; 28 in new buildings and 40 in converted old buildings.

Description.   In 1952 Mr. Roberts was commissioned to prepare a 15–20 year plan for Benson and Mallory Courts, and for Tan Yard behind Mallory

Court. Only Tan Yard now remains to be done.

The site is bounded by the old Magdalene Street shops and Sir Edwin Lutyens's brick range, with the converted factory of Mallory Court to the north (see plan). There are three entrances from Magdalene Street, of which the first runs into Mallory Court between two small rows of cottages. These were converted into undergraduate rooms in 1954–5 and 1958, with the cottage front doors imitating the traditional staircase pattern.

Behind the old shops is a small enclosed court, completed by the erection of the first of Mr. Roberts's new buildings, a three-storey terrace in yellow brick. Along one side of the court runs an open gallery, giving access to rooms on the upper floors of the three old ranges. These are mainly white-plastered, with exposed timbers left natural, but one house is painted a deep pink.

The second, and principal, entrance from Magdalene Street leads under a former innyard arch into Benson Court. This is a large and grassy court stretching down to the river. On its west side is the long Lutyens building; to the east are a large half-timbered house, new bicycle sheds, and three remaining cottages right by the river on the site of Fisher's Wharf. A paved towpath leads back again into the street. Next to a giant weeping willow near the river stands Mr. Roberts's second new building, a four-

Magdalene College, Benson Court; looking towards River building and the Cam

storey tower of 1957–8, on concrete piles and faced in red-brown Essex brick. It has square bay windows which form continuous verticals. Within, a flying staircase around a circular well lit from a skylight leads to 16 sets, four on each floor. Underneath there is a basement punthouse opening onto the river.

Comment.   In its quiet diversity, Benson Court has a paradoxical character entirely its own which demands enjoyment at length. Mr. Roberts has carefully kept his modern buildings simple to balance the twisting complexity of the old cottages. As in his Clare Hostel nearby (see page 114), he has achieved a flexible and relaxed atmosphere by concentrating on undergraduate needs—rooms, meeting-places and services—and letting these determine the scale and pattern of building. Only the signwriting of the shops and the anaemic furniture of the rooms seem less than happy. The materials—different coloured bricks, white plaster, green grass—achieve clean colour and textural contrasts without striving for effect. Mr. Roberts has eschewed both rusticity and

Civic Trust smartness. His neat pathways successfully link space with space to give unity to the court. A particularly good feature is the way in which Mr. Roberts has used Sir Edwin Lutyens's over-formal and unfashionable building as a continuous backdrop to the animated scenes on the other parts of the site. Above all, Benson Court shows that the frankly modern cannot merely coexist with, but positively enrich ancient work adjoining it. Two hundred and forty years ago at King's, Gibbs demonstrated this in the grand manner, and here Mr. Roberts has proved it on the domestic scale.

Here, as in his other buildings in Cambridge, Mr. Roberts has worked with associates, Christophe Grillet and Geoffrey Clarke (1952–60) and Geoffrey Clarke and Peter Hall (1959–64).

Buckingham Court

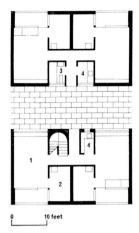

0   10 feet

Plan at deck level
1 Study **2** Bedroom **3** Bathroom **4** Gyproom

Date.   1968–9

Architects.   David Roberts & Geoffrey Clarke

Cost.   £200,000

Requirement.   Forty sets for graduates and under-graduates, car-parking and cycle sheds.

Description.   This latest addition by David Roberts and Geoffrey Clarke to Magdalene is to be sited at the southern side of Mallory Court and Tan Yard, facing the Cripps Building of St. John's from across the St. John's car park. The design shows three two-storey, and three single-storey blocks which are grouped in pairs and raised on a podium over a car park and cycle sheds. At the raised level is an open concourse between the blocks from which there is access to the rooms. The westernmost pair of blocks is stepped forward by the width of one block and the concourse: and in each case the single-storey block is on the north side. The sets are arranged in pairs and each pair has its own door onto the concourse; to the left and right of the entry are bathrooms and gyprooms, and beyond, again to left and right, at the end of two short lobbies, the door to each set. The two-storey blocks differ only in that there is one bathroom and gyproom to four sets, and a staircase occupying the extra space.

Each room has its own balcony in the depth of the block, those on the ground floor looking southwards, but those on the first floor facing north. The construction is to be of brick cross-walls and expressed concrete floor slabs.

Comment.   The idea of the concourse seems a good one and ought to help avoid the problems of an internal corridor by creating what is in effect a street, which will be pleasant to linger in. But its siting is such that it may well induce unpleasant draughts; and the relationship of the 'street' to the rest of the college is not altogether a clear one. The drawings show a use of brick structure similar to that already employed in the Churchill Graduate Flats, and as with that building, the differentiation between loadbearing and panel walls is not altogether apparent. This may yet prove an interesting scheme, in spite of these criticisms.

Master's Lodge

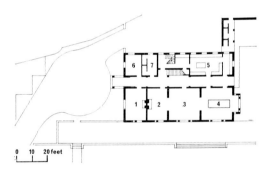

0   10   20 feet

Ground floor plan
1 Study **2** Sitting room **3** Drawing room **4** Dining room
5 Kitchen **6** Cloaks **7** Secretary

Date.   1966–7

Architects.   David Roberts & Geoffrey Clarke

Contractor.   Kerridge

Cost.   £41,000

Description.   This plain, rectangular brick box sits modestly back on the corner of Magdalene

Magdalene College, Master's Lodge

painted; flooring is of hardwood blocks, vinyl tiles in service areas, and white vitrified tiles in the main corridor, and windows are of teak. Except on the north side, all the windows are full-height and are varied in width according to the room size.

Comment.   From the south, this curious building is strongly neo-classical in form with the brick columns looking like pilasters rather than structural members. Unfortunately, this highly formalized approach is spoilt by various discrepancies both in planning and detail. There is, first of all, the use of brick mullions between windows on the south side, which reach with equal intensity to the more important structural members; and where in the drawing-room and dining-room windows one such mullion is structural and the other not, there is considerable confusion, in spite of the projection of the main member. More importantly, there is a certain confusion in the planning. On the ground floor there is a very clear division into two halves by the wide corridor, and although the recession of the wall at this point on the upper floor seems to imply a similar organization, in fact this is not the case: it is instead a centroidal pattern around the three-sided gallery onto which most of the rooms open. The ground floor corridor itself is a curious feature, launching one headlong across the building, and, but for the window at the far end, outside again. Not even the double-height space in the centre can properly divert such a persuasive movement.

The building is not without its good points. Its relationship to the college as a whole is well handled, standing detached, yet with its principal rooms opening south towards the college, and its broad flight of steps from the terrace inviting entry (or perhaps expressing a certain condescension). The whole south façade, in spite of the confusion already noted, has a noble serenity, befitting a Master's lodge.

Street and Chesterton Lane. Its long side faces the garden, at the far side of which is the college itself. A square brick porch leads straight into a corridor running the full length of the ground floor. On the north side of this corridor is the service area— kitchen, utilities, cloakroom and secretary's office— and to the south, the four principal rooms. From the west these are the Master's study, then a sitting-room opening into a drawing room which in its turn opens into the dining room at the far end, with its small rectangular bay projecting eastwards into the garden. All these four rooms open onto a reconstructed York stone terrace; opposite the dining- and drawing-room windows is a broad flight of steps down to the lawn. To one side of the corridor is a single flight of stairs leading to the first floor. Here the organization is different, with a three-sided gallery running around a double-height space over the corridor below. The principal bedrooms, of which there are five, open onto this landing, another two being reached from a corridor behind the stairs. Over the corridor, the external walls have been slightly recessed at either end to emphasize this basic division. The structure is loadbearing brick columns supporting reinforced concrete slabs, and all the rooms conform to this structural grid. It is faced in Himley handmade bricks and the structural piers are projected slightly from the face of the building. Internally, walls are plastered and white-

Pembroke College   b

338 undergraduates, 86 postgraduates, 48 fellows.

Pembroke is a college where the existence of modern architecture has only recently been recognized. The only complete new building since the war is an anaemic neo-Georgian design: Orchard Building of 1957–8, by Marshall Sisson. Its pale brickwork, Gibbsian doorways and gaudy coat-of-arms are ostentatiously set a little apart from the other buildings. It contains rooms for 30 undergraduates and two fellows on its three staircases.

In furnishings, the college has been more fortunate. The new Master's chair, of 1953, is an excellent design in black bean and rosewood by David Pye. In 1963, the new junior parlour was converted from rooms in Waterhouse's former Master's lodge, with furnishings and decoration of good quality, designed by Alec Crook.

In 1947–9, Old Court and the chapel were cleaned and Waterhouse's hall, which had had a storey added before the war, was finally purged of its external ornament. David Kindersley sculpted the heraldry. Since 1959, a ten-year programme of restoration has started with the overhaul of the Old Library (1961) by David Croghan, which included double-glazing and the installation of air-conditioning. In 1962–4 David Roberts undertook the reconstruction of the Hitcham Building. He inserted attractive oak staircases and fitted out the Thomas Gray Room with chairs by Owen Owen and a carpet woven by Marlene Hutton. The whole restoration has been done with commendable restraint. On the far side of the court the Ivy Building is now being restored by David Roberts & Geoffrey Clarke.

Peterhouse   a

212 undergraduates, 44 postgraduates, 39 fellows.

Peterhouse has twice been in the forefront of modern architecture in Cambridge, first with Hughes & Bicknell's Fen Court of 1939–40, and now with the New Building by Sir Leslie Martin & Colin Wilson, described below.

The first post-war building (1953–4) was an extension to the kitchens, hiding part of the medieval south wall. The architect was Alec C. Crook and here his mixed semi-Georgian modern was quite happily ex-

pressed in pale brick and golden Ketton stone with a flat roof and a classical inscription. However, it clashes with the nearby medieval wall. Old Court was cleaned and well restored in 1947.

Fen Court, with its elegantly asymmetrical courtyard and charming Dutch modern details, exhausted the land available on the college side of the deer park. Recent developments have treated the park as a central campus by enclosing St. Peter's Terrace at its south-west corner as part of the college. In 1961–2 the inelegant, institutional railings were replaced along the Trumpington Street front. The New Building stands in the deer park behind.

William Stone Building

Behind St. Peter's Terrace.

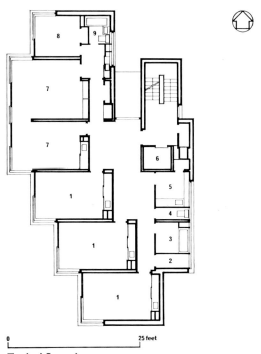

0   25 feet

Typical floor plan

1 Undergraduate's room **2** Shower **3** Bath **4** W.C.
5 Kitchen **6** Lift **7** Fellow's living room
8 Fellow's bedroom **9** Fellow's bathroom

Date.	1963–4
Architects.	Sir Leslie Martin & Colin St. J. Wilson
Contractor.	Kerridge Ltd.
Cost.	£100,000

Requirement. Rooms for eight fellows and 24 undergraduates. Landscaping and other work towards St. Peter's Terrace.

Description. This compact, yet irregular, eight-storey block stands near the southern end of Peterhouse's former deer park, close to St. Peter's Terrace, which is now also part of the college. It was decided not to adopt a courtyard plan for the new building, but to erect an isolated block with a landscaped garden flowing round it and so visually connecting the terrace with the college.

The planning of the block is like a human hand, the palm consisting of a landing on each floor, with the five rooms on its western side arranged in echelon with a continuous window band providing south as well as west light. The rooms overlook the garden and the river. Three of them on each floor are bed-sitters with built-in cupboards and basins. The other two form a fellow's set (alternatively they can be used by two undergraduates, the double size living room being virtually divided in two by a wall and sliding door).

On the other side of the landing are service rooms, store-room, bathroom, lavatory and kitchen. On the north side a tall window looks back towards the college, and in the north-east corner is the lift-tower and projecting staircase. This is the first residential college building in Cambridge with a lift.

The structure is entirely of loadbearing brick, with cross-walls between rooms, external cavity walls around the services and solid brick round the staircase tower. The facings are of brown Stamfordstone brick. External sills to the rooms are splayed inwards with bull-nosed bricks (c.f. parapets at Harvey Court). The roof garden has a deep parapet fascia of lead-coated copper. There is double glazing in all main rooms.

Comment. No less rigorous intellectually and in its use of materials than Professor Martin and Mr. Wilson's Harvey Court, this splendid building shows a

William Stone Building from approach road

far greater understanding both of its site and of the needs of student living. It *is* an expensive building, made possible by Mr. Stone's legacy. There is no reason, however, why brick should not bear a multi-storey load—calculated brickwork can be modern and technological as well as 'traditional'. Its particular value here is that the cross walls subdivide the rooms evenly and with excellent sound insulation (always difficult in frame construction).

Certainly this is a great remove from the enforced sociability of Harvey Court at one extreme, and the confined, arrow-slitted rooms of Fitzwilliam at the other. The privacy of the rooms is conditioned partly by the generous landings, with their piquant view back to the old college, and partly by the overlooking at the other corner of each window section.

Aesthetically the building is comparable with the recent work of Aalto. Only when seen 'full face' from the garden does it appear curiously squat and ungainly. This could well be Cambridge's masterpiece of the sixties, rather than the three new colleges, which all seem overburdened with the heritage of the medieval court. Here, in contrast, there is a frankly suburban relationship with the garden. These Peterhouse bed-sitters are civilized flats and suggest a new independence and freedom of student life.

Queens' College   q

407 undergraduates, 68 postgraduates, 38 fellows.

The Tudor brickwork of Queens', with its warm and massive enclosure, has been an inspiration to recent Cambridge architects, such as Sheppard and Lasdun. It has also presented a great temptation to dabblers in the picturesque, such as Drinkwater, who designed the terrible Fisher Building of 1932 across the river. Since the war, Queens' has been more fortunate.

Sir Albert Richardson restored the library (the old chapel) in 1950–1, inserting an attractive wooden gallery. Stephen Dykes Bower, the surveyor to Westminster Abbey, has excellently restored Bodley's Victorian decorative work in the chapel (1955) and the medieval hall (1961–2). The Morris patterns in the hall perhaps need to re-mellow a bit. The Erasmus Building might originally also have been designed by Mr. Dykes Bower, but fortunately his neo-Jacobean design was narrowly rejected and Sir Basil Spence was commissioned instead. Even he did not wholly escape the temptations of the picturesque, as will be seen.

Erasmus Building

Date.   1959–60

Architect.   Basil Spence & Partners

Contractor.   William Sindall Ltd.

Cost.   £100,000

Requirement. Study–bedrooms for 43 undergraduates and two fellows' sets.

Description. Erasmus Building forms a four-storeyed east side to the Victorian Friars' Court and is set back from the river behind the fifteenth-century Fellows' Bowling Green. The paved terrace at ground level, continued beneath the projecting south-west wing, is left open for the view through to the river, for bicycle parking and for use during May Balls and other entertainments.

The massive bush-hammered reinforced concrete columns and brick arches support a cantilevered first floor slab. Above this are three floors of rooms with concrete floors on loadbearing brick cross-walls. Facing bricks are red-blue Keymer below, yellow-brown Stamfordstone above.

The rooms are on the corridor system, reached by two staircases, that to the south rising direct from the open terrace, that towards King's from an enclosed entrance hall. At the top these staircases open onto a flat roof terrace, with all round views beneath a concrete pergola.

In the study–bedrooms, all furniture, except the armchairs, was chosen by the architects, the desk, table and coffee tables being from their own standard university range. The divan beds were specially designed. The study–bedroom windows, of anodised aluminium, slide horizontally. Floors are of afzelia strip, with black quarry tiles in the service rooms. Heating is by small bore hot water pipes serving radiant panels and convectors in each room, with electric fires as boosters and for making toast.

Comment. Erasmus is a handsomely detailed and beautifully furnished building, which shows all Sir Basil's skill in siting the new next to the old (cf. Coventry Cathedral, Rome Embassy). Reassuringly massive in outline and warm in tone, it differentiates clearly its loadbearing brick rooms and its reinforced

Queens', Erasmus Building, from the Backs

concrete public spaces. It is marred if anything by too great a desire to conform to the rest of Queens'. The admirable flow of space from the court through to the river is interrupted by pseudo-Tudor brick arches, which spoil the consistency of the concrete pilotis.

More seriously, the artful window pattern of window-slit-slit-window has no very clear relationship to what happens within. Larger windows, particularly in the corridors, would have helped to unite the building with Friars' Court. On the other hand, the panoramic sheath of glass enclosing the northern staircase affords a view only of bicycle sheds and back yards. The Cotswold stone wall towards the river is framed by curious vertical slits. There are superb views from the roof terrace of King's and the Backs, from which Erasmus's own brickwork looks pleasantly meaty. But the useless roof-top pergola fails to mask the gable end of Fawcett's building (the extra two storeys originally designed are needed) and does not relate to the structure below.

It seems grotesque that this moderate, conformist design once caused such a furore among *The Times* letter-writers, but in 1958 this was a test case for modern architecture in Cambridge, even though such battles had been won ten years or more earlier in the design, say, of primary schools.

St. Catharine's College   p

375 undergraduates, 92 postgraduates, 27 fellows.

St. Catharine's had little building activity since the war on its hemmed-in central site until 1965.

In 1951 Woodlark Building was completed. It contains the porter's lodge and storerooms, with three storeys of undergraduate rooms above. Hobson's opposite was built in 1930. 'Both are nearly identical in design and of an imitation early-eighteenth-century Baroque, by no means unappealing, chiefly because set back slightly from Principal Court so as to give an effect of side wings on a stage' (Pevsner). The careful landscaping included the repainting of two of the college's early nineteenth century lamp posts, made from cannons captured at Waterloo. The architect was G. L. Kennedy.

South of the 1951 block a new court has been created (1956) with the neo-Grumboldian Johns Building of 1936 facing a fifteenth-century cottage at the back of the Trumpington Street and Silver Street shops, carefully brightened with whitewash and black paint. A utilitarian addition to Johns Building (1952) in the angle with Silver Street effectively hampered the success of this court.

The major work carried out since 1965 has been the joint development of the King's Lane area with King's College to the design of Fello Atkinson of James Cubitt and Partners (see page 31).

St. John's College i

525 undergraduates, 177 postgraduates, 96 fellows.

Not surprisingly for a foundation of its size, St. John's has been building on a massive scale over the past 30 years. Maufe's large development of Chapel and North Courts in 1938–9 was perhaps the best of the semi-modern in Cambridge. It is carefully analysed by Pevsner (*Cambridgeshire*, pp. 130–1). For the Backs a comprehensive landscaping plan was prepared in 1951 by Dr. Thomas Sharp, better known as a town planner. The death of the trees leading from the Grumbold bridge to Queens' Road gave Dr. Sharp the opportunity to open up the view of Rickman's 'wedding cake' from Trinity Library. Otherwise he respected the existing layout. To the west of Rickman, contrasting with the nearby Wilderness, Dr. Sharp created a new formal garden, with shrubs selected by the landscape architect, Sylvia Crowe. The Garden Shelter added in 1954 was designed by David Roberts. It has a tubular frame and copper roof.

Drastic restoration has been carried out since 1957 of Second and Third Courts. The kitchen and buttery block has been reconstructed from ground level with facings of a particularly loud red brick, specially made at Reading. Re-used Tudor bricks of a sensitive dark brown have been used on the Second Court façade of the Shrewsbury Tower, which has been reconstructed from first-floor level with Reading brick facing Third Court. On the ranges either side of the gateway, both bricks are used: red in the gables and brown in the main walls, with purple Dorking bricks on the plinth. This restoration, Cambridge's largest since the war, has respected neither the intrinsic merit of Second Court's architecture nor the texture of mature brickwork.[1] The interior of the hall, however, was pleasantly redecorated (1963) by S. E. Dykes Bower in harmony with Clayton and Bell's work of 1868.

St. John's have now turned to the development of the large area behind New Court, towards Magdalene, part of which was recently acquired from Merton College, Oxford. Several architects were considered, Denys Lasdun submitted a design, and finally Powell and Moya (famous for their Pimlico housing, Chichester theatre and Swindon hospital) were chosen. They have provided a memorable building on this demanding site. In connection with this, the remarkable late twelfth century Norman

School of Pythagoras is being converted by Alec Crook to form a first floor hall for music and drama, and large area below for entertaining.

Cripps Building

Between New Court and Magdalene.

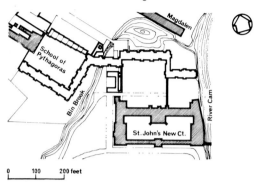

Date.	1963–6
Architects.	Powell & Moya
Contractor.	John Laing Construction Ltd.
Cost.	£1,000,000 (a single benefaction)

Requirement. Rooms for 191 undergraduates, eight fellows' sets, new J.C.R. and seminar rooms; squash courts and workshops.

Description. Lying between Rickman's 'wedding-cake' and Lutyens's red-brick building at Magdalene, the building has been laid out as a continuous, bent ribbon, stretching from the river in the east to the School of Pythagoras in the west. In doing so, it forms two three-sided courts, with the white brick back of New Court at one end, and with the School of Pythagoras at the other. Framing the east side of the western court is the single-storey J.C.R. building, which looks westwards onto a terrace and a grass slope down to Bin Brook, a tributary of the Cam. Bin Brook passes under the main building and, before joining the Cam, flows into a new lake, formed between the Lutyens building and the Cripps building. Here, there are two landing stages and moorings for punts. There is pedestrian access both from New Court and from Northampton Street:

---

1. Admittedly, few original bricks existed, as the core is of rubble, and certainly the new Clipsham stone dressings are a fair exchange for the stucco patching of 1793.

43

Cripps Building, roofscape

at this end there is also a car-park for 48 cars. At the Northampton Street entrance, at the opposite side of the building from the J.C.R., is a porter's lodge: here, too, is a ramp leading to the basement cycle sheds and boiler rooms. The building is four-storeyed throughout, with a roof terrace and an additional penthouse. Along the ground floor is a continuous promenade, sometimes the whole width of the building, and sometimes backed by ground floor rooms. The promenade is punctuated by large, Portland stone-faced column-ducts within which are reinforced concrete L-shaped structural piers. The rooms are organized round eight staircases—the traditional Cambridge layout which has yet to be faulted. A single flight leads to a half-landing where it divides and two half-flights rise in opposite directions, to serve two more landings giving access to four rooms each. From one of these landings, a single flight rises to the half-landing above, where the pattern is repeated, and only the final flight to the roof terrace does not divide in this manner. The typical floor consists of six sets and two study–bedrooms: of these, the end room runs the width of the block, the two middle rooms have large square bay windows (giving additional east and west light for those facing north), and the study–bedrooms are on one side only, having the desirable outlook. In the case of the sets, the bedrooms are divided by sliding screens which are covered with hessian to give pin-board space. There is a shower, a bath and a gyp-room to every four rooms. On two staircases there are fellows' sets: each set has a small hall into which the living room, study, bedroom and kitchen all open. The penthouse bedrooms are reached by a steep stair internal to some of the third floor rooms. Between and above each pair of penthouses are lead sheathed water-tanks.

The construction consists of the reinforced concrete piers and in situ floor slabs with a white flint aggregate finish where they are exposed. Window mullions are white polished concrete, and the windowframes are bronze, with lead spandrel panels below. External walling, for example at the promenade-side of the ground floor rooms, is in Roachbed Portland stone with Whitbed Portland stone quoins. Internal finishes include rough-textured plaster and wood-block flooring: under-floor heating is used to provide background heat, and each room has a fan-assisted storage heater.

The J.C.R. building is L-shaped; at the far end, bounding the southern side of the terrace is a seminar room. A covered way connects both rooms to the promenade. The J.C.R. is finished inside in hardwood boarding, with a carpeted floor. There is much black leather upholstery and soft spot-lighting to create atmosphere; three roof-lights in the form of truncated pyramids in the northern arm help define smaller spaces within the room.

The squash courts and workshop building is entirely separate, at the north-west corner of the School of Pythagoras. It is reached by a path bounding the north side of the western court. Three warehouse-like glazed roofs cover the squash courts; internally there is a first-floor spectators' gallery.

Comment. The most exciting feature of this new building is the way in which it has been fitted into this difficult site. Powell and Moya have made a virtue out of necessity and have managed to fulfil the promise of their first sketches. Much of the success is due to the repetition of each staircase unit time and again, so that in unfamiliar situations, this remains a point of reference. How different this is from the straining at picturesque effects and the development of the particular situation without reference to the whole, which characterizes many other Cambridge buildings (is it unfair to instance the King's Lane Courts, which make an interesting comparison?) At the same time there is considerable, necessary articulation provided by the expression of each room, reflecting a rational arrangement of different room types around each staircase. Then, too, there is the successful use of landscaping to provide variety within the framework: perhaps best of all is the punt lake dividing the building from Magdalene, but the exploitation of Bin Brook or the retention of the existing trees in the western court are equally praiseworthy for their simplicity and broad scale. Only the eastern court, facing the prison-like white brick rear of New Court is, in contrast, austere and almost forbidding.

Inevitably, there are reservations. One of the most curious features is the means of access. The broad promenade implies an east/west link route through the college. Indeed, the eastern end seems poised to leap across the Cam (there would seem to be some point in allowing the same architects to develop the Master's Lodge site and create a new Bridge of Sighs). How odd it is, then, to discover that the western access is half way along the length of the building, that the west end of the building peters out at Merton Hall, and that the eastern access is through

Cripps Building, with punt lake in foreground

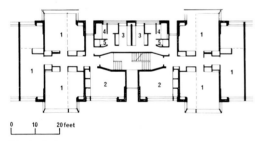

0 10 20 feet

Typical plan
1 Undergraduate set **2** Undergraduate study-bedroom
3 Gyproom **4** Bathroom **5** Shower

a very tortuous passage from New Court. Then there is the question of the massive hollow columns, which, to the casual observer, appear to keep the whole building up. It is a disturbing irrationality that within the rooms, these columns are displaced by cupboards and basins and that the structure is in fact an L-shaped pier, not even expressed within the room. Their size cannot be justified by calling them service ducts for each column cannot surely contain so many pipes. There are other criticisms of detail, too. The penthouse rooms are in the one part of the building which curiously aims at overtly picturesque effects. They are, of course, a repetitive unit, like the

staircases, and it was felt that a broken sky-line was needed to harmonize with the existing buildings. But was there really a need for the kind of sculptural effects aimed at, which is not entirely in accordance with the drier detailing of the rest? As for the arrangement of the rooms, in itself rational, one is tempted to question the differences between the room types. There does not seem to be any significant reason for this, other than the concept of variety for its own sake. It underlines the fact that all too little is known about student needs or the way in which the rooms are used.

But the biggest question this building poses, as do the three new colleges, is this: was there a real understanding by client and architect of the basic assumptions behind such a building as this? It has been built at great cost of beautiful materials to last a long time; by its very nature it reinforces the glorious tradition of Cambridge, and in so doing it has fossilized a situation irrevocably that in the not so distant future may seem intolerable. Let us be clear that this is a building of which St. John's and Cambridge can be proud and which will be visited, and rightly admired, by many people. Let us also be clear that the attitude which created this building may ultimately accelerate Cambridge's decline.

Sidney Sussex College new building: model

Sidney Sussex College   f

242 undergraduates, 32 postgraduates, 38 fellows.

There has been little new building at Sidney Sussex, except for a boathouse, shared with Corpus Christi College (see page 116). In 1948–50 the kitchens were reconstructed by Basil Ward. The porter's lodge, by the main gateway, was remodelled in an institutional manner in 1958 by H. H. Parker. In 1954, restoration of Wyatville's two courts started under the direction of Marshall Sisson with the misguided replacement of stucco with Ketton and Weldon stone on the chapel front. The heavy stonework loses all Wyatville's frivolous Gothick atmosphere. Fortunately the stucco has been renewed properly in the wings facing the street (1962–3). The redecoration (1959) by the bursar and two fellows of Burrough's and Essex's fine Georgian hall interior is one of the most successful works of its kind in Cambridge. The latest addition to the college, at present under construction, is a new undergraduate block at the corner of Malcolm Street designed by Howell, Killick, Partridge & Amis. It is described below.

New Buildings

Between Garden Court and Malcolm Street.

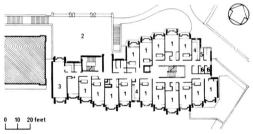

0 10 20 feet

First floor plan
1 Undergraduates **2** Terrace over common room
3 Fellow's set **4** Gyproom **5** Shower **6** Bathroom

Date.   1967–

Architects.   Howell, Killick, Partridge & Amis

Contractor.   Marshall-Andrew Ltd.

Cost.   £325,000

Requirement. 65 rooms for undergraduates, four fellows' sets, common rooms, and a caretaker's flat.

Description. In this irregularly shaped, five-storeyed block, the rooms are placed in echelon and swell in and out around the staircases. Nearest Garden Court, the rooms face south only and the swelling is slight, around a staircase and entry on the north side. The main staircase is placed centrally and the rooms are double-banked around it, overlooking the college garden to the north. Here the swelling is more marked. The vertical divisions are marked by pairs of inward-bending brick ribs, each pair embracing a single window on each floor. The deep-splayed window reveals and the spandrel panels are to be of lead. At the eastern end are the fellows' sets, one to a floor which run the full width of the building. Also at the eastern end is a one-storey common-room block, projecting northward into the gardens, which is reached from a cloister in front of Garden Court. Over it is a terrace reached by an external staircase; there is also a door leading off it into the building. The arrangement of the rooms seems a good one, and should provide an interestingly modelled exterior. What is rather disturbing is the vertical emphasis of the brick ribs and the general bulkiness of the exterior. Surely such a highly sculptural building is questionable on this restricted site. Its relationship to Malcolm Street and Ivor Smith's King Street project (see page 68) is also unresolved. It can only be hoped that, in practice, it works out.

Trinity College   j

654 undergraduates, 192 postgraduates, 109 fellows.

Trinity, Cambridge's largest and perhaps most influential college, has also had the worst recent building history.

Bevan Hostel (1949, architect Ian Forbes) occupies an obscure site in Green Street with no problems of 'keeping in keeping'. Yet it is a fussy little house with 18 bed-sitters, pale rusticated brickwork and a heavy mansard roof. It cost £28,000.

In 1954, Powell and Moya were commissioned to design a building for the derelict Brewhouse site (next to Garret Hostel Lane). The plan was narrowly approved by the college council, never implemented and is still unpublished. Judging by this firm's outstanding reputation and its later work for Brasenose and St. John's (see page 43) it is regrettable that this project should never see the light of day. It is still more regrettable that its alternative should have been Angel Court (see below).

Restoration has been carried out in New Court, the north and east sides of Great Court, the hall and Nevile's Court by H. C. Husband & Co. They have also been responsible for the reconstruction of the kitchens (the old kitchen is now a private dining room) and the restoration of Bishop's Hostel. A reading room has been added to the library by Donald Macleod. It is a pleasant series of irregular spaces punctuated by square columns, and rooflit. The fellow's parlour has been redesigned by Anthony Mauduit. Sir Albert Richardson was responsible for the cleaning and whitening of the ante-chapel, and in 1963 the rest of the chapel was whitened, in place of poor Victorian murals.

In 1965, Trinity launched an appeal, not only to finance work then being undertaken and the restoration of the Wren Library, but also for the development of the 'Matthew's' site, south of Whewell's Court, the Brewhouse site and Burrell's Field. The Architects' Co-Partnership is preparing designs for the first of these; but over the other two, the college is remaining secretive. It is to be hoped that these three sites will redeem Trinity's past record.

Elsewhere in Cambridge, Trinity have built nine graduate flats by Eric Lyons in Newton Road (1966–7) and sports pavilions by Lyster & Grillet in Grange Road. They were also responsible for commissioning the Conran Design Group to suggest a colour scheme for Nos. 1–7 Bridge Street (see page 70).

Angel Court

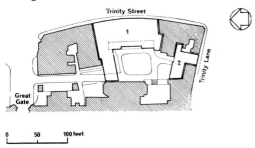

Trinity Street

Trinity Lane

Great Gate

0   50   100 feet

1 Undergraduates' rooms (large block)
2 Undergraduates' rooms (small block)
Shaded areas indicate existing buildings

Trinity, Angel Court

Date.	1957–9
Architects.	H. C. Husband & Co., Sheffield. R. Broadbent and J. E. T. Littler, architects-in-charge
Contractor.	Youngs of Norwich
Cost.	£170,000
Requirement.	Rooms for 50 undergraduates.

Description.   Angel Court occupies a 100 ft wide strip between the back of Great Court and Trinity Street, a site first suggested for a court (five-storey) in 1899. Husband's design meticulously preserves the four-storey Georgian brick façades of Trinity Street and their ground floor shops. These have rear pedestrian access at basement level and the ventilation space for this projects into the Court behind as a podium. Over and behind this rises the main block of three floors of undergraduate rooms, planned on the corridor system with a staircase at each end. The upper floors have fine views towards King's and Trinity Library. The steel frame is threaded down through the shops below. Secondary three-storey blocks join up with the stuccoed (1833) lecture room building at the back of Great Court which had been remodelled from the string-course upwards by David Roberts in 1953–4. Facing materials are specially selected red brick, with Ketton stone for the south-east staircase and for the bow-window above the arched entrance from the northern forecourt. A quarter of the accommodation is in two-room sets, the rest being bed-sitters, of which a few

are used as fellows' teaching rooms. The court has been laid out with stone paving, lawns and flower-beds.

Comment.   Cambridge's largest college, the patron of Wren, went to a firm of Sheffield engineers for its first important new building this century. Angel Court is a monument of subtopian banality. Its mildly semi-modern brick buildings with their windows of semi-Georgian pattern show no particular confidence in either style.

A valid and illuminating comparison can be made with David Roberts's similar conversion work at Magdalene (see page 35). Roberts's buildings are married subtly on several levels to the old shops; Husband's completely smother them and have little organic relationship with Great Court. Roberts provides straightforward structural materials as a foil to the equally direct ancient materials; Husband decks out his design with ornamental criss-cross ironwork, little plaster star patterns and a large irrelevant coat of arms. The mawkish sculpture is by David Wynne.

The landscaping of Angel Court, with its flowerbeds and artistic stone steps, is worthily municipal. The interior of the staircases and the furnishings of the rooms are institutional and dull. One corner of the Court is filled with a massive 10 ft high curved wall which looks as if it might conceal dustbins. As can be seen from the upstairs rooms, it does.

Angel Court is not the fault of its architects—they clearly did what they were asked to do. The responsibility lies squarely on Trinity's dons.

Trinity Hall   k

315 undergraduates, 73 postgraduates, 41 fellows.

Trinity Hall has fortunately preserved and enhanced its delightfully intimate scale. Sir Albert Richardson's bursary in North Court (1949–51) successfully fills the gap between Sir Giles Scott's two pre-war blocks. It has a plain façade with tripartite Ketton stone windows; its rear, towards Garret Hostel Lane, has brown brick pilasters and virtually no windows. But Sir Albert's single-storey rooms in South Court are sadly artificial in their neo-Georgian details and did not blend with the court until 1963, when it was thoroughly cleaned and whitewashed.

Alec Crook's river terrace of 1957, with its formal walls and seats is a successful termination of the picturesque and informal gardens. W. F. Haslop of Rattee and Kett supervised the cleaning of Waterhouse's South Court building in 1961–2 and in 1965 the hall was repainted. At present Trevor Dannatt's interesting new senior combination room has gone up on a narrow site south of the hall. Finally, in 1962 a boldly modelled bronze sculpture by the local John Smith was placed in North Court; it fits in surprisingly well with Scott's and Richardson's brown brickwork. Trinity Hall's latest new building is going up on their Wychfield site, west of Fitzwilliam. This is a promising design by Philip Dowson of Arup Associates.

New Combination Rooms

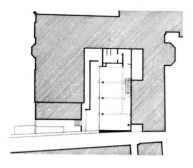

Date.   1963–5

Architect.   Trevor Dannatt

Contractor.   Coulson & Son Ltd.

Trinity Hall new Combination Rooms: roof terrace

Cost.   £30,000

Requirement.   New Combination Room, parlour and terrace.

Description.   The old, single-storey S.C.R. (1892, by Grayson and Ould) had become inadequate and Trevor Dannatt was selected to design a replacement largely on the strength of his Laslett House interior (see page 189). The site is south of the hall and east of the Master's Lodge; it is largely enclosed and very cramped, but it proved adequate to provide a generous Combination Room on the ground floor and a parlour above, with an adjacent roof terrace. The lower room is used for dinners, meetings and various social occasions, and has a table placed on the long north–south axis. Three reinforced concrete beams span the short dimension and are supported by columns on the west side; the beams cantilever beyond to form a glazed bay running the full length of the room. This bay space is divided horizontally by a concrete slab above head level which helps screen the room from overlooking windows and creates an interesting subspace. Spanning between the reinforced concrete beams are joists of Oregon pine between which are randomly-placed lights, shielded by louvres. Along the east wall is the leisurely flight of stairs to the parlour which is used as a relaxation area, and contains the famous Port Table of 1838. Internally, the walls are plastered and white painted; on both floors there is hardwood boarding. The upper walls are faced in pale brown brick. A brick wall protects the building from the Master's Lodge, and the narrow patio it forms has been richly planted.

Comment. The exterior of this excellent little building is hardly visible from the outside, but displays characteristic Dannatt motifs—the brick cladding of the walls, long box-like chimneys and windows wrapped around the corners. But for all that it is hardly visible, it is well worth visiting for its delightful interior spaces which show sensitive handling in difficult circumstances. The use, for example, of the slab to create a lowered bay zone helps the modulation from interior to exterior space, and the patio becomes an effective part of the interior, rather than a grubby little court outside. If the lighting of the combination room seems just a little artful in comparison with the rest of the building it provides a pleasant and lively light which enhances the space. Dannatt also chose the furnishings which are agreeably unostentatious, like the rest of the building.

Planning for Science: C
The New Museums site

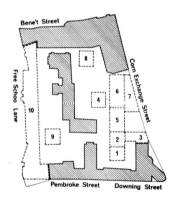

Site-plan with November 1962 proposals

1 Zoology (2 storeys) **2** Zoology (5 storeys) **3** Zoology (2 storeys + basement) **4** Mathematics (10 storeys) **5** Mathematics laboratory (5 storeys) and Physics (10 storeys), total 15 storeys **6** Metallurgy (5 storeys) **7** Metallurgy (1 storey + basement) **8** Physics (5 storeys) **9** 15 storeys **10** 4 storeys

Those of us who still adhere to that passionate discovery of English architectural philosophers a century ago, that the quality of buildings is closely related to the quality of thought and organization,

even of morality, of the society which produces them, are floored completely by the dark and sordid muddle which is the physical expression of Thomson, Rutherford and Cockcroft. Why did Cambridge science, or even Cambridge physics by itself, not reflect in its labs and lecture theatres some of the lucid passion of experiment that possessed those for whom they were built? The Cavendish's most recent Nobel prize winners, the molecular biologists Kendrew and Crick, used to work in conditions of cramp and confinement in a group of prefab huts scattered round the Austin Wing. They have now moved out to the new Addenbrooke's site (see page 82). Only now does the rest of the Cavendish seem to be emerging from years of squalor and uncertainty.

In December 1965 Professor Deer presented his report on the long-term needs of the scientific departments: this called for the transfer of physical sciences to the vast western Cambridge site, for which a plan has now been prepared by Matthew, Johnson-Marshall & Partners (see page 183; and for the immediate preparation of a plan of the Addenbrooke's site, see below). This would in effect liberate the New Museums site for logical redevelopment, and Stage I, now under construction, was designed by Philip Dowson of Arup Associates. But the prehistory of this redevelopment has been a long and stormy battle.

This site was already built up by 1910. The 1930's added two good 'early modern' buildings, the Workshop and Mond Laboratory by H. C. Hughes, and saw the rebuilding of Zoology by Murray Easton. Since 1945 there have been several minor alterations. The Physical Chemistry extension of 1952 is a small work by Basil Ward (of more recent fame at Oxford). In 1958–9 the Shell Company donated a four-storey block for Chemical Engineering, sited so as to close the courtyard formed by the earlier Zoology buildings by the same architect, Murray Easton. The building is concrete framed with an infill of golden yellow brick. Easton's architecture, while fairly fresh and uncomplicated, has declined since the 1930's, as can be seen here. In 1959–60 Alec Crook designed yet another storey to be stuck on top of the already overtall Austin Wing. Next, in 1960–1, an extra storey was added to the southern end of the old Chemical Laboratory (now Metallurgy). This addition, faced expensively but insensitively in Ketton stone, is horridly visible from such nearby spots as St. Botolph's Churchyard. Lastly, in 1961–3, with the comprehensive redevelopment plan in the offing, a massive reconstruction on the cheapest lines was carried out on the Cavendish and the H.T. Laboratory next to it, by Alec Crook again. The rebuilding created a whole new teaching wing which was incorporated in Denys Lasdun's master plan.

Lasdun's plan was originally published in May 1961 and almost immediately rejected by both city and county on grounds of over-congestion on the site, the height of the three towers (two of 205 ft for Physics), and the lack of relationship to either city or university overall plans. Revisions made in November 1962 met many of the criticisms. Physics was to be removed to Addenbrooke's, and only one tower (Mathematics, 13 storeys, 151 ft) remained. The rest of the buildings (see plan) were of four and five storeys, with basement and sub-basement for parking and services. Vertical segregation of pedestrians and vehicles would ease congestion enormously. Within the concrete-framed buildings there were to be no permanent partitions, with all vertical circulation in a series of external towers. On the Maths tower these rose as eight pinnacles, giving a richly moulded silhouette. The external concrete finish was to be an exposed aggregate of light-coloured stone. Altogether the scheme, with its open, flexible spaces and attractive upper level 'hanging courtyards' for pedestrians showed Lasdun at his best. Possibly the Kahnian aesthetic of the tower had led to too great a compromise with the medieval. Meanwhile, with planning permission still withheld, Physics has taken over the Examination Schools, which were refitted by Alec Crook (1964–5).

The university put forward Mr. Lasdun's third scheme at a public inquiry in February 1964. By this time, the Cavendish Laboratory had decided to move elsewhere: not only was there too little room for expansion but tower blocks would have been quite unsuited for the needs of Physics. The towers for the remaining departments were to be of 95 ft and 110 ft (only 23 ft higher than the existing Austin Wing). Two of them were to be in the first stage, nearest Corn Exchange Street. At the end of this inquiry, the county was still opposed to the plan, and Denys Lasdun retired. To carry on the detailed planning, Philip Dowson was appointed. His first building for Zoology, Mathematics and Metallurgy, will be only some 75 ft high and was started in 1966. It follows the general outlines of Lasdun's proposals, which, so it is now said, were never supposed to be more than an outline.

The Downing site   D

If the Cavendish is a medieval slum, the Downing site is the scientific equivalent of the Peabody tenements. The first grey stirrings of enlightenment are shown in the overall layout of formal courtyards which, however, bear little relation to the functions and needs of their inhabitants. From 1906 onwards, big blocks of elephantine scale arose in every style imaginable. Because the plan was so irrelevant and the buildings so inflexible, hutment extensions soon appeared to clutter the ornamental courtyards long before the permanent buildings had all been erected. If it were not for the fact that so many of the same errors have recently been repeated, albeit in a different guise, both in the Chemistry Laboratories and on the Sidgwick Avenue development (see page 174), it would surely be unnecessary to repeat that flexibility, flexibility and flexibility are the only three real criteria for the architecture of university teaching and research. There are obvious modern solutions using broad concrete frames, non-loadbearing and easily demountable walls and standardization of parts that make conversion and extension convenient and aesthetically satisfying.

The Downing site has had four additions since the war. T. S. S. Dale's Public Health Laboratory of 1950, at the southern end of the site, is a mild little two-storey brick building in a symmetrical semi-Georgian, semi-modern manner. Close to it is J. Murray Easton's Veterinary Anatomy building, a five-storey extension to his successful Anatomy building of 1938. To the south-east is the new Psychology building of 1961–3 by Alec Crook, a big three-storey utilitarian lump in pink brick. The copper clad top floor added to the adjoining block is quite impressive. Finally, in 1962–3, has appeared the pleasant building with the title 'Biochemistry Stage III'. It deserves special treatment.

The Addenbrooke's site E

One of the recommendations made by the Deer Report was that the most urgent need, apart from Physics, was for more Biochemistry, and it would be best sited on the old Addenbrooke's Hospital land, the first part of which becomes available to the university in 1968. To this end, Philip Dowson of Arup Associates, who had already designed the first stage of the New Museums site (see above), proposed a report for the development of the whole site, and for the Biochemistry building in particular, which was published in 1966.

The development of the site has almost as involved a history as the New Museums site. Already in 1955, Richard Sheppard carried out preliminary researches for the university in land use here, but in 1962 Peter Chamberlin, planner of Leeds University, the Barbican and designer of New Hall, was appointed architectural overlord of all the university's science sites, to work in collaboration with Sir Leslie Martin and with the appointed architects for the Cavendish (then Lasdun) and Mill Lane (Howell). This bore no fruit, however, and nothing further happened until the publishing of the Deer Report in 1965. It was subsequent to this that Philip Dowson was adopted as architect, and it will mean that both sites will be developed consistently with each other.

Their project was evolved on a grid plan, comparable to their laboratories at Loughborough, Birmingham and, of course, the Mathematics and Metallurgy building. Here, the grid consists of major bays which will be the laboratories and minor bays between, which take all the services and circulation. Vertical services will be accommodated in the width of the columns, but circulation and horizontal services will occupy the full width of each minor bay and will alternate.

The first part of the site to be relinquished by the hospital is at the southern end and this will extend northwards until the main buildings are handed over in 1980. Tennis Court Road will be used both as a service road for the site and as a pedestrian and cyclist link between all the sites. Main access points will occur at the north end of the site and to the north of the first phase. In the report, the architects state the importance of the Trumpington Street row of houses which they propose to retain, and behind it, the new buildings will not rise much above the existing sky-line, with a maximum of four floors.

The plan should produce a sensitive and flexible group of buildings and provide Cambridge with its best set of laboratories. The attempt to relate the building to the existing scale of development is admirable: it is to be hoped that the final result will have the clarity of the report.

The Mill Lane site F

The removal of the University Press to the suburbs has released this valuable site for university use. The Press are keeping the Pitt Building in Trumpington Street (Blore's Freshers' King's Chapel) for prestige offices, which were remodelled by Lyster & Grillet 1964–5, but everything behind, down to Laundress Lane, will be cleared. In 1961, the university appointed Howell, Killick, Partridge & Amis to draw up plans for the area, but so far nothing has come of this. Instead, Alec Crook has converted the premises to provide accommodation for Mathematics and Theoretical Physics, for Pure Mathematics, for the Department of Engineering, pending the completion of their buildings, and for the Board of Research Studies.

Laboratories for Mathematics, Metallurgy and Zoology

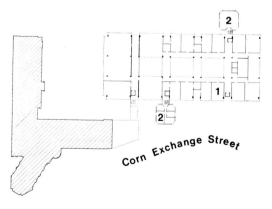

1 Laboratories 2 Offices

Mathematics and Zoology laboratory, model

Date.	1966–8
Architect.	Philip Dowson of Arup Associates
Contractor.	Trollope & Colls, in association with William Sindall Ltd.
Cost.	£1,522,010

Description. Because of the proximity of Lion Yard, this building was designed in close consultation with Gordon Logie, the city architect, and the result is a building which will both serve as an efficient laboratory and relate to its future neighbours. It has been raised on an *in situ* concrete podium, 12 ft above ground level, and at the same height as the proposed Lion Yard podium. Below this level are the Zoological Museum and workshops. On Corn Exchange Street are unloading bays, ultimately to be a part of the whole Lion Yard servicing area, but at present to be served from street level. The main pedestrian access is from the deck level, above which will rise a precast concrete structure of four floors. The design is divided into a grid of major and minor bays, which will take the laboratory spaces, and services and circulation respectively. The width of the building increases from 76 ft to 100 ft, on the top floor, where additional lighting and ventilation is provided by three internal courts. These also provide a valuable amenity in an area badly lacking in open space. There are offices in two 'satellite' towers to east and west, which plug into two of the main building's service bays. For every two laboratory floors, there are three office floors. This should prove a most acceptable solution and provide the basis for a rational development of this muddled site. The plan shows a lucidity of thought which will surely make a fitting environment for Cambridge's scientists.

Biochemistry Stage III

Date.   1962–3

Architects.   Hammett & Norton

Contractor.   Kerridge Ltd.

Cost.   £330,000 (including equipment)

Description.   Grafted onto the back of Sir Edwin Cooper's 1923–4 building, the new four-storey wing provided by the Wellcome Foundation continues the same floor levels. It provides animal houses in the semi-basement. Part I teaching laboratories on the ground floor and two upper floors of research space. The penthouse contains ventilation and lift plant. The structure is largely of precast concrete. Pre-cast 'T' space frames at 4 ft 6 in centres span the full 48 ft width of the building and are carried on edge beams between *in situ* bush-hammered concrete columns at 9 ft centres. The tall windows on the north and south elevations have precast spandrels with exposed aggregate. The bare east wall is clad with storey-height precast panels, again with an exposed aggregate. The colour of the aggregate varies from light (east wall) to medium (spandrels) to dark (edge beams). Purple brick is used on the lift tower and in the concrete-canopied bicycle shed.

Comment.   This is an acceptable building, appallingly sited in the middle of a courtyard on the Downing site. However hard the architects have tried to use light-coloured reflective surfaces on this building, with much glass, the fact remains that it deprives the blocks around it of their fair share of natural light and views. In itself it has many virtues. Because of other architects' pre-occupation with brickwork, it has been left to Hammett and Norton to demonstrate in Cambridge the coming-of-age of concrete as a building material. Techniques of pre-casting and mass-producing large units under ideal factory conditions means not only that concrete can now weather as attractively as stone, but also that it can be produced with infinite flexibility of composition, texture and colour. These laboratories provide a good example of the surprising richness of texture which can be obtained with exposed aggregate panels. In addition, the windows here are boldly modelled, the opening panel at the top of each window being inset several inches, thus producing

the effect of corbelling each bay outwards. The bicycle shed is rather over-emphatic.

Chemical Laboratories   G

Lensfield Road.

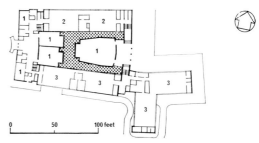

Ground floor plan
1 Lecture halls **2** Physical Chemistry
3 Organic and Inorganic Chemistry
Dotted area indicates enclosed open spaces

Date.   1953–60

Architects.   Easton & Robertson, Cusdin, Preston & Smith. J. Murray Easton, partner-in-charge

Contractors.   Stage I, Kerridge Ltd.; II and III, Rattee & Kett Ltd.; IV, Johnson & Bailey Ltd.

Cost.   Stage I, £972, 600; II, £831,000; III, £129, 000; IV, £405,000; Total, £2,250,000

Description.   Rehousing both Chemistry departments and the Statistical Laboratory, this building accommodates over 200 research students and teaching staff, and provides practical classrooms and lecture rooms for 500 undergraduates.
It is disposed round a single large courtyard which is itself entirely filled with three auditoria. The largest of these seats 450 and is entered through a low one-storey foyer to the east of the courtyard. The west block, with the main entrance, is built on a slight curve. It has a semi-basement and six storeys. In order, the functions are: basement, research; ground, seminar rooms and foyer leading to the two smaller (150-seat) lecture rooms; 1–3, research and

Chemistry laboratories: roof of large lecture hall

staff offices; 4, library, with picture-frame windows; 5 (slightly recessed), canteens and services. The north and south blocks contain research laboratories and practical classrooms.

The structure throughout is a steel frame, faced with brick, the most impressive feature being the 45 ft steel floor ribs that span the width of both wings. These leave the classroom spaces unobstructed by columns and allow the research space above to be flexibly partitioned. There are five lifts in the building. A stone sculpture at the north-west corner depicts alchemical symbols. All parking is outside, on ground level.

Next door, an extension to the Scott Polar Research Institute has been built by Hughes & Bicknell (1966–8) providing an extension to the library, laboratories, offices and workshops. Tucked behind the existing building to which it is linked by a two-storey entrance hall, it is an utterly unremarkable building built in pale brown brick. It does not draw attention to itself.

Comment. This is the largest and most complex building of its date in Cambridge, and one of the largest laboratories in Europe. On a straightforward functional level the buildings have so far been a marked success.

The form chosen—the covering of the site by connected buildings of medium height—was largely dictated by local planning regulations. The buildings face into an inner courtyard which is not merely aesthetically unpleasant as a rather grim light well, but also functionally wasted. Why couldn't the roofs of the auditoria have been used as a piazza at first floor level? They could have been planted with grass and even small trees, with out-door seats. The space could also have been used as an extra concourse to relieve pressure on internal spaces, for example, for conferences.

Even an imaginative piazza (as at Sheffield University) would not have outweighed the overall inflexibility and bleakness of these six- and seven-storey peripheral blocks. A tall tower might never have been accepted. However, Mr. Easton's other works prove that he likes big rectangular blocks arranged with a fair degree of symmetry, possibly as a result of a pre-1914 Beaux Arts type of training. A tower here would have released ground for better circulation, better all-round lighting, and better provision for the inevitable modification and expansion in the future. (For most chemists, unlike physicists, tower-top vibration does not matter.) Furthermore, a tower could have grouped well on the bottom with those of the Catholic Church.

The detailing throughout is monotonously conventional. Variations in detail are somewhat arbitrary: for example, the dramatic vertical windows, with stone fins and excessive use of different materials at the north-west and south-west corners, light a series of staff offices, not a grand staircase, as might have been expected. Above all, by its bulk and massive scale, pregnant for some future southward sprawl, this laboratory does great damage to the surrounding neighbourhood of small, intimate terrace houses. The site chosen was far too small. Chemistry should have gone beyond the Backs.

Engineering Laboratories H

Trumpington Street.

Site plan
1 Stage I 2 Stage II, central wing 3 Stage II, mechanics lab
4 Stage II, south wing 5 Stage III, north wing 6 Stage IV

Date. 1948 (Workshops), 1949–52 (Baker Building, Stage I), 1956–8 (Baker Building, Stage II), 1962–4 (Stage III), 1965–6 (Stage IV–Inglis 'A')

Architects. Easton & Robertson, Cusdin, Preston & Smith. J. Murray Easton, partner-in-charge. (Stages I–III). Cusdin, Burden & Howitt (Stage IV)

Contractors. Rattee & Kett Ltd.; William Sindall Ltd.; Kerridge Ltd.

Cost. Workshops and Baker Building (Stage I): £412,000. Stage II: £408,000

Requirement. Workshops and laboratories to accommodate the steady growth of the department up to c. 1970.

Description. The department of engineering, the largest in the university, commissioned plans from

J. M. Easton in 1945. They allow for an eventual floor area of 286,000 sq ft (compared with Chemistry's 238,000 sq ft) accommodating 1,000 undergraduates and 200 research students. The site is a small rectangle bounded by Scroope Terrace, Fen Causeway, Coe Fen and Peterhouse garden. The first building on the site, the Inglis Building next to Coe Fen, appeared in 1930–1. To it was added in 1948 a two-storey block of workshops facing Fen Causeway. It is a steel-framed structure and supports a low tower at one end which contains research rooms and the photographic darkroom. There is a decorative sculpture on the east wall by Siegfried Charoux and a mural in the students' entrance by Toni Bartl.

The Baker Building, the first half of the total redevelopment of the site, has been built in three stages. The main east wing, which is the administrative centre of the department, is 70 ft high (five storeys plus basement). The double-height ground floor, containing the entrance hall and a large lecture room, is partially divided by a mezzanine floor of offices above a covered car park. Upper floors contain three more lecture rooms, offices for teaching staff, two common rooms and a library. The top floor is used for research and the flat roof can be used for radar experiments. The right-hand part of the front curves slightly forward and then drops back to reveal the glazed sheath of the main staircase. The structure is a steel frame on a regular 11 ft grid, with concrete floors and $13\frac{1}{2}$ in solid external brickwork. Further laboratories have been added at the back of the Baker Building, and a south wing (research laboratories) and centre wing (offices) have been built. Stage III, the north wing, has recently been finished and forms a link with the Inglis building. Stage IV will be built in five sections, making 158,000 sq ft in all and replacing everything (including the 1948 workshops) west of the Baker Building, from which it will be separated by a central service road. The first part of Stage IV, the replacement for the Inglis building, has already been completed. The first plans for this stage, produced in 1961, were rejected by the planning authority on grounds of plot ratio, traffic circulation to Fen Causeway and the bulk of the buildings, some of which were multi-storeyed. In the accepted proposal, the same plot ratio (2:1) was kept but the building arranged in a dense four-storey complex not exceeding 48 ft. On the ground floor, there is considerable car parking space and the Structures Laboratory, with a mezzanine gallery, which is designed to withstand very heavy loads. Above the ground floor the building is curtain-walled; on the Coe Fen front, the top floor is stepped back. All the floors have artificial lighting, because of the depth of the building, with the exception of the top floor, which is roof-lit.

At the Trumpington Street entry to the laboratories is a curious sculpture designed by Kenneth Martin and built under the direction of Clive King at the laboratories. It consists of a series of aluminium box-sections arranged in a rippling, irregular cruciform, placed on a stone podium.

Comment. As with the same architect's Chemistry Laboratory, it is clear that an efficient job has been done, but as laboratory architecture this is fairly primitive stuff. Admittedly it is an advance on the Downing site: there are no giant colonnades, no meaningless friezes. But the general layout is not very different; large blocks of medium height, entirely closed in, with heavy brick facings, disposed around monumental courtyards. There is little flexibility or room for expansion, partly for geographical reasons, but partly because Mr. Easton's structure has little idea of modular planning and standardized prefabrication. The spectacular glazed staircase and the smoothly curved façade are gimmicks, of no particular functional relevance, and the sculptures are stuck on like postage stamps. The new Inglis building is a marginal improvement, with its curtain walling, and shows the influence of a more rational approach. It helps to lighten the mass of brickwork that clothes the Baker building. Curiously, underneath all this there is an engineering achievement of real interest; Stages II and III have been constructed according to Professor Baker's plastic theory, whereby a steel frame will support far more load than was previously thought possible. There is thus an economy of 30 per cent in structural steelwork in the Baker building. Stage III was worth visiting before brickwork covered it all.

School of Architecture Extension

Scroope Terrace.

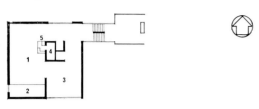

First floor plan
1 Lecture room **2** Speaker's platform (removable)
3 Criticism room **4** Rewind room **5** Projection pulpit

0   50 feet

Date.   1958–9

Architects.   Colin St. J. Wilson & Alex Hardy

Contractor.   Coulson & Son Ltd.

Cost.   £12,000

Requirement.   Exhibition and lecture space, tuition rooms.

Description.   The new two-storey block with its small garden lies at the back of the existing school in Scroope Terrace, and is overlooked by the Engineering Laboratory. It is approached through a passageway and a staircase which acts as a 'scrambler' of the change of floor levels, from three in the old building to two in the new. The extension has a square plan, built round a 9 ft 9 in square service core. The two floor heights are proportionately related (7 ft 6 in to 12 ft) as in the golden section. This perfection of modular geometry is carried through into every detail.

The ground floor contains four tuition rooms and a central staff common room. The upper floor is divided into a lecture room and a criticism room, but swing doors open to create a single exhibition space. The lecturer has press-button rooflight control. The structure is of loadbearing brickwork (second-hand fair-faced Cambridge stocks). The floor slab and roof beams are exposed concrete.

In the garden next to the extension an 'artificial sky'

School of Architecture extension

has been erected (1958–62) to the design of David Croghan. It consists of a geodesic dome, based on Archimedes' truncated icosahedron, with an outer skin of anodized aluminium and an inner skin of plastic through which light is diffused from 184 fluorescent lamps in the interdome space. The dome is used for teaching and research into levels of daylight in buildings by the study of models.

Comment.   Designed by two lecturers at the school, this was treated as a 'live project' with students doing the survey and working drawings. The instructional quality is emphasized by the exposure of all structural elements. Paint and plaster which normally cover inaccuracies and birthmarks of building are excluded and even bolt-holes for shuttering are left exposed.

To the architect, this building exudes geometric refinement. He will study the golden section, the modular relationships of shelf to blackboard to window. He will rejoice over the purity of the structure. The layman sees almost exactly the opposite: the deliberate (and very attractive) crudity of the massive brickwork, the rough-shuttered concrete and the self-consciously massive pulpit, which juts out into the lecture room and turns out to be merely a table for the slide projector.

The contradictions of this building are perhaps characteristic of the present state of intellectual architecture in England. It is a modular structure, using the mathematical relationships which are the basis of recent developments in mass produced schools and housing. Yet it is essentially a one-off job, with $13\frac{1}{2}$ in external brick walls and specially designed furnishings.

School of Architecture: projection pulpit in lecture room

Fitzwilliam Museum Extension

J

Trumpington Street.

Date. 1959, 1963–5

Architect. David Roberts & Partners

Contractor. Johnson and Bailey Ltd.

Cost. £100,000 (Stage I)

Requirement. Architecture and Fine Arts library, reserve galleries, reception and handling facilities, loan exhibition room, offices, work rooms.

Description. Only one side of Dunbar Smith's new court next to the Courtauld Gallery was completed (1924–36). Better facilities and more space have become increasingly necessary,[1] especially to house the Clarke and Beves bequests and an anonymous offer of 137 paintings and over 500 drawings, which is conditional on the building of an extension. It has been decided to build reserve galleries (accessible on request), and to have constantly changing exhibits in the main galleries.

In 1959 Grove Lodge was connected to the main building by a crescent-shaped corridor, designed by David Roberts. Mr. Roberts was then commissioned in 1961 to build from the south-west stump of the Courtauld Gallery, behind Grove Lodge and towards the Peterhouse tower. He has taken the set-back of Smith's wing behind the Courtauld gallery as a cue for a series of three square pavilions in echelon. They will be faced with precast units with a white stone aggregate. Stage I contains a ceramic reserve gallery and a receiving room on the ground floor. A monopitch roofed loading bay projects westwards. Above is the library, which is top lit. The deep waffle slab was specially designed in the sky dome at the School of Architecture, under David Croghan, to give even lighting. There is a large goods lift. Ground floor windows are of thick glass set directly into a grid of precast members. So far, only Stage I has been built.

Comment. David Roberts has proved before his skill at adding to existing buildings while retaining a positive character; and this pristine little cube is externally no exception. It is fortunate the Fitz-

Fitzwilliam Museum, extension with service entry

william was spared another dose of pomp and circumstance like the Dunbar Smith extension. Because of this, it is particularly unfortunate that the building itself has proved a considerable embarrassment. The brief for the reading room stated that it should have totally even, natural lighting and to that end, the highly complicated waffle slab with its deep reveals was designed. The end was achieved; and the result is disastrous. Instead of the variations of light and shade, which are essential, not only in giving interest, but in aiding concentration or focusing attention, there is here a monotony, which, apart from being quite unnatural, is totally unsuited for any purpose. Moreover, the effect could probably have been achieved much more simply with artificial lighting. Externally, it seems very curious that the openings are not more closely related to the grid of square precast panels: although the modulor has been used, it has not been used to give a really intelligible set of relationships. Maybe both these weaknesses will be cleared up in future stages.

---

1. In the main building the Watercolour Room was designed in 1955 by Robert Atkinson & Partners.

University Centre, across the river

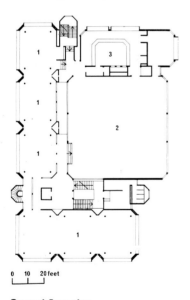

0 10 20 feet

Second floor plan
1 Common rooms **2** Dining hall **3** Servery

The University Centre   K

Granta Place.

Date.	1964–7
Architects.	Howell, Killick, Partridge & Amis
Contractor.	William Sindall Ltd.
Cost.	£320,000

Requirement. Graduate and staff club and centre for university entertaining and social life.

Description. The site, between the Mill pub and Little St. Mary's Lane is rather restricted, but offers superb views over both the upper and lower rivers. The building is four-storeyed and the principal rooms are on the upper three floors. On each of these three floors are six common rooms, three on the south side, and three on the west: these can be divided by sliding glass screens, across which curtains are drawn, to provide a variety of different spaces. Each of these common rooms is rectangular with splayed corners: externally, this results in three long, shallow bays on the south and west sides. Within these rectangles, the four hexagonal precast concrete columns, supporting a complicated roof structure, stand free. One set of three rooms is used as a small dining room. Behind the common rooms, on the second floor, is the main double-height dining-hall, which is covered by a timber pyramidal roof with pyramidal roof-light on top. Here, the structural columns stand within the thickness of the fair-faced blockwork walls. Below the hall are the kitchens. On the ground floor, are games rooms, a bar, cloak-rooms and offices. Under the southern end is a small car park. The entrance hall, running the full depth of the building, divides the two sets of common rooms, and lies at the south side of the hall. It is punctuated on the front by an external stair leading from the first-floor balcony to the roof terrace, but the main staircase is nearer the back. Another staircase at the northern end gives external expression to the corridor between the hall and the western set of common rooms. The southern and western sides are clad in Roach-bed Portland stone panels with the fixing bolts exposed. The long bay windows which project slightly beyond the face of the panels are sheathed in lead. Internally on the upper floors, except in the hall, many wall surfaces are plastered: there has also been considerable use of mirrors, on the splayed corners and at the back of the main staircase. Floors are wood block or carpeted. On the ground floor a dark yellow brick has been used inside and out: the lower half of the external walls are battered back to recess them behind the plane of the stone panels, from which they are divided by continuous clerestory.

Comment. There can be no question that the planning of this building is well worked out and admirably achieves its end. The common rooms, in particular, are eminently suited both as general common rooms, and, divided off, as rooms for private meetings and entertaining. Here, above all, the complicated structure seems to be a reasonable way of framing the space. Externally, the organization is expressed with clarity, and in this respect it is a pity that there is very little evidence of the hall, which internally is the major space. In relation to the existing buildings, the architects have successfully carried off a difficult operation. There was no possibility of 'harmonizing' with the diminutive Mill pub

University Centre, common rooms

or even developing the pattern it establishes, as the same architects have done at Darwin College (see page 149). By deliberately using large-scaled elements they have achieved a splendid contrast with the cottages behind and the adjoining pub. But there are criticisms, largely of detail, which mar this scheme. In spite of the much-exposed fixing bolts, the stone panels do not look very readily de-mountable, and together with the boldly expressed window cladding take on an almost structural significance which is misleading. This is not helped by the flower-boxes on the roof terrace which are clad in the same stone and have a monumental solidity. The same applies to the brick wall at ground floor with its battered sides; and even the clerestory does not break the illusion of a structural element. The battering has the added disadvantage of causing some curious window glazing. Internally, the simple decor of the hall and common rooms is sadly upset by an apparent inability to let well alone in the entrance hall. The stairs, with their lead-covered treads, the lights set into the underside of the concrete bearer, and the mirror-clad end wall disturb the basic attractiveness of the space created. The mirror-cladding, in particular, is an annoying device which sets the lavatory doors on the landings into sharp relief. There is, here, an overt attempt at modishness which is in conflict with a rational idea. Mercifully, the idea is still very much apparent.

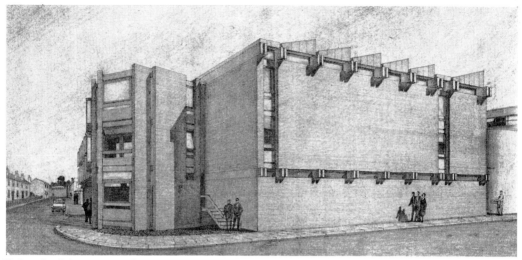

Union Society, proposed extension

Union Society

Proposed remodelling and extension.

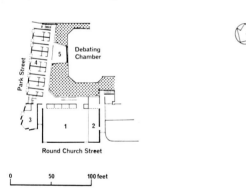

First floor plan
1 Multi-purpose hall 2 Stage 3 Clerk's maisonette
4 Visitors' bedrooms 5 Committee room
Dotted areas indicate enclosed open spaces

Proposed.   1962

Architects.   Howell, Killick, Partridge & Amis

Cost.   £142,000 (extension only)

Requirement.   Multi-purpose hall, guest bed-

L rooms, garages, clerk's flat, and new squash courts. Also reorganization of existing building.

Description. The remodelling of Waterhouse's 1866 building[1] can be carried out separately from the expensive extensions along Round Church Street and Park Street. It consists mainly of the replacement of the present staircase and well by a straight stair running up to the left of the main entrance to give direct access to the library. The gallery of the debating chamber would then be reached by way of an open exhibition area. Above the chamber existing store rooms could be converted into music rooms. Reorganization of the library would increase its importance and also open up the fine Waterhouse interior in the present stack room.

The new extension will be of loadbearing brick with exposed concrete beam ends on each floor. It is L-shaped (see plan) and surrounds the debating chamber, with a narrow courtyard between. On the Round Church Street side, opposite the new multi-storey car park (below), are squash courts as a semi-basement, with a two-storey hall above, to be used as a gymnasium or as a 200-seat auditorium. This will be roof-lit to avoid street noise. Facing Park Street are the bay windows of 18 bedrooms, nine on each floor, with private baths or showers, and covered parking spaces below. In the angle is the clerk's three-bedroom maisonette, above the

1. Which was restored in 1949 after war damage.

64

entrance to the extension. Next to the existing building will be lavatories and changing rooms; and in a wing on stilts across the courtyard will be smaller general purpose rooms for television and reading.

The Union may never carry out the project because the 150th anniversary appeal was not very successful. This is a pity, for such an excellent scheme could revitalize the society and make it more relevant to the present-day university. The planning is sensible and the architects have responded to Waterhouse's style with a wholesome brutalism. Only the small rooms straddling the L-shaped interior courtyard threaten to make it a depressing light-well.

City Churches

In spite of mutterings about redundancy, Cambridge's central parish churches have flourished since the war, apart from Bodley's All Saints, which, according to the Bishop of Ely's report on redundant churches (1958) will eventually be moved, stone by stone, to the suburbs. St. Clement's and St. Botolph's are also said to be redundant. St. Michael's has been converted into a parish hall and offices for Great St. Mary's to the designs of George Pace, the restorer of Llandaff Cathedral. His scheme, costing £10,000, is most ingenious. The chancel, with its fifteenth-century stalls, has been kept as a chapel, as has the Founder's Chapel on the south side. The Nave has been turned into the parish hall, with its stage platform on the south side and the audience at right-angles to the existing axis. Also on the south is a storeroom, and an upper floor with a club-room has been added; on the north will be the kitchen, cloak-rooms and offices. The chancel arch has been filled with a screen of re-used stock bricks in the centre of which is a timber-framed window with glazed doors below. The lights have been leaded in rectangular panes which provide sufficient enclosure for the chapel and the hall alike, while maintaining a sense of inter-communication.

Mr. Pace[1] carried out a complete interior redecoration of Great St. Mary's in 1960-1. Gilbert Scott's heavy Lightfoot reredos was removed from the high altar and, with the walls whitened, some statues and stained glass expelled and Hardman's east window of 1869 cleaned, the effect is now one of lightness and simplicity. Unfortunately Mr. Pace introduced his own idea of a reredos, a wooden carving of Christ in Majesty by Alan Durst, A.R.A., lathered in

gold leaf. This is neither large enough to dominate the church, as a Majestas should and as Epstein's sculpture for Mr. Pace at Llandaff magnificently does, nor small enough to avoid diverting attention from the altar, which has been given a fine abstract frontal, designed by Mr. Pace himself.

Four other central churches have been restored. Sir Albert Richardson redesigned the Victorian window tracery in the aisles of St. Edward's in 1946, and added heraldic glass by James Hogan of Powell's. St. Bene't's interior has been pleasantly whitened, spoilt only by the gilt baroque reredos to the side altar. Since 1959, Stephen Dykes Bower has been restoring Little St. Mary's beautiful interior, with a little too much whitewash and good taste. He has opened out the vaulted charnel house crypt in the south-east corner. Holy Sepulchre was restored in 1950 after war damage with an anaemic neo-Gothic east window from Gerald Smith's studio.

Street Furniture

It is now widely accepted that street furniture is as important in its effect on a town as the largest single buildings. In Cambridge, the Preservation Society (founded in 1927) has done much to prevent eyesores, but its function has been largely negative. In 1955-8, when the old street lamps in the centre of the city came to be replaced, the Society were consulted at length. Sir Albert Richardson, then P.R.A., was commissioned to design them.[1] The result is vertical cylinders which shine more brightly into bedrooms than onto streets, seated on fluted bronze columns of an old-world monumentality. However, since then the side streets (1959-62) have been lit by graceful and efficient light aluminium standards. Both these, and the timber-slatted litter baskets are Design Centre approved.

Public conveniences, built mainly in the early fifties, are pleasantly unobtrusive little brick buildings. A recent example (1961-2) on Victoria Avenue, is in the current brutalist vogue, faced with blue brick under an overhanging concrete roof slab. Bus shelters, erected in 1962-3, in Peas Hill, St. Andrew's Street and Sidney Street provide an excellent foil to surrounding buildings with their light and graceful steel framing. Equally successful was the widening of Park Street in 1962, with walls of re-used stock bricks and clear signposts using the Kinneir typeface seen on motorways.

1. Alec C. Crook has converted vestries from the west end of the south aisle, marked by a row of square windows outside, also in 1960-1.

1. Since he lived much of his own life by candlelight, he was hardly a rational choice.

Garret Hostel Bridge　　　M

Garret Hostel Lane.

Date.	1960
Architect.	Timothy G. Morgan of Guy Morgan & Partners
Structural consultants.	J. L. Kier & Co. Ltd., with T. V. Burrows (city surveyor)
Contractor.	J. L. Kier & Co. Ltd.
Cost.	£35,000

Requirement. Footbridge to replace Chadwell Mylne's cast-iron Gothic of 1837, to be capable of withstanding occasional motor traffic.

Description. The new bridge is higher and longer than the old one, with a clear span of 80 ft. The concrete portal frame is supported on a concrete hinge at one end and steel rollers at the other, a structure which minimizes the depth (only 1 ft 9 in at the crown). Embedded within the frame are two 8 in water mains and two 3 in ducts for electric cables. The concrete has an aggregate of Cornish granite, exposed by pneumatic hammering. However, the legs of the portal frame are concealed by walls faced in York stone, which is also used for the paving stones. The handrails are of satin-polished bronze.

Comment. The bridge was presented to the city by the Trusted family, who are connected with nearby Trinity Hall. The designer, Timothy Morgan, was an undergraduate at the school of architecture who died in 1960. We must be grateful that he was able to complete this, one of Cambridge's best post-war works of architecture.

The high-arched bridge is graceful, serene and beautifully constructed. With its clean lines and sparkling concrete finish it shows up most strikingly the clumsiness of Silver Street bridge upstream.[1] Only in the stone-clad pseudo-abutments are there signs of a desire to cover up engineering with a veneer of art. There has been some criticism of the slippery surface of the paving in wet weather. The steep pitch of the arch, however, is necessary to prevent it becoming a cyclist's speed track.

1. A design of 1932 by Sir Edwin Lutyens, resurrected in 1958–9 by the Ministry of Transport, complete with Portland Stone balustrade.

Multi-storey car park　　　N

Park Street.

Date.	1962–3, 1967–8
Architect.	De St-Croix of Truscon Ltd., with T. V. Burrows (city surveyor)
Contractor.	Truscon Ltd.
Cost.	£154,000

Requirement. Accommodation for 319 cars, being extended for 440.

Description Cambridge's first multi-storey car park is a five-storey structure, with a semi-basement on the Round Church Street side. There are thus 11 levels in all (of which the upper two are uncovered) opening alternately off the central ramps. It is entered and left by openings on the Park Street side. Pedestrians use the staircase tower there with its two lifts, or a smaller tower at the other end. The time-keeper's booth is manned from 7 a.m. to 1 a.m. The structure is a concrete frame, with a continuous slab forming ramps and floors. The sides are screened partly with precast railings of triangular section and partly with armour glass to waist level. The staircase towers are clad in red-brown brick, and the concave corner at the junction of Park Street and Round Church Street has precast panels with an exposed aggregate of large pebbles. The second stage of the car park is now being built, filling the U-shape to form a rhomboid plan.

Comment. As a first step in removing the private car from Cambridge's choked centre, this building must be unreservedly welcomed. As an individual structure, moreover, the Park Street car park has much to recommend it, with its use of Truscon's simplified concrete construction. It is a pity that an over-luxurious variety in facing materials has tended to disguise the simplicity. The railings are busily over-detailed; the brickwork is far too massive for its non-structural function; and the municipal lawn and shrub[1] on the pebble-faced concave corner are absurdly suburban in character. Ultimately more car parks of this kind will have to be built farther out, connected to the centre by an improved system of public transport. Although the

1. Which has since died.

Park Street car park

charges (1/– for 4 hours) are very reasonable, it is improbable that the Park Street park will be used fully until cars are proscribed in central Cambridge.

Lion Yard   O

This much-discussed area of Cambridge has remained in a state of flux ever since Sir William Holford's plan for the city was accepted by the Minister in 1954 (see page 10). The area in question is bounded by Petty Cury, Downing, Corn Exchange and St. Andrew's Streets. Any redevelopment would involve the demolition of the south side of Petty Cury, and the site includes St. Andrew's church, the Post Office and Fisher House, none of which are likely to be moved. At present, much of the site is cleared and used as a car park, a grey vacuum in the heart of Cambridge's commercial area. After an initial proposal in 1963, Gordon Logie, the city architect, produced a second solution which was embodied in the report of June, 1965, following the Minister's decision to cut the shopping space to 30,000 sq ft. As in the 1963 proposal, there is vertical segregation of traffic and pedestrians and again there is car-parking provided under the site. The main feature of the scheme is the pedestrian podium raised 12 ft above ground level, below which is the

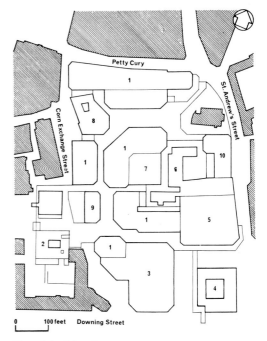

Plan at deck level

1 Shops **2** Mathematics and Zoology building **3** Large hall **4** Hotel **5** Department store **6** Post Office buildings **7** Library **8** Fisher House **9** Arts centre **10** Offices

car-parking and servicing area. (It is this podium which connects with the concourse in Philip Dowson's building for Mathematics and Metallurgy; see page 53.) The main road access to the site is along Emmanuel Street; and while Downing and St. Andrew's Streets are shown as open to traffic, it is intended to make Petty Cury, Wheeler Street and Market Hill pedestrian precincts. Pedestrian access to the podium is along the edge of St. Andrew's churchyard, by the side of Fisher House and through the range of shops along Petty Cury and St. Andrew's Street. Above the podium level, there is provision for a wide range of uses. At the southern end, there are two assembly halls and space for an hotel; at the centre of the site is the library and an Arts Centre. Shops flank the main pedestrian route running south at the west side of the site and over these there is residential accommodation and space for the university Music School, a new Y.M.C.A. building, and the International Centre for foreign students. From the sketches, the scale of this development should be excellent, but until more detailed plans are published, it is impossible to comment further. Preliminary plans for the assembly halls have been drawn for the city council by Llewellyn-Davies, Weeks, Forestier-Walker, & Bor; and the same firm has prepared for City Centre Properties a detailed design for the Petty Cury shops, the first phase is likely to be started in 1970.

The planning of traffic routes relates to Logie's plan for Cambridge published in 1966, and it suggests that the whole of central Cambridge could be a unified, largely traffic-free zone. The Minister, in 1967, named Lion Yard as one of several town centre schemes which would receive government support, so that it seems probable that it will now go ahead. But however admirable it is that the future of Lion Yard should for the first time appear settled, and however admirable the planning of the scheme is in itself, there is real doubt that it may still detract from the as yet unpublished proposals for development east of Parker's Piece, also prepared by Llewellyn-Davies, Weeks, Forestier-Walker & Bor. And the next problem that will face Cambridge is the relationship of the two developments.

King Street Redevelopment

North side of King Street.

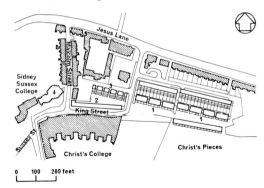

1 Three- and four-storey flats over parking area
2 Two-storey flats over shops 3 Three-storey flats over parking 4 Sidney Sussex new building

Designed. 1966

Architects. Ivor Smith Architects

Requirements. Stage I: 119 flats, seven shops, public house, car parking
Stage II: 112 flats, car parking

Description. King Street is a ramshackle but picturesque street of slightly seedy early nineteenth century shops, cottages and pubs, these latter being famed for the now forbidden 'King Street run'. To the north of King Street the land is owned by Jesus College who commissioned Ivor Smith to redesign the whole area. He considered the Malcolm Street and Jesus Lane terraces of the 1830s well worth preserving—as indeed they are—and turned his attention to the King Street housing. Because the site is bounded by open space—Christ's Pieces, Jesus College grounds, Midsummer Common—he felt a high density solution was acceptable. His proposals include closing King Street at Milton's Walk and diverting traffic back to Jesus Lane. West of Milton's Walk he has placed two rows of flats, one of three, and the other of two storeys. Both these are raised one floor over garages and shops on the King Street side. The rear block has a stepped section to give views over to Christ's Pieces, and between the two is a pedestrian deck. East of Milton's Walk, there is a similar arrangement, but the rear block is four storeys high and the lowest flat has a private court at deck level. A further two-storey block has been designed for the south side of King Street at this point. Unlike an earlier design, the scale is identical to that of the existing buildings and will fit well into its surroundings. There is unfortunately one snag to all this, which is that at the same time Christ's have commissioned Denys Lasdun to design an as yet unpublished scheme for the southern side of King Street and Howell, Killick, Partridge & Amis have designed a new residential block for Sidney Sussex on the corner of Malcolm Street (see page 47). How will these relate?—or will this be another corner of Cambridge fragmented by good intentions working at cross purposes?

Commercial Buildings

Apart from Bradwell's Court (described below), the quality of post-war commercial architecture in Cambridge's centre has been generally abysmal. The problem is basically one of planning. Unless some decisive contrary action is taken, the multiples will continue to pull down and amalgamate outworn cottage property so as to erect acres of uniform sales space. Dr. Thomas Sharp's plea for comprehensive redevelopment in small, intimately-scaled units is irrelevant, unless the large stores and multiples can be shifted either to Lion Yard or to City Road or to both. Only small shops can look like small shops.

The multiples, in crowded Sidney Street, have failed the city badly in their architecture. Much of it was done before the war. Woolworth's extended with three more semi-Tudor windows in 1959–60. Boots built (1959–61) a three-storey, Ketton stone-faced extension cruelly overlooking Holy Trinity Church to the designs of Colin St. Clair Oakes. The dashing window display of Wallis Shops underneath merely heightens the anachronism of the terrible minimum Tudor details. More recently, Marks & Spencer's next door to Woolworth's, have more than doubled their sales area by building a second floor at the rear and opening the first floor for sales. This was designed by Monro & Partners of Watford in 1966 and the new rear elevation on Hobson Street is in a lumpish neo-Georgian.

Worse still, because of its prominence, is Prudential House in St. Andrew's Street (1957–9), designed by F. J. Doyle, the company's staff architect, with the late Louis de Soissons, R.A., as consultant. The semi-Georgian façade sits in sublime alienation upon the broad expanses of plate glass beneath. De Soissons, in younger and wiser days, was the architect–planner of Welwyn Garden City. In fact, the Pru has a concrete frame underneath the dressing. The Post Office opposite has extended into the Lion Yard with the clean but colourless automatic telephone exchange (1962–3).

At 16 Trumpington Street, the Cambridge Building Centre opened in April, 1963, in converted premises, well designed by Cassidy, Farrington and Dennys, apart from the unnecessarily large shop window. It consists of a large enquiry hall leading through to an 80-seat meeting room, suitable for exhibitions. This is the first of a series of regional building centres set up by the parent body in London. Bursars might do well to consult it. The Building Centre are now engaged upon a further extension designed by T. F. Morris & Partners. Next to Bowes and Bowes, in Market Hill, the Bournemouth architects, Jackson and Greenen, have converted a Georgian house for the Leicester Temperance Building Society (1963–4). James & Bywaters, architects of Sherlock Close (see page 130) have designed a pleasant four-storey T-shaped block for Douglas January's offices in Downing Street which provides a lively façade between the Presbyterian Church and the Royal Insurance Group offices. It is faced on the first and second floors in Roachbed Portland stone panels (which surely must be *the* material of 1967) and aluminium windows. The top floor is set back and is clad in timber, while the ground floor is also recessed. Here, the exposed columns are clad in slate, and there is floor-to-ceiling glazing.

There remained one large gap in the centre, Mackintosh's site at the north-east corner of Market Hill, which lay empty for over a year. No. 9 Rose Crescent had also been demolished. The whole site is now occupied by Radcliffe Court, a part-residential, part-commercial development designed by Stanley R. Nevell & Partners. The maisonettes on the top two floors and the courts at the back (there is access through to Green Street) are pedestrian in the extreme. Mercifully, the city architect's department intervened in the design of the elevation on Market Hill, and the end result is suitable. Above the shops is a floor of offices, and above this are two floors of four maisonettes. The maisonettes are set in

Joshua Taylor Interiors, Bridge Street façade

echelon and face sympathetically back towards Market Hill, though seen from the Guildhall the effect is less successful than from Market Street. The façade is finished in white mosaic. 9 Rose Crescent has been cleverly rebuilt to match the rest of the row.

A second smaller gap—the site of the former New Theatre—has been plugged by Janus House (1964–6), a four-storey office block by Fitzroy Robinson & Partners. There are shops on the ground floor forming a one-storey annexe at the rear, with a roof-top car park. With its five bays set in echelon this is a lively addition to Regent Street.

Next door but one to Janus House, The University Arms Hotel have rebuilt their Regent Street front, designed by Feilden & Mawson of Norwich (1965–6). It is a four-storey block whose basement and ground floor are largely devoted to car-park. Fifty-nine rooms have been added, and four on each floor in the front have windows in echelon—a motif which is becoming well-worn in Cambridge. The building is in dark brick with expressed floor slabs; on the ground floor is the boarded 'Hobson's Choice' bar.

One of the most recent conversions is by Rodney Fitch of Conran Designs for Joshua Taylor Interiors Ltd. (1966). He has turned the old King & Harper garage, 1–7 Bridge Street into furniture showrooms. The exterior has been painted deep blue with a white

fascia and string-courses. The interior has been opened into one large space divided into a lobby and main showroom largely defined by different floor and ceiling treatments. The existing steel joists are painted bright red and a nineteenth-century spiral staircase has been renovated and placed at the rear of the shop. A new concrete stair serves the first floor which is used as a gallery. This is a clever, modish design which no doubt warms the hearts of the younger dons' wives. Fitch also designed the colour scheme for the shop fronts southward from Joshua Taylor as far as Jesus Lane.

There are one or two other small buildings in the centre which are an encouraging improvement on the rest. Peter Barefoot of Ipswich has designed two premises for the Trustee Savings Bank (1966–7) in Jesus Lane and Victoria Avenue. Both rely for their success on large black slate surfaces, broad expanses of glass and bold lettering. The interiors are also designed by the architect. G. M. Vickers has also completed two buildings, for the Belfast Linen Warehouse Co., with a simple four-arched façade reminiscent of nineteenth-century American commercial architecture (but now being given a white mineralite finish which spoils the allusion), and the Pagoda Restaurant, a not unattractive piece of pop-Oriental, with a façade of closely-spaced timber studs randomly placed. Both are in Regent Street. Lanchester & Lodge, a London firm, are building an extension for Eaden Lilley's store: the only visible part of this is a single window next to the Arts Cinema in Market Passage.

Bradwell's Court from Drummer Street

Bradwell's Court

St. Andrew's Street/Drummer Street.

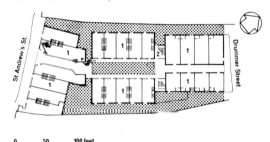

```
0      50      100 feet
```

1 Shops **2** Stairs to offices above
Dotted areas indicate enclosed open spaces

Date.	1960–2
Architects.	Hughes & Bicknell
Contractor.	William Sindall Ltd.
Cost.	£170,000

Requirement.‡ Comprehensive redevelopment, with 14,000 sq ft of offices and 21 shops around a pedestrian precinct.

Q

Description. Occupied previously by cottages and shops, this site borders the main pedestrian link between the historic centre and the newer residential areas to the east of the town. Redevelopment was carried out for Christ's and Jesus Colleges by Ravenseft Properties Ltd. At the west end there is a two-storey parade of six shops, set back from the original St. Andrew's Street building line, at the request of the county planning authorities, in order to relieve congestion and provide a bus-stop bay. At the east end three-storey showrooms and bus offices face Christ's Pieces and the Drummer Street bus station. Connecting these two blocks down the centre of the site is the pedestrian thoroughfare, which broadens into a long rectangular piazza lined with shops with continuous shallow canopies. The structural frame is of concrete faced with granite, terrazzo and Clipsham stone, with a dark blue curtain wall towards Drummer Street and a smaller area of light-blue glass towards the precinct. The shops are serviced from two private roads: that on the east drops steeply to an underground park for 100 bicycles and 20 cars.

Comment. This is a self-effacing design, particularly in view of the forebodings aroused by the collaboration of colleges with speculative developers. In contrast to the Prudential building next door, the temptations of multi-storey profiteering have been resisted and the shops are sensitive to the small scale of a pedestrian precinct. The details, however, are crude: the pseudo-Tudor diapering of the service rooms on the St. Andrew's Street front, the ragged relationship of the shopping canopies to each other (they are in any case too narrow to give shelter), the apologetic appearance of gratings in the midst of artistic paving—above all, the rigid parallel lines of the piazza, which emphasize that the space is too narrow to give real urban relaxation and yet too wide to recapture the intimacy of Cambridge's older pedestrian shopping alleys (Rose Crescent, St. Edward's Passage). Only the Drummer Street curtain wall has a certain elegance when seen from the trees of Milton's Walk. The St. Andrew's Street front sensibly carries on the low roofline of Christ's and it is not the architects' fault that the domineering Pru crushes it. Few of the shops have shown any flair for display on their new site, except perhaps the brassy Kenya.

Southern Area

Hills Road, Trumpington

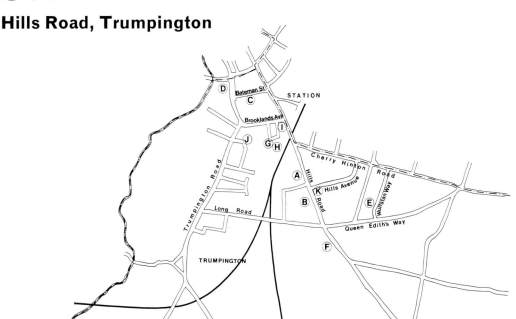

Southern Cambridge consists of two long ribbons of post-1880 private housing along Trumpington Road (to London) and Hills Road (to Haverhill), connected at their base by Lensfield Road. Between them is first the attractive early-to-mid-nineteenth century terrace housing in Panton Street and Bateman Street; then Brooklands Avenue and the railway; and finally, a broad area of playing fields and post-war spec building, across which runs Long Road, intended to be part of the pre-war outer by-pass. Apart from the Panton Street–Bateman Street neighbourhood, which deserves preservation and rehabilitation as a whole (in spite of the blighting influence of the Chemistry Laboratory), the character of the area is one of high-class suburbia, with many 'villas of character' and private schools. Trumpington has been largely spoilt, particularly by the horrid pre-war ribbon development which connects it to Shelford and Stapleford and was largely promoted by the colleges who owned the land. Fortunately the 1947 Planning Act prevented any repetition of this.

Homerton College   A

Hills Road.

Founded in 1876 as Cavendish College for boy undergraduates in the medieval tradition, Homerton has been a teachers' training college since 1894. Its main buildings are an unprepossessing Tudor, but there are interesting additions in 'Arts and Crafts' (gymnasium of 1913 by Herbert Ibberson) and 'Early Modern' (nursery school by Maxwell Fry, 1940). Its two post-war buildings illustrate perfectly the encouraging changes in Cambridge architecture. The three-storey residential and lecture block, including the gateway and porter's lodge, was added in 1955 to a deplorable semi-Tudor design by Seely and Paget, the ecclesiastical architects. Ketton stone and pretty heraldry do nothing to mitigate its banality. The science building and music cells, by Ellis & Gardner, described below, are a refreshing contrast, though badly sited. Better still, in 1962 the college appointed the ubiquitous David Roberts to draw up a master plan for future extensions. In 1964 he relinquished the job to his former assistant, Christophe Grillet, whose scheme is under construction and is described below.

the side walls and red brick for the end walls. The basement or plinth level is painted black and the staircase is fully glazed. On the top floor are three tutorial rooms, panelled in teak. A bronze sculpture by Geoffrey Clarke has been placed next to the main entrance.

On an isolated site nearby are the Music Cells by the same architects, providing five carefully insulated practice rooms in a one-storey building clad in timber, with prominent roof-lights. It is now linked to the extensions by Grillet described below.

Comment.   This is a successful building from the architects of Tillotson's factory at Burwell. Accommodation is straightforward, with natural lighting and split levels carefully handled. The detailing and facing materials are in sharp contrast to the rest of Homerton, being reminiscent in their crispness of the 1930s. It is encouraging to see one of Geoffrey Clarke's vigorous bronzes in Cambridge, which has far too little modern sculpture. However, its position under the staircase is clumsy and gives it no clear relevance.

The Music Cells form an attractive bungalow in rich brown timber, though its siting is inexplicably awkward.

Homerton College Science Building

Date.	1960–1
Architects.	Ellis & Gardner
Contractor.	Johnson & Bailey Ltd.
Cost.	£40,000
Requirement.	Laboratories for physics and chemistry.

Description.   The site is restricted and awkwardly placed on the northern boundary of the college. These limitations have been exploited by dividing the 2,000 sq ft of accommodation into two small blocks, of two and three storeys, which meet at right-angles. The split levels are united in the central staircase, from which the rooms open directly off landings. The structure is a reinforced concrete frame with Portland stone faced concrete slabs for

New Buildings

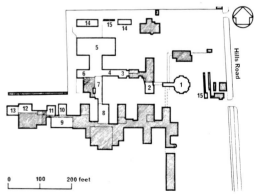

1 Library 2 Geography 3 Mathematics 4 Common room
5 Kitchen/dining 6 Workshop 7 Exhibitions/lecture
8 Student cloakrooms 9 Senior common room 10 Staff cloakrooms 11 Sculpture 12 Graphics 13 Pottery
14 Garages 15 Bicycles

Homerton College extensions

Date. 1965–8

Architects. Lyster & Grillet

Contractor. Kidman & Son Ltd.

Requirement. New kitchen, dining rooms, common rooms, library, classrooms and exhibition rooms.

Description. The architects were asked to provide accommodation to meet the requirements of a change from two- to three-year teacher training. The site for the extensions was an awkward one to the north of the main buildings, dotted by the sporadic extensions by Ellis & Gardner and Maxwell Fry and by Trumpington House. The main part of the new buildings is cruciform in plan and consists of the kitchen and dining rooms in the northern arm, a common room and space for Mathematics in the eastern arm, which links with the Ellis and Gardner block, exhibition and lecture rooms in the southern arm, which joins to the main building and a workshop to the west. The science block is extended southwards for Geography, and free-standing to its east side is the octagonal library. On the western arm of the old building have been added studios for sculpture, graphics and pottery and a senior common room and staff cloakroom. It is built on a 14 ft

module in a black-painted steel frame with white-painted precast concrete infill panels. Each bay is topped with a pyramidal roof clad in 'natural'-coloured asbestos slates, the apex of which is covered by a perspex skylight. The larger spaces, lecture- and dining-rooms, have larger pyramids spanning three bays.

The building is being carried out in overlapping stages so that teaching can continue as normal throughout the development.

Comment. When the first pyramids began to appear, nestling against the red brick of the older buildings, it seemed that the new buildings might provide an attractively scaled series of buildings to give a coherence to this existing jumble. Unhappily, as pyramid has succeeded to pyramid, the scheme has developed an irritating fussiness, heightened by the black and white painting. Is each individual unit so important in this building that it merits this individual treatment? The structure of the larger pyramids, too, is far too complex for so small a scheme. Nor can it be said that this fussiness of detail blinds one to any essential quality in the scheme, for the planning does not show any great virtues, nor provides any agreeable new spaces, or a sense of a coherent whole to the college. Rather, the pyramid-roofed pavilions break up the unity and give the appearance of greater muddle. It was not an easy task, but no real solution has been found.

Perse School, view from Long Road

Schools

Southern Cambridge is the city's primary and secondary school centre. The leading boys' school, the direct-grant Perse (founded 1615), moved to its third site in 1960 with a complete new set of buildings by Stirrat Johnson-Marshall (see below). The Perse girls' school, with an inadequate site in Panton Street, has added the Holland Library (1954–5), a pleasant building by James MacGregor and David Roberts. In Hills Road, the Cambridgeshire High School for Boys is also hemmed in, and successive county architects have added single-storey classrooms and science buildings. In Trumpington, the Fawcett Schools are early post-war city surveyor's work. However, the best L.E.A. building remains the Cambridgeshire Girls' High School on Long Road, an excellent pre-war Dutch-modern design by S. E. Urwin (see Appendix B). Three private schools deserve mention. Hughes and Bicknell in 1960–1 joined two Trumpington Road polychromatic villas with a dining hall block for St. Faith's preparatory school. The attempt to 'harmonize' with self-effacing patterns of red and yellow brick results visually in a hiatus rather than a link. St. Mary's Convent has been extended by David Roberts and deserves special treatment. Finally, the Leys School has erected several new buildings by Beard, Bennett, Wilkins and Partners, which are dealt with below.

Perse School for Boys   B

Hills Road, opposite Glebe Road.

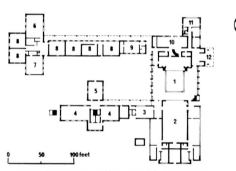

1 Hall 2 Gymnasium 3 Kitchens 4 Laboratories
5 Science lecture theatre 6 and 7 Specialist rooms
8 Classrooms 9 Staff room 10 Library
11 Headmaster's study 12 Main entrance

Date.	1958–60
Architect.	Robert Matthew, Johnson-Marshall and Partners. Stirrat Johnson-Marshall, partner-in-charge
Contractor.	Rattee & Kett Ltd.
Cost.	£205,000
Requirement.	Grammar school for 420 boys.

76

Perse School hall from the north west

Description. The Perse sold its previous central but cramped site to the university in 1957 and prepared to rebuild on the 28-acre playing fields two miles south. The main entrance, with the 1953 War Memorial Gates (neo-Georgian, by Messrs. George Lister), is opposite Glebe Road, in which are the two boarding houses. The new buildings consist of a large range of public rooms in the front, with two cruciform class room wings enclosing small courts to the rear. All buildings are in loadbearing brick, with low pitched slated roofs and timber windows. The central block has four strongly emphasized transverse gables, with clerestory windows. The two to the left light the gymnasium, which has changing rooms on either side and can be united with the hall, through folding doors. The hall is spanned by a complex wooden truss roof supported only at the corners and enclosing fully glazed curtain walls. The floor is on two levels, the sunken centre for assembly and the sides and back for dining. The upper gallery, with folding study cubicles, communicates on either side of the stage with the reading room of the library, which is also seen through the glass screen behind the stage, through which the view extends to the playing fields.

The classroom blocks are on two floors, grouped round central staircases. Science, with elementary and advanced labs for physics and biology, together with preparation rooms and a lecture hall, is on the south. Arts is on the north side, with 12 classrooms seating 20–30 and four specialist rooms—geography and music, art and mummery (drama).

Throughout, extensive use is made of timber, especially African hardwoods; gurjun and danta in the public rooms and ground-floor classrooms, sapele and iroko on the stairs, guarea in the offices and acid-resistant missanda in the laboratories. The vestibules, however, have studded rubber flooring and the upstairs classrooms soft Bulgomme.

Comment. Stirrat Johnson-Marshall was formerly deputy architect of Herts and chief architect to the Ministry of Education. The Perse deserves much credit for commissioning him to design its new buildings. His task was difficult—the total of £205,000 is astonishingly small for a school of this size. But his plan, compact and clear, is well managed, and the structure is simple and consistent. A choice of priorities had to be made, and the client expressly chose the sort of monumental timber-roofed hall which the school had had at Free School Lane (1615) and Hills Road (1890). So in the central block there is a sense of transparency and space and a splendid roof. But the stage is not really suitable for drama nor the dining area for lunches. Moreover, the classrooms, as a corollary, had to be severely reduced in size, and the geography and art rooms, and the changing rooms in particular, are decidedly cramped.

Within these restrictions, the craftsmanship and detailing in the classroom blocks are excellent, and the informal courts are delightful. By contrast, the hall assumes a slightly phoney monumentality, with its flèche and weathercock and African hardwoods. Perhaps it mirrors the ambiguous status of the direct-grant school.

St. Mary's Convent: internal courtyard

78

Saint Mary's Convent School

C

Bateman Street.

Dates. 1953–4; 1959–60; 1962–4

Architect. David Roberts

Contractors. Johnson & Bailey Ltd. (Stage I)
Kerridge Ltd. (Stage II)
Rattee & Kett Ltd. (Stage III)

Costs. £28,000 (Stage I)
£28,000 (Stage II)
£73,000 (Stage III)

Requirement. Extensions to convent and school to provide assembly hall, dining hall, library, classrooms and laboratories.

Description. St. Mary's Convent and its school have previously occupied two Victorian villas about 100 ft apart, with pre-war extensions. Mr. Roberts's three-phase development has formed a central courtyard around which all buildings, new and existing, are grouped.
The first stage consists of the dining hall, and the assembly hall, a simple structure of concrete portal frames and brick infill, which forms the southern side of the central court. Stage II consists of the three-storey buildings of the west and north sides, with the main entrance from the street on the north. This entrance leads into the broad fully glazed corridor which extends round three sides of the court. Above are the library and classrooms. The building is concrete-framed, with brick infill panels and floor slabs clad in slate.
Stage III is a long block, similar in structure and finishes to Stage II and extending along Bateman Street. From the cycle park on the ground floor rises the main staircase, which is fully glazed, with precast concrete mullions. On the upper floors are classrooms and laboratories.
A fourth floor has been added to stages II and III, and here the long band of glazing is recessed behind the slate-faced fascia.

Comment. This is a particularly interesting and attractive example of David Roberts's personal yet functional design. The assembly hall of 1953–4,

St. Mary's Convent: detail of façade

in spite of its simple structure, has brick decoration (diapering), which lacks the refinement of Mr. Roberts's later work. The newer buildings have a restrained, precise formality that exactly suits a convent. The planning is excellent and the relationship with the Victorian villas and their neo-Georgian extensions is managed with great delicacy. Stage II, with its symmetrical formality about the entrance, is a little unbalanced by the adjoining bulk of Stage III in the same materials. The glazed staircase is an insufficient separation. However, the new buildings keep in scale with and enhance the surrounding early Victorian streets. Only with the latest addition have the buildings begun to seem too high, despite the device of recessing the top windows.

The Leys School

D

At the corner of Fen Causeway and Trumpington Road.

The first building put up by the school after the war was the new West House by Beard, Bennett, Wilkins and Partners of 1959–61. Rigidly axial about a glazed central staircase this brick-faced block emphasizes its isolation from the school without adding any particular character of its own. The second set of buildings by the same architects is infinitely more successful.

Leys School, new theatre block

Fen House, Theatre and Sports Pavilion

Date. 1965–6

Architects. Beard, Bennett, Wilkins & Partners

Contractor. Coulson & Son Ltd.

Cost. £157,000

Requirement. New house for 65 pupils, accommodation for housemaster, sports pavilion, theatre and music rooms.

Description. The new buildings are to the west side of the site nearest the river. Fen House is a four-storey block with a spine corridor on each floor serving changing rooms and classrooms on the ground floor, study–bedrooms and common rooms on first and second floors with dormitories on the top floor. At right-angles to it, at the north-east corner, and linked by a bridge at first floor level, is the three-bedroomed housemaster's house in a two-storey block. Beyond it lies the sports pavilion with a main room which uses fine oak panelling taken from the old pavilion, on a semi-basement containing changing rooms and groundsman's store. A scorers' look-out is provided in a mansard over the main room. All three levels are joined by a spiral staircase. The theatre is to the north of Fen House which it

faces across a paved court. It seats 460 people, including a gallery. The seats are not raked, but movable boxes are provided when this is required. The auditorium has saw-tooth side walls with vertical windows directed towards the stage, which are invisible from the auditorium. The brick panels between the windows are curved inwards. A double-height foyer with a glazed screen on to the court serves both levels; the final brick panel on the west wall curves round the staircase to form a tower at the south-west corner. To the rear of the stage, and under it, are music cubicles which double as dressing-rooms, seminar rooms and workshops. The cubicles are capped by pyramidal roofs. The structure is loadbearing brickwork with concrete slabs, and steel joists in the theatre. The slabs are expressed externally in Fen House. The brickwork externally is High Broom handmade dark greys, but internally Staffordshire strawthatch facings with engineering brick skirtings have been used.

Comment. This is a vast improvement on the same architects' West House and more in line with their achievement in the University Press building (see page 84), although there is an irritating lack of co-ordination. The theatre building is probably best of the three and the sculptural treatment of the brickwork on the west wall is admirable, particularly where the corner is rounded off to guide one into the paved court. It is sad that in the event the curved corner is not fully exploited internally. But at the north end the pyramidal roofs seem to bear little relationship to the sensuous detailing of the auditorium, just as in its turn Fen House seems blockish in comparison. Yet Fen House seems to be striving at a different kind of order: the lower façades change by degrees from top to bottom from a solid wall with openings to a glazed screen with brick piers, and yet the relationship of the openings is confused and the pattern blurred. Then, too, the spry little pavilion with its deep fascia is out of scale with more diminutive housemaster's house, which in its turn butts awkwardly onto Fen House. The internal planning of Fen House is dominated to too great an extent by the wide corridors on each floor. They make the study-bedrooms seem mean and dark, generous as those are by public school standards; and they do not make for a coherent community. The craftsmanship is, by and large, good although the painted concrete ceilings internally leave much to be desired. The internal brickwork, too, makes a pleasant finish, supposedly resilient to grubby hands.

Saint James's Church   E

Wulfstan Way.

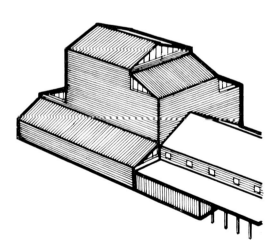

St. James's Church: isometric sketch looking south east

Proposed.   1963

Architects.   Robert Maguire & Keith Murray

Description.   This church will show the first decisive impact on Cambridge of the Liturgical Movement, the re-appraisal of Christian worship which has been going on in Europe during the last two generations and has contributed towards the movement for church unity. Anglican churches have changed from the medieval pattern to the simplified one-room plan, seen in Cambridge at St. Martin's and St. Stephen's (page 93). Maguire and Murray's St. Paul's Bow Common (1958–60), in Stepney, was the first English church to express fully the new insights, in particular the corporate quality of worship around a central altar.

St. James's is a development from Maguire and Murray's second church, St. Matthew, Perry Beeches, at Birmingham. The altar stands with the pulpit on a central platform (expressing the unity of Word and Sacrament). This is set within a tall central space, square in plan, supported on four concrete columns, with sheer brick walls above, surmounted by a clerestory window under the low-pitched roof. Around this central space runs a continuous ambulatory, with its roof rising a storey on each side, forming a kind of spiral with rooflights. Entered on the east side, which has the lowest roof and contains the font and the side-altar, this ambulatory forms both a processional way and an extension of the central space, when needed. Seating in the church will be completely flexible, depending on the size of the congregation and the type of service. The windowless outer walls will be of local Burwell white gault brick, exposed internally, with grey pantiled roofs. Outside the entrance is a new covered way, alongside the existing church hall, by David Roberts, who also designed the vicarage. The hall is faced with red-brown brick and has a tall side window lighting the temporary sanctuary.

Comment.   This should be a most beautiful church, its stark outline in local brickwork providing a focus for an unprepossessing area of council estates. The re-examination of fundamental ideas by Maguire and Murray results in a direct, worshipful enclosure which is far removed from the beautiful overwrought details on a medieval plan, characteristic of Coventry Cathedral. Only the pantiled roof seems a trifle self-conscious. The simplicity of this church is perhaps best comparable with Llewelyn-Davies's research laboratory (see page 116), which also had a fundamental appraisal of its programme.

Addenbrooke's Hospital　F

Red Cross.

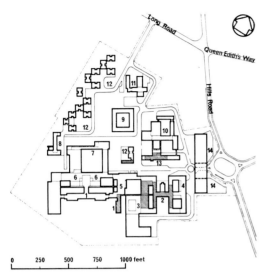

0   250   500   750   1000 feet

1 Ward blocks **2** Out-patients **3** Radiology **4** Artificial limb and appliance centre **5** Laboratories **6** Operating theatre **7** Supplies centre **8** Training school **9** Special hospital **10** Medical school **11** Blood transfusion centre **12** Residential accommodation **13** Radiotherapeutics and Molecular Biology **14** Car park

Date.	1960–2 (Stage I)
	1966–　(Stage II)
Architects.	Easton & Robertson, Cusdin, Preston & Smith. S. E. T. Cusdin, partner-in-charge (Stage I). Cusdin, Burden & Howitt (Stage II)
Contractors.	Kerridge Ltd.
Cost	£1,134,000 (Stage I)
	£9,800,000 (Stage II)

Requirement. A teaching hospital of 1,000–1,200 beds. Stage I to contain a ward block of 94 beds, with associated neurosurgical and orthopaedic theatres; out-patient department and accident service; radiology department and staff residence.

Description. Because of the confined site and poor quality of the existing buildings in Trumpington Street, the Minister of Health acquired the Hills Road site of 41 acres, for which a comprehensive plan was drawn up in 1958–9. It is hoped to complete Stage II in 1970–1 and Stage III soon after.

The whole site is to be covered by buildings of not more than nine storeys with a central axis leading from Hills Road. In the main entrance concourse will be parking, shops and a porter's lodge; then on the left hand the large two-storey out-patients' department in a double H-shape, with artificial limb and appliances department and a crèche; the four-storey buildings for the X-ray department and accident service, behind which is the radiotherapy centre; and finally the long seven-storey ward block stretching westwards with three cross wings, one of which contains accommodation for teaching and clinical research. At the end of the central axis is the surgical block, running parallel with the ward block. Next to it is the main entrance, leading to the administration block, which has a nine-storey engineering services tower and central dining room and kitchens. On the right-hand side of the axis are the medical staff residence and the five-acre site for the university medical school, on which has so far been built the laboratory of molecular biology. From Hills Road the service road leads to the right, behind the university buildings, to the residential 'village', which includes low terraced courts for senior medical and nursing staff, tower blocks of six and nine storeys for the nurses and a block for domestic staff. From here the road continues to the Long Road entrance.

The first stage, opened in 1962, consists of three buildings: most of the out-patients' department and the accident section; one cross wing of the ward block, and the medical staff residence. The buildings are of contrasting materials. The out-patients' building is of loadbearing brick, faced in brown and with a large timber entrance canopy. The other buildings are concrete-framed, with stone and red brick facings. The M.R.C. laboratory has a flat roof and glazed staircase. Stage II will consist of laboratories, the radio-therapeutic centre, operating theatres, supplies centre and training schools for the nurses, and some residential accommodation. There is also a ward block of 426 beds.

Comment. Although only one-fifteenth of the ultimate development has so far been opened, there

Addenbrooke's Hospital: ward block

is painfully little to say in praise of the new Addenbrooke's, which will be by far the largest and most costly building scheme in Cambridge since the war. No doubt these bleak buildings work efficiently. The architects were among the pioneers of hospital design in the thirties. But there is little indication of the new ideas of the 1950s, embodied in the Nuffield researches and in such buildings as Powell and Moya's Swindon, in which the needs of both patients and traffic are met by clustering the wards around low, intimate courtyards. At Addenbrooke's, medium-sized blocks, of depressingly conventional detail, have been dispersed all over the site, with excessively narrow service roads. Even the bungaloid growth of the out-patients' building does nothing to mitigate the overall barrack-like atmosphere.

Cambridge Institute of Education G

Fitzwilliam Road.

Date. 1963–4

Architect. Ralph Tubbs

Contractor. Kerridge Ltd.

Cost. £100,000

Requirement. New premises for the Institute, including library, common rooms, offices, lecture rooms, seminar rooms and a caretaker's flat.

Description. The building consists of a main three-storey block, and a one-storey range linked to its north side by the foyer. Entry is directly into the foyer which runs at right-angles to it. At the southern end of the foyer is the three-storey block whose rooms are arranged around the top-lit staircase well; at its northern end, the library and conference room which are grouped around an internal court. The caretaker's flat lies directly beyond cloakrooms on the east side of the foyer. The buildings are of brick; the conference hall has a deep, white-painted fascia and a glazed screen towards the west. In the main block, there are triangular bay windows on the upper floors.

Comment. Amidst the gimmicks of other Cambridge buildings this old-fashioned brick box is a refreshing change. The main building exudes an almost Georgian good taste, reminiscent of the better work of the fifties, coupled with a certain genteel artiness in the bay windows which so often typified the decade. Certainly the differing window heights is straight transcription from eighteenth century practice, and to a certain extent it is justified, reflecting, as it does, the differing uses of the rooms behind. The common and lecture rooms on the first floor clearly need the larger windows they are provided with. Also typical of the fifties is the loose planning, the difficulty in treating the larger glazed or plain areas, the restrained, but weak, lettering, and the poor landscaping. Yet it is not to be scorned, for all that it is something of an oddity: there is a crispness of outline and general unpretentiousness which is all too often lacking in its contemporaries.

Cambridge University Press, printing block (left) and offices

University Press   H

Date.   1961–3

Architects.   Beard, Bennett, Wilkins & Partners

Contractor.   Johnson & Bailey Ltd.

Cost.   £1,000,000

Requirement.   New printing works, with an area of 210,000 sq ft.

Cambridge University Press, spiral ramp

Description.   These long-delayed new buildings house a complete letterpress and binding plant with warehouse and administrative offices, on a large open site, 1½ miles south of the city centre. The adjoining railway is not at present used by the firm. The new press is planned for economic work flow, flexible expansion and good working conditions. All production areas are on a single level and are tightly planned around a central spine, which also acts as a central core for the service ducts. At the south end of the spine is the printing block, consisting of seven bays spanned by a steel ribbed roof, curved in both directions, with 150 ft span longitudinal ridge girders. The curved area accommodates the service ducts; the large working areas beneath are sub-divided for increased intimacy and sound proofing and have a flat acoustic ceiling. The long horizontal windows are not required for illumination, but to give a restful all-round view of trees and playing fields. At the north end of the spine is a court enclosed by the offices and the well-lit proof-reading block (both concrete framed), and the composition and canteen blocks, which are steel-framed and clad with alu-

minium. The offices have an infill of blue ceramic panels, a top floor devoted to lift motors and plant, and a connection at first floor level to the canteen which lies above the despatch department and unloading area. The powerhouse is by the railway. The broad forecourt and car parks are landscaped with trees, lawns and pools.

Comment.   If some of Cambridge's newest buildings are too much 'architects' architecture', this is a refreshing contrast: a printers' printing house. Every possible care has been given to the design of the working areas, which combine most satisfactorily a giant steel framework and open flexible spaces with the intimate, secluded silence required for concentration in work. The introverted plan, leaving plenty of room for expansion outwards in all directions, is excellently handled. However, the client's interest seems to have flagged when it came to the offices; these are depressingly conventional in detail, and externally the five buildings do not group well together, except from the railway. The ragged edges are partially smoothed by the attractive landscaping.

84

Great Ouse House   I

Clarendon Road.

Date.   1965–6

Architect.   Edward D. Mills & Partners

Contractor.   Johnson & Bailey Ltd.

Requirement. Offices and laboratories for the Great Ouse River Authority.

Description. The building is on five floors and consists of groups of laboratories and offices arranged around a central service core containing stairs, stores and cloakrooms. There are tank and plant rooms over the service core on the roof. The structure is *in situ* reinforced concrete perimeter columns and slabs. The concrete walls of the service core are also loadbearing. The ground floor is recessed behind the structural columns; above this, each floor has continuous bands of window with a brick spandrel band below, and the floors are expressed as independent units by a continuous clerestory recessed behind the columns above each band of windows. Where the columns are exposed, they are faced with a black asbestos cement cladding and the ground floor is faced in reconstructed Portland stone. Vinyl fabrics are used internally for wall surfaces and vinyl tiles and carpet are used on the floors. Columbian and Oregon pine are used for panelling, door finishes and frames, and for the staircase.

Comment. This is the most accomplished office block Cambridge possesses. It has a neatness of detail and a clarity of expression which none of the others quite match. One's first regret is that it has got five, not twenty-five floors, for here, surely is a building whose potential is not fully developed. But the appearance of the block still poses certain awkward questions. The plant room, to start with, is a totally extraneous element, and it is not improved by being painted white: it sits winking maliciously from the roof top, and is visible from almost every angle. The recessing of the ground floor is another uneasy feature: is the function of the ground floor so very different that it merits different treatment? It is not as though it was entirely devoted to reception and public rooms: indeed many of the rooms recur

Great Ouse House

on higher floors. There the regular window bands are effectively separated out from the structure; and these upper floors as a whole are a forceful, stylish solution to a common problem.

Applecourt   J

Newton Road.

Date.   1959

Architect.   Eric Lyons

Contractor.   Wates Ltd.

Requirement. 24 flats for Span Developments Ltd.

Description. The first of the Span developments in Cambridge, this adopts a different solution from their well-known courtyard plans. It consists of two identical three-storey blocks, H-shaped, with staircases in the centre of the crossbar of the H. From the staircase access galleries lead east and west past utility rooms to two flats at each end. The structure is of loadbearing brick, with tile-hanging and brown brick end walls. The roofs are flat. The utility rooms have unglazed louvres of hollow tile. Around the blocks is a carefully tended garden across which they are linked by a paved forecourt. Garages are in a group at the back of the site.

Comment.   Although less ambitious than Highsett (see page 110). Applecourt has a sufficiently different solution to be worth a visit. In place of an urban courtyard, the paved forecourt successfully unites the two blocks within the garden, preserving suburban privacy. The detailing is in several respects superior to Highsett, particularly the spacious glazed staircases and the careful use of colour, as in the blue steel handrails and grey terrazzo stair treads.

Keelson   K

8a, Hills Avenue.

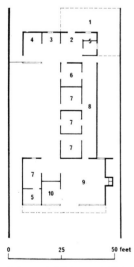

0   25   50 feet

1 Car port **2** Entrance **3** Dining **4** Kitchen **5** Bathroom
6 Nursery **7** Bedroom **8** Gallery **9** Living room **10** Study

Date   1960–1

Architect.   Eric Sørensen

Contractor.   M. J. Allen & Sons of
Brampton, Hunts.

Cost.   £8,500

Requirement.   House for Dr. and Mrs. Kennard.

Description.   The site is a narrow strip, 120 ft by 50 ft. The house is all one-storeyed and is divided into three parts, reflecting the needs of the clients, who are away during the day, but whose children live here permanently with a maid. Towards the front are the car-port, entrance hall, dining-kitchen and cloakrooms. Beyond is the paved and grassed courtyard leading to the third part of the house—living room, study, sleeping area and bathroom—looking south into the main garden. In between is a connecting wing containing the playroom and three bedroom-cabins (children, guestroom and maid), behind which is a long book-lined gallery, rooflit and enclosing a small herb garden. The fourth side of the courtyard is closed by the garden wall.
The structure, partly of non-loadbearing white bricks and partly of timber, stained dark brown, is on a module 7 ft by 9 ft 6 in. The dining-kitchen is divided by built-in cupboards. The cabin-bedrooms have demountable fibreboard partitioning, to allow for the changing needs of the family. The living area has pine panelling, an open fireplace with a tall brick chimney painted black and a mixture of modern Danish, old English and Oriental furniture and rugs. The heated floors are of small red ceramic tiles throughout. The roof is edged with copper.

Comment.   This Danish-designed house has the same purgative effect on the visitor who is used to the picturesque eccentricities of most English design that Arne Jacobsen's college at Oxford has on a larger scale. Planning is rational, structure is clearly expressed, colours are few (white, brown, black, red) and the union of internal and external space is brilliantly achieved, with a characteristically Scandinavian transparency and sparseness of furnishing. The effects of light and shade are wholly delightful, and any impression of clinical precision is softened by the dignity of the book-lined gallery. The long, narrow site is used to the greatest advantage by dividing it into three main areas and by making good use of existing trees and walls. This is one of the two or three best buildings in post-war Cambridge.

Keelson, Hills Avenue: living room

Work by the City in the Southern Area

The city are undertaking two projects in the area, the most extensive of which is the first stage of the Newtown redevelopment. Work started on this at the end of 1966 and the first slab blocks have appeared. The first stage will comprise 127 flats and parking for 134 cars, and the contract is valued at £398,940. Already it is apparent that the small-scale streets of this part of Cambridge have been disrupted irrevocably, and the new blocks do not look as though they will provide a convincing alternative. The brick cladding seems to echo rather than counter the depressing bulk of the Chemical Laboratories just behind. The other scheme the city has promoted is the development of flatlets for old people at Whitelock's Yard, Trumpington. There are 28 flatlets, accommodation for the warden, and a common room. The block is L-shaped with a long-terraced three-storey range running east/west and a short range facing the road containing the warden's flat and common room. Each flatlet has its own south-facing balcony shielded by screen walls. Advantage has been taken of the levels to provide access to the first two floors without steps. The arrangement is a subtle and clever one and is worthy of the best the architect's department have done. The cost will be £60,000.

City housing in the area comprises a couple of large estates. The first was that at Trumpington of 1946-7 where 383 dwellings were put up and at Queen Edith's Way in 1951-4 where 466 houses and flats were built. Both estates are typical of the worst type of council housing. At Trumpington there is a

crescent-shaped shopping parade, with two storeys of flats above the shops. The flats have prominent balconies. All three projects were designed by the City Surveyor's department.

Miscellaneous work in the Southern Area

The main university area south of the Chemistry Laboratories is the Botanic Gardens. Sir Albert Richardson's proposed library of 1946 was fortunately shelved, as its precise Georgian formality would not have suited the winding Victorian paths and exotic planting. The laboratories of 1957 are a symmetrical semi-modern design by Alec Crook. In December 1962 an admirable plan by Lyster & Grillet for an £8,000 entrance gate and circular public convenience for Hills Road was non-placeted by the Regent House, amid exaggerated controversy worthy of 'Clochemerle'. In Latham Road is Southacre, a four-storey group of university staff flats built in 1951-2 by Robert Atkinson & Partners.

Tayler & Green also designed flats and houses for the Southacre site but Regent House non-placeted these also, in 1965. The drawings show three-storey terraces of houses, tile-hung above first-floor level and three-storey blocks of flats.

In Trumpington, there is a Shell service station by Hughes & Bicknell, to which has now been added a two-storey garage in purple brick with chamfered corners. The Plant Breeding Institute in the grounds of Anstey Hall has a prominent laboratory close to the road, in pink brick, designed in 1951 by J. B. F. Cowper & Poole.

There are several adequate commercial buildings: Heffer's Printing Works, with curtain-walled offices of 1956 by Hughes & Bicknell; Rattee & Kett's new offices next to the railway, another curtain-walled block of 1960-1 by John Mowlem's architects' department; and the trunk telephone exchange in Long Road, a clean and well-detailed Ministry of Public Building and Works design of 1960-2, with three concrete-framed wings of different heights and an attractive white-painted bicycle shed.

Private housing in Porson and Rutherford Roads is typically suburban; 33 Porson Road (architect, D. O. Cole) was published in *The Daily Mail Book of House Plans*, 1961. 21 Trumpington Road, by Ellis & Gardner, is a well-designed house (1961-2); they have also designed a house at 17a Hills Avenue in pink brick with cedar boarding, and a block of flats at 273 Hills Road. Also off Trumpington Road is a T-shaped bungalow, Menai, in Gazeley Road, by David Roberts. At 39 Newton Road, D. C. Croghan is building a house for himself. Other private work includes houses by David Roberts at 34 Barrow Road (1956–7), by Roger Scott in Edendale Close (1958), by Donald Macleod (1964) at 319a Hills Road, and by T. F. Morris & Partners at 283 Queen Edith's Way. Cound, Page have built an attractive house in Hills Road ('Inner-berth') in dark grey brick with a deep, white fascia at first-floor level. The drab Edwardian Hope Nursing Home has been extended by Douglas Lowkes (1949–52) and Cedric Brown (1964–6). Both architects have succeeded tolerably in harmonizing with the existing building. There is a modish bungalow by D. C. Denton-Smith and Partners in Hauxton Road, Trumpington, close to six little white bungalows for retired clergy by Lyster & Grillet. These are built around a paved court which each bungalow faces; and they all have private front and back gardens. Connecting each building is a concrete screen wall pierced in a Mexican pattern, an unfortunately irritating device which mars an otherwise well-thought out scheme. Galewood, a timber-framed bungalow on the edge of the Gog Magog hills, is an excellent design (1959–60) by Felix Walter, informally grouped around a central patio. To the north of Bateman Street are a number of little new houses by Christophe Grillet (142 Pemberton Place and 1 St. Eligius Street) and Oliver Churchill (3 St. Eligius Street and 20 Panton Street) which fit well into the existing pattern of narrow Victorian streets. Extensive speculative developments have taken place off Babraham Road in the south-east corner of the city by J. R. Stott of Trend Housing Ltd., which follow weakly in the wake of Eric Lyons's work for Span. Nevertheless 'Georgian-style' houses are still being put up in Bishops Road, Trumpington, designed by G. G. Miller.

Bungalows for retired clergy on the Hauxton Road, by Lyster and Grillet

Eastern Area

Newmarket Road, Romsey Town, Cherry Hinton, Fen Ditton

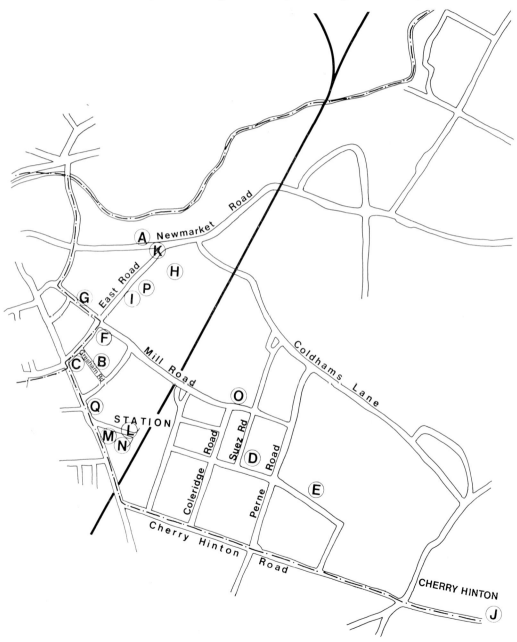

Eastern Cambridge has the city's main modern development, partly because of the railway, partly because of the university barrier to the west, but also because it has always been an extramural centre of commerce. The medieval Stourbridge Fair was one of the largest in the country. Barnwell Abbey and the Leper Chapel are survivals of the ancient ribbon development which has given Newmarket Road something of a country high street character at its western end. Barnwell developed in 1820–60 from Christ's Pieces to East Road with pleasantly small-scale cottages (Orchard Street, Prospect Row), the grander houses of the Warkworth Terrace and a number of squalid back streets. West of Mill Road, middle-class villas were built in Newtown. The humane proportions and landscape of these areas with many alleyways for pedestrians only have recently been perpetuated in the excellent East Road and Highsett flats, and could well be incorporated into any new system of decks spreading from the proposed City Road shopping centre. If City Road comes true (for doubts about this, see page 12) urban renewal of the mostly radical kind will be possible.

Romsey Town, the railway throw-up of the 1860–70's, is a twilight area of a kind even drabber than the close-knit slum. Sooner or later it will need comprehensive redevelopment—and bright new supermarkets along Mill Road only postpone the day of decision. A tightly planned first stage could perhaps use surplus railway land.

Farther out, post-1918 ribbon development reaches as far as Cherry Hinton, with Perne and Fendon Roads as cheerless fragments of the projected 1938 by-pass. The nearby cement works overshadows wasted land with an aloofness peculiar to itself (see photo, page 96). Cherry Hinton village has been almost wrecked by untidy infill and post-war sprawl, though three recent city architect jobs are at least interesting in isolation.

Another fragment of by-pass forms the centre of the Meadowlands council estate at Fen Ditton, concluding Newmarket Road's long line of pre-war villas and filling stations. This area badly needs pulling together with higher density housing and vehicular segregation—there is so much waste space that much can still be done. Just outside the city, preserved from depredation, is the old village centre of Fen Ditton, beside the river, the towpath of which forms an invaluable and attractive northern promenade for the whole area.

Barnwell Hostel; 'Cambridge News' building at left

Emmanuel Barnwell Hostel A

Newmarket Road.

Date. 1960

Architects. T. A. Bird & R. M. T. Tyler

Contractor. Kidman & Sons Ltd.

Cost. £63,000

Requirement. Hostel for 29 undergraduates of Emmanuel College.

Description. This small out-of-town hostel is a three-storey L-shaped block, overlooking a small grass court at the back of a house owned by the college and with views down to the river. It is on a modified staircase plan with access to short lengths of corridor around which are grouped bed-sitters and service rooms. The staircases are lit by polygonal glazed turrets. The structure is of loadbearing brickwork, with yellow facings and some white rendering, bay windows being weatherboarded.

Comment. This is the kind of building that offends by its very inoffensiveness. Only the site layout, with a pleasantly scaled courtyard opened up behind an existing house, has the courage of its convictions. Otherwise everything conforms to the little England which the newspapers usually call 'Swedish': bland and timid by turns, with the river front crushed by an out-of-scale (yet still timid) staircase turret. Something strong was needed on this suburban site to stand up to the bulk of the 'Cambridge News' next door.

University Health Centre Fenner's B

Gresham Road.

Date.	1950–1
Architects.	J. M. MacGregor & David Roberts
Contractor.	Coulson & Son Ltd.
Cost.	£44,625

Requirement. Accommodation for department of Human Ecology, University Health Service, and gymnasium.

Description. The narrow site between the cricket field and a suburban road dictated the form of the building: a long central block with short wings, all two-storeyed. The north wing contains Human Ecology, with rooms for the professor, reader and secretary, offices, library and store. The central link contains the U.H.S.'s X-ray rooms on the ground floor, with consulting rooms opening off a corridor on the far side. At the junction with the south wing is the entrance foyer, with stairs to the gymnasium (back) and boxing room (front) on the first floor. The structure is of loadbearing brick walls with Berkshire red facings and concrete floors.

Comment. This building arouses little comment now, but when the 'Architectural Review' surveyed Cambridge in 1951, it was almost the only non-traditional post-war design. More important, it was the first appearance in Cambridge of David Roberts. Perhaps the Berkshire brick (the same as at St. John's, page 43) is a bit too red for an infill site among white brick Gothic villas; the interior is an appropriately clinical contrast. Nevertheless, at a time of shortage and restriction, the Health Centre was a considerable achievement. Its relationship to both the cricket field and Gresham Road is informal but strong.

Local Examinations Syndicate Offices C

Hills Road, opposite Roman Catholic Church

Date.	1960–4.
Architects.	Robert Matthew, Johnson-Marshall & Partners; Peter Newnham, partner-in-charge
Contractor.	Rattee & Kett Ltd.
Cost.	£259,579

Requirement. Offices for the Syndicate.

Description. Previously scattered round the city, the syndicate's expansion and progressive switch to automatic data-processing made central offices necessary. The Perse site of $1\frac{1}{3}$ acres was bought in 1960 and everything was demolished except the science building of 1934 which was converted into offices immediately. The next two stages, built in 1961–2 (northern part) and 1962–4 (southern part), consist of a long three-storey office block along Hills Road and a short two-storey link, forming two open courtyards, set well back from Gonville Place. There were three main requirements: flexibility, insulation from traffic noise and space for machinery, including a computer. Therefore planning to a square 4 ft $10\frac{1}{2}$ in module was adopted to allow flexible partitioning (offices are four modules deep). The walls are of $13\frac{1}{2}$ in loadbearing brick, with windows double-glazed. Each window fits into a module width but three different types, all tall and thin, are used in a random pattern. The concrete floors are also supported on two rows of widely spaced central columns and beams, which carry separate ventilation and strip lighting for each modular unit. The computer room is on the ground floor.

Comment. This is a functional, modular building, which attempts a certain rationalism of planning yet which defeats its own ends by the random window pattern, which has produced some curious results within, especially in the two-storey link block. Mercifully, perhaps, the strongly expressed floor slabs help play down this irrationality from the outside. As for its relationship to the admittedly difficult site, the long southern wing does not make

Local Examinations Syndicate, offices

a really convincing street front, nor does it provide a hard outside edge in contrast to the quiet entry court from which one penetrates the building. Internally, there are depressing corridors which make it unfortunately institutional. The craftsmanship is good, and the choice of finishes (including extensive use of timber) excellent, except in the entrance foyer. This has a profusion of different materials which do battle with each other in an effort to attract notice.

Churches

As a result of the Bishop of Ely's appeal, five new Anglican churches are being built in Cambridge, three in the eastern area. Holy Cross, Fen Ditton, on the Newmarket Road, has been designed by Dr. M. E. Little, lecturer in structures at the School of Architecture. The hall and vestries were built first in 1961–2 at the surprisingly high cost of £17,200, considering their utilitarian character. The present sanctuary will become the baptistery of the permanent church, the folding doors to the hall being left open on special occasions. The first centralized plan to be approved by the diocese, the church will have a

Greek cross plan with tapered arms, the altar standing just 'east' (in fact, north) of the centrepoint. A reredos wall flanked by pulpit and lectern screens a low Lady Chapel with meeting room over. The tapering mitigates the dividing effect of the internal corners on the congregation in the other three arms. Lighting is all at high level, through a continuous strip of clerestory over the plain brick walls and through a cruciform arrangement of tapered gables in folded concrete over the crossing. As yet the details of the scheme show no sign of being better than routine Anglican. Close to it is the unassuming Meadowlands Methodist Church, by Hughes and Bicknell, a steel-framed dual purpose hall of 1960, costing £4,370, which will similarly be used for worship until a permanent church is built.

The other two Anglican churches have used an inexpensive bay system of transverse arches in laminated wood. St. Stephen's, Crooks Road, of 1962–3, designed by C. J. Bourne, looks cheap (in the wrong sense) externally—it is hard to see how the future bell tower and chancel can remedy the deadness of the yellow brick walls. The interior, however, has a decent simplicity in the Cambridge Evangelical tradition.

St. Martin's Church: forecourt from south west and interior looking east

Saint Martin's Church   D

Suez Road

Date.   1960–2

Architects.   Paterson & Macaulay of Bebington, Cheshire

Contractor.   Johnson & Bailey Ltd.

Cost.   £36,500 (including vicarage)

Requirement.   Church to seat 300, with vicarage and parish rooms.

Description.   Built behind the pre-war dual-purpose parish hall, which was then demolished, this church has a narrow paved entrance court flanked by the new vicarage and a block containing a kitchen and meeting room. The church is a single rectangular room spanned by 11 pairs of laminated timber beams, each 50 ft long. Outside these are narrow side-aisles only 10 ft high. The altar is brought well forward from the east end and close to the congregation, with choir and organ accommodated at the west end. Also at the west end, raised on steps, is the font. All furniture is in light-coloured wood. Windows are cedar-framed. Services can be relayed to the hall, which is united with the church by a broad window. A vestry and Sunday School room will be added later at the east end.

Comment.   Although keeping a rigidly axial plan, exaggerated by the very steep pitch of the roof, this church shows the influence of the Liturgical Movement in the closeness of altar to congregation. It is an inexpensive building, but has a surprising spaciousness, even grandeur, in its graceful timber framework. It is a great pity that this liturgical and structural directness is masked by jazziness in furnishings and decoration: the diapered brickwork and triangular frames for the Creed and Commandments, the busy window tracery and tinted glass, the intricate carpentry of the Holy Table itself. The porch, courtyard and communal rooms are well-planned for formal or informal meetings.

Public Buildings
south-east of Parker's Piece

While arguments still fly back and forth about the 'historic centre' of Lion Yard and the 'new centre' of City Road—neither of which yet exist—a new civic centre for Cambridge has actually been created piecemeal beside the East Road roundabout, not far from City Road. The two best designs, the city surveyor's swimming pool (1961–3) and the county architect's police headquarters (1968–), both described below, have shown an imaginative sympathy with their situation on the perimeter of Parker's Piece—one of those vast Cambridge spaces defined by low terraces (cf. Trinity Great Court, New Square, Downing College). The Fire Brigade Headquarters, however, standing between them on the corner of Parkside and East Road, is a crude rebuff to its environment. As a property development in a back street, 'liquorice allsorts' architecture would be passed over resignedly; put up by the county council in 1963–4 on one of the best sites in Cambridge, it excites nightmarish disbelief. Lacking any sense of visual good manners the architects, S. N. Cooke & Partners of Birmingham, have concentrated on finicky detail, splitting up the accommodation into its parts and decorating them with various stale clichés (the building was first designed as long ago as 1949). From left to right, we see the domestic quarters and rest rooms (three storeys, slate mullions and grey mosaic panels) the appliance room (six bays, purple brick piers) with the control room projecting over (Georgian-shaped windows, yellow brick walling), and the offices (three storeys, red brick piers, grey mosaic panels, yellow brick gable wall and two curious sun-breakers connecting to the control room); round the corner in East Road is the single-storey stores and workshop block, with garages and practice tower in the training courtyard behind.

Across East Road, as a backcloth to the small park of Peter's Field, is the long pre-war flank in Lutyens-Georgian of the Post Office Sorting Office. This was extended through to Mill Road in 1963–4, replacing a vividly polychromatic Gothic villa, by the Ministry of Public Building and Works (architect in charge Morris Williams). It is a sensible design: the frame picked out in stone, the infill panels of brown Stamfordstone brick with raked joints. The upper floor canteen is cantilevered over the side access for vehicles.

Technical College: temporary and permanent buildings

Behind the Sorting Office, in Collier Road off Mill Road, is concealed the largest public building of all, the Cambridgeshire College of Arts and Technology, which has 7,500 full and part-time students. Anyone who visits Cambridge to study the architecture of higher education should trek here to see the difference between private (Oxbridge) affluence and public (technological) squalor. Poverty of funds means that behind the Tech's 1909 building a wide area is littered with prefabricated huts of ancient (wartime) and modern (Terrapin) vintages. The latter compare very favourably with the recent permanent buildings—the result of another inexplicable choice by the county council of an outside architect, this time Alister MacDonald & Partners. The north wing of 1929–31 forms one side of a new back courtyard formed by MacDonald, with three buildings of 1955–60: a large and terrible four-storey block for English and Science faced with brown brick and panels of red tiling; a four-storey wing with north-lit workshops behind; and a two-storey Engineering block, slightly more humane, with facings in brown and purple bricks and also red colour-wash. This last building faces a desert of slum clearance (and more

Terrapin) stretching to the East Road frontage—all eventually to be covered with new buildings for the Tech. Meanwhile a fourth MacDonald building has been added (1965–6) at the opposite end, between the 1909 building and the cemetery. A considerable improvement on earlier work, it still falls far short of the proper ambitions of an expanding college of technology (and one which has a deserved reputation for teaching the fine arts). L-shaped and five-storeyed, this steel-framed block with *pilotis* cased in concrete has the fashionable mannerism of brick panels separated by clerestory gaps instead of by solid floor slabs—the windows being shuffled irregularly and the brick being in curious bands of white and pale yellow. The purple brick boiler house beneath the south-west corner has a well-detailed concrete chimney.

Also next to the cemetery (a typical Benthamite position) is the Maternity Hospital. Towards Mill Road is the first stage of the staff residency (1963–4), by Hughes & Bicknell, a simple brick structure (purple sides, yellow gables) containing 22 bed-sitters in all, for doctors (ground floor) and sisters and pupil midwives (upper floor). The next of three stages is to replace the original Poor Law block of 1838—but eventually the whole hospital will move to the Addenbrooke's site (see page 82).

Saint Bede's   E
Secondary School

Birdwood Road

Date.   1961–2

Architect.   David Roberts

Contractor.   William Sindall Ltd.

Cost.   £120,000

Requirement. Co-educational Roman Catholic secondary modern school for 262 pupils.

Description. St. Bede's had to be built to the stringent cost limits of the Ministry. It stands on an open flat site beyond the eastern suburbia, with nothing between it and the cement works except open playing fields. It is planned as a single rectangular group around a central courtyard, mostly

two storeys high, entered by an open arch under the west wing. Opposite is the double-height hall, lit by all-round glazing at the upper level. The hall is also used as a chapel and gymnasium and has a stage at one end where an altar can be set up. Swedish beams and ropes hang near the centre. East of the hall are three single-storey wings—boiler and stores, changing rooms and kitchen—around two small yards. The north and south classroom wings have balconies (or open corridors) at first floor level. The structure is a steel frame, faced with bright red brick below sill level, with details in black-painted copper. Curtains are also black.

Comment. This is probably Roberts's best building in Cambridge, though few find their way to visit it. So sensitive to *genius loci* in a medieval college such as Magdalene, he shows here that on a bleak open site, he can be bold, almost defiant, in his use of a compact form, ruthless Miesian proportions and two contrasting colours (red and black). The narrow approach between bicycle sheds from the dull suburban housing estate emphasizes the dramatic openness of the site, in which Mr. Roberts pulls off an unlikely *coup de théâtre* by echoing the forms of the distant cement works in his strip windows and free-standing boiler house chimney. If gossip be true which attributes the uncompromising quality of the detailing to certain of Mr. Roberts's students at the School of Architecture, then that is to his credit as much to theirs.

It is remarkable how much has been achieved within the cost limits—after all, when Mies plays this kind of game, he has an American benefactor or business house to support him. Five years after completion, the brickwork of St. Bede's is still perfect and the black paint is chipped only on the tubular supports of the bicycle sheds; the formal approach incidentally is marred by the asymmetrical placing of the lamp standards.

The corroding of the silver-painted chimney is disappointing but the beach pebbles which set off the base of the outside walls remain miraculously unthrown and unswept away. Only in the abrupt junction of the classroom wings with the hall and in the vicissitudes of the hall's multi-purpose use does the skeleton of poverty poke through.

St. Bede's School and the nearby cement works

Parkside Swimming Pool   F

Mill Road

Date.	1961–3
Architect.	R. J. Wyatt of the city surveyor's department
Contractor.	Rattee & Kett Ltd.
Cost.	£224,620

Description. First demanded in 1950 and held up by delays in loan sanction, the indoor swimming pool was finally begun to a specification slightly below the new Olympic standard: main pool 110 ft by 42 ft, learners' pool 36 ft by 20 ft, seating for 752 maximum. The rectangular hall presents a symmetrical end to Mill Road, flanked by single-storey wings containing women's changing rooms and laundry (left) and men's changing rooms with offices, club room and judges' room (right). Swimmers can walk directly to the pool through the spacious glazed foyer; but spectators have to go up some stairs to the upper foyer, containing the cafeteria, which connects to the main 532-seat gallery on the south side of the pool. The north wall is wholly glazed with an aluminium curtain wall, giving a panoramic view of Parker's Piece. The west wall behind the diving boards is windowless, but opposite there is another glazed curtain to the cafeteria.

The bath, itself of concrete, is spanned by the 81 ft roof trusses of a steel frame, which is faced externally in purple London bricks, with vitreous-enamel fascias and aluminium windows. Internal finishes are intended to be corrosion resistant and sound absorbent: the broken surfaces of the cedar-slatted ceiling, the hollow clay blocks on the west wall and the grey acoustic plaster over the spectators' gallery. The heated water circulates on the Surflo system; filtration plant, boiler and plenum system are accommodated below the gallery, with service access screened from Mortimer Road by a mound. There is parking space on that side for 125 cars and 180 bicycles. Next to the pool is Parkside House, for the superintendent, which is faced in the same purple bricks, with some panels of grey rendering on the ground floor.

Comment. By far the best of the city surveyor's department's work, this is an impressively restrained solution to a complex problem within rigid cost limits. Few buildings in Cambridge have been better value for money or more appreciated by users. The use of materials externally is unpretentiously excel-

Swimming pool: Mill Road entrance

lent: the large north-facing curtain wall establishes a delightful two-way relationship between the naked bodies in the pool and the natural world of grass and trees outside—not least when lit up after dark. Internally the yellow clay blocks and dark brown cedar slatting provide an unusual richness of texture for such a building, while successfully reconciling the demands of durability with those of acoustics. A continuous strip of clerestory window separates crisply the 'floating' ceiling from the solid walls, in which only the single windows behind the gallery seem indecisive.

The lower level of changing rooms is prolonged at the opposite end by walls which effectively link the superintendent's house to the main building and give a sense of enclosure to the spacious lawn. Deposited on the grass with the best of intentions is a sadly underscaled group of bronze figures by the late Betty Rea.

Besides the loss of flexibility in separating male and female changing rooms symmetrically, the entrance is misleadingly formal for what is in fact an asymmetrical building. The gracefully bifurcated entrance porch of steel and timber (the pay box was resited in its present central alcove from an uncontrollable position on the other side of the foyer) is unpleasantly jarred by the diagonal teeth, in gold and grey terrazzo, of the staircase up to the cafeteria; and access to the gallery is far too circuitous, with spectators threading round behind the kitchen and servery. Each of the changing rooms, however, is admirably laid out in a V-shape around a central timber-slatted hanger store for clothes. Cubicles have curtains instead of doors.

Police Headquarters   G

Parkside

Proposed.   1966

Architects.   P. R. Arthur, county architect; M. R. Francis, project architect.

Cost.   £521,790

Requirement. Combined divisional headquarters for 'A' division (Cambridge City) and 'B' Division (rural Cambridgeshire) of new Mid-Anglia Police Authority.

Description. The site faces west across the vast open space of Parker's Piece and is being developed in depth around an open entrance courtyard along Warkworth Terrace, which may eventually form part of the re-aligned inner relief road. There are to be three separate buildings: an L-shaped administrative block of 47,400 sq ft, with the main enquiry office, operational group and cells accessible both from the courtyard and from Parker's Piece; a separate gymnasium block with the main hall over a ground floor containing changing rooms and the traffic wardens' section; and, on the site of the famous cycle pound at the back of the site, a multi-storey garage for 85 cars and 800 'found' cycles, with a maintenance section on the ground floor. In the basement of the office block are parade and locker rooms, stores, fall-out shelter and boiler house, the triple chimney stack of which projects with the water tank above the roofline.

The architects have aligned the principal offices in a regular terrace along Parkside, consciously rebuking the strident variety of the adjoining fire station. The almost Beaux Arts *parti* is taken from Andrew Renton's St. Katharine Dock House in London: a structural wall system of storey-height precast concrete panels for the offices and common rooms, topped on the Parkside frontage by a residential penthouse for single officers, cadets and caretaker. The penthouse is a functionally logical excuse for providing in different materials—a steel frame with battered walls of lightweight concrete—a strong cornice and attic similar to the servants' bedrooms of the nearby Regency terraces. Much less happy is the introduction of stilted arches of *in situ* concrete for the ground floor cloister, with an appliqué entrance canopy in a kind of jazz-Tudor. Individual expression for the gymnasium and car park by contrast was inevitable: the former in panels of loadbearing brick supporting concrete troughs and skylights, the latter in a split-level concrete frame similar to Park Street (see page 66) but more fully enclosed at the sides. The crowding of these various buildings is the result of using a site selected 20 years for the City police only and further limited by the setback along Warkworth Terrace. Much will depend on the architects' ability to control scale at ground level: the visitors' cars in the courtyard, for example, shaded by a giant chestnut but probably hemmed in by ill-designed police notices. It is hoped to start work in 1968.

Regional Police Headquarters from Parkside

Youth Centre H

St. Matthew's Piece and Sturton Street

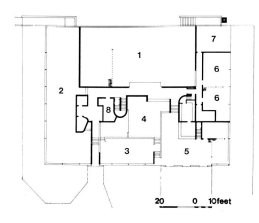

1 Upper part of hall **2** Upper part of craft room
3 Games area **4** Upper part of dance floor **5** Coffee bar
6 Group rooms **7** Music room **8** Leader's room

Date. 1967–8

Architects. J. C. Williams and John Barrow of the city architect's department.

Contractor. Grant & Dobson Ltd.

Cost. £58,000

Requirement. Multi-purpose youth centre, open seven days a week throughout the year, with average nightly attendance of 300.

Description. This glittering temple of communal activity, replacing part of a drab playground, was ironically delayed by legal difficulties over building on common land. It is situated close to the future ring road in a twilight area of light industry and decayed housing beyond the new East Road flats. Externally it is a steel-framed workshop in the James Stirling manner, with aluminium patent glazing on a grassed plinth; on one side light buff brickwork forms the backcloth to a netball pitch. The timber-joisted roof of asphalt-covered flaxboard has a pressed metal fascia. Within this shed is a completely separate internal structure of fairfaced and painted brick, defining a wide variety of spaces based on the requirements of the Department of Education's post-Albemarle youth club at Withywood, Bristol. The whole building has been sunk 4 ft into the ground to make a two-storey interior (hence the grassed plinth). Three main spaces run through both levels: a craft room across the northern end, a large hall with a folding screen to divide a small hall off from it, and a central dance floor with band platform. The visitor, entering on a 'bridge' at the north-west corner, follows an irregular route which 'discovers' for him areas of activity along it: first, up six steps, the control point and leader's room; then, turning at right angles, the gallery level of the main spaces; down steps to the right, the games area and coffee bar (with folding partitions to a group room and girls' sitting-room) which occupy only a single level, unexcavated beneath; and finally a relatively private cross corridor with large group, small group, music and dark rooms placed over lavatories, general purpose room and oil-fired boiler.

Comment.   In spite of the Ministry's excellent Withywood bulletin, youth centres are an adventure for the architect as well. On a small budget there are inherent contradictions in attempting to provide both the special spaces and corners with which disorientated youths can identify and also a structure sufficiently flexible to regroup itself round each particular phase of teenage fashion. Whatever the initial cost, a great deal of money will be needed for subsequent pushing around. Williams and Barrow have courageously attempted to solve the contradictions by separating completely the external and internal structures. The former may not be sufficiently sophisticated in finish and insulation (double glazing?); the latter's Corbusian curvatures may prove excessively immobile. Again, the equally courageous attempt at architectural control by the Smithsonian development of the 'route' may simply encourage by-passes via the coffee bar terrace and netball pitch entrance. Besides the central staircase, there are three different flights of steps up to the coffee bar and games area from the dance floor and large hall below; but one can still fear hideous congestion. As architecture for youth, this building tackles problems of gregariousness and individualism at a more fundamental level than anything the university has put up; it is exceedingly promising and deserves the success of being used and hacked to pieces (if it is preserved spotless as an architectural monument, it will have failed).

St. Matthew's Primary School I

East Road.

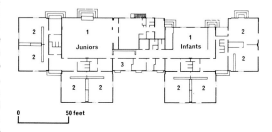

1 Halls **2** Classrooms **3** Staff rooms

Date.   1965–7

Architects.   Lyster & Grillet

Contractor.   R. Slingsby & Son Ltd.

Cost.   £66,000

Requirement.   Infants and junior mixed school for 240 pupils, plus nursery school.

Description.   Replacing an old school and some slum housing in three continuous phases, this Church of England school lies just south of the East Road development area. The infants and junior departments are placed at either end of the building and are linked by the staff areas and kitchen. Each department consists of four classrooms in pairs grouped around two sides of separate halls, but divided from them in each case by cloakrooms. A wide corridor links the two halls; this is used along its length as library, medical inspection room and waiting room. To the south, the building is symmetrical, with two equal projecting pairs of classrooms, but to the north, the façade is asymmetrical, reflecting the much smaller size of the infants' hall. Hyperbolic paraboloid roofs in pairs cover the main areas, forming triangular clerestory windows. The circulation areas are flat-roofed. The school is built of loadbearing blockwork fair-faced inside and out.

Comment.   This makes an interesting comparison with the City Architect's King's Hedges

Fulbourn Hospital, Kent House from Fulbourn Road

School (see page 126) with which it has much in common. But it is inferior in several respects. The basic layout adheres to the traditional concept of individual classrooms without the relieving feature of a shared activities space: this, it should be pointed out, is the clients' fault more than the architects'. Then there is the symmetrical south side conflicting with the north side: should there really be any symmetricality at all, since the needs of five-year-olds must surely differ radically from those in the older age group? Again, this is a fault in the brief, but one which has been allowed to enter far too readily into the architecture. The use of the hyperbolic paraboloid roofs seems an irritating device, like the pyramids at Homerton, which neither clarifies the function (identical roofs cover classrooms, kitchens and halls alike) nor adds much to the interior spaces. The system was devised originally by Christophe Grillet and Cedric Price for a competition entry.

Fulbourn and Ida Darwin   J Hospitals

Situated on a bleak hill between Cherry Hinton and Fulbourn, this curious agglomeration of nineteenth-century institutional buildings looks almost noble in its setting. There were no new buildings until, in 1957, Edgington, Spink & Hyne were commissioned to design a self-contained psychiatric unit, described below. Other additions include a sports pavilion and staff social club by Douglas Harding of Hughes & Bicknell, containing changing rooms, bar, lounge and games room in eight little pavilions. Edgington, Spink & Hyne have also built a boiler house and stores for the hospitals which include a dominant water tower clad in the same ribbed precast concrete slabs as Kent House. A group of single-storey wards for Ida Darwin Hospital was added in 1966–7 by A. F. Scott & Partners (of Norwich).

Kent House Admissions Villa

Date.   1963–4

Architects.   Edgington, Spink & Hyne.
H. J. Villet, partner-in-charge

Contractors.   Coulson & Son Ltd.

Cost.   £238,348

Requirement. Self-contained admissions and short-term psychiatric unit.

Description. Kent House is entirely independent of the main structure of the hospital, to the extent of having its own entrance from the Cambridge–Fulbourn road. It is T-shaped in plan, with recreational and communal facilities in the long arm and a treatment and administrative area in the short arm. Across the long arm straddles a dominant two-storey block in which there is accommodation for 95 patients, divided into male and female sections. On the ground floor of this block are two ten-bed dormitories; the rest of the accommodation is provided in one- or four-bed rooms. At each end of the block there are terraces, part uncovered, part sheltered by a canopy, and enclosed gardens. The building is largely prefabricated, with concrete H-frames for the two-storey block, and simple beams and columns for the rest. On these, are fixed precast ribbed concrete panels. The two-storey block has a 'butterfly' section roof and a ribbed aluminium fascia, but elsewhere the roofs are flat and there is no fascia. All the windows are double-glazed, in timber frames. Internally surfaces are generally plastered or tiled, but the ceilings are boarded in the circulation areas and are designed to reduce noise.

Comment. This is a good building by a firm which had not practised in Cambridge before. Its long bland façades and the slight rhythmic play of the windows create a coolness which might help to calm the patients. What is not so good is the disruption of the extreme regularity of south front by the low one-storey T-block projecting forward, and by a slight setting back of the west wing, or dislocation, which does not seem entirely justified in the organization, but which nevertheless has a disturbing effect on this otherwise deadpan façade. Nor is the (comparatively) jazzy tank-room roof altogether a welcome feature. The external finishes are crisp, and the ribbed panels provide an attractive texture; internally, too, the architects have avoided too institutional a manner, although the long corridors are not altogether welcome.

Commercial Buildings

In view of the interest of planners in the City Road area, there is surprisingly little to report. Fitzroy Street, largely owned by Jesus College, has the first two buildings of a comprehensive redevelopment. Reston House of 1957, by Cecil Elsom & Partners, is an admirable two-storey shopping block grouping with New Square. Concrete-framed, it is faced in yellow brick, with dark-blue ceramic infill panels and ceramic covered columns, free-standing at either end. The newspaper kiosk against the end wall towards New Square links new to old with notable success. The other building, Nos. 31–9 Fitzroy Street, of 1959–60, by Hughes & Bicknell, is much less happy, with an arty diapered and bow-windowed first floor visually unconnected with the plate glass beneath.

In Newmarket Road there has been more activity: the pleasant S.R.C.R.A. offices (see below), the small granite clad Lloyd's Bank of 1963 by Hughes & Bicknell and, opposite, the new 'Cambridge News' offices and press built in 1960–1 to the design of Jeffrey Lyde of L. A. Culliford & Partners. This is a straightforward commercial solution of a complex planning problem, with details no better than average. The entrance hall of the three-storey office block, which is faced with yellow brick, is distinguished by a cantilevered exposed staircase and some potted plants. Further east in Newmarket Road is a motley collection of garages and showrooms of little merit (J. H. Cooper & Son, 1963–4, is by C. J.

Bourne). A belated effort to stiffen the street frontage has been made in the new depot of Greene King (1966–7) by Lyster & Grillet. To Newmarket Road this presents a solid wall (with no entrance) in a decent industrial vernacular of blue engineering bricks, with a continuous clerestory and a fascia of sheet aluminium. This screens the three stores for bottles, for casks and for wines, spirits and tobacco, which are spanned by broad structural space frames. The entrance, on the southern side towards New Road, has a two-storey office block slotted in beneath the same level roofline, with blue bricks and aluminium windows again. The nearby Gas Works, which recently lost a splendid Piranesian façade of *c.* 1875 to River Lane, is now dominated by a shapeless 'brick cathedral' of Battersea vintage, with sub-Dudokian window details—designed in 1957 by Woodall-Duckham Ltd.

In Mill Road piecemeal improvements are merely delaying badly needed redevelopment, but the Magnet Bowl (see below) is a bright newcomer on a larger scale. Beside the gloomy station yards, the offices of the Cambridge University & Town Waterworks Co. (1957–8), by Bird & Tyler, are simple and unaffected, with yellow brick facings and a flat roof. The front side of the station, which was redecorated admirably in 1959, does not yet have its promised forecourt, but only a makeshift roundabout. Opposite the excellent Great Eastern House in Station Road (see below) are the laboratories of Spiller's: two depressing brick buildings by Lanchester & Lodge, with a sculpture of Ceres, and a yellow curtain-walled block of 1959 next to the former flour mills, by Oscar Faber & Partners. Further down Station Road the bulk of Kett House may be joined by a comprehensive office development sketched for St. John's College by Viscount Esher (both schemes are described below).

S.R.C.R.A. Building   K

Newmarket Road

Date.   1960–1

Architects.   Feilden & Mawson of Norwich.

Contractor.   William Sindall Ltd.

Cost.   £22,850

Requirement.   Offices and laboratory for Shipowners Refrigerated Cargo Research Association.

Description.   This small two-storeyed T-shaped building contains offices, library, store and two small laboratories in the arm of the T, facing Newmarket Road across a small forecourt, and a single large laboratory running through both storeys in the stem of the T. Work carried out includes the testing of materials used in the insulation and construction of refrigerated cargo space and the products carried in them. The building has an exposed concrete frame, designed to carry an extra floor if required. Infill walls are generally of red facing bricks, and there is green tile cladding to the first floor spandrels on the street front. All windows are double-glazed.

Comment.   This pleasant little building is one of two buildings in Cambridge by one of the better East Anglian firms of architects. It is easily missed, being set back behind a small forecourt which unfortunately breaks the street line, but it well repays a glance for the intimate quality of its detailing. Its crispness can be compared with the flabbiness of Barnwell Hostel (see page 9) on the other side of the road. This kind of street architecture, rational and repetitive like a Georgian terrace, can do more ultimately for Cambridge's background beauty than the expressive masterpieces by the big names from London. There is a strong case for mediocrity in ordinary workplaces—the Functional Tradition as it is sometimes called.

Great Eastern House   L

Station Road and Tenison Road

Date.   1956–7

Architect.   H. H. Powell, chief architect, B.R. Eastern Region

Contractor.   Gilbert-Ash Ltd.

Cost.   £85,256

Requirement.   Offices for Regional Traffic Manager and social club for Railway Institute.

Description.   This grey concrete block close to the railway station was Cambridge's first example of the new industrialized methods of prefabricated construction. The reinforced concrete columns and first-floor slab, poured in situ, support three floors of offices which were built dry, using the patent Intergrid system. The factory-made parts are joined like a Meccano set without the use of mortar. The prestressed concrete frame is faced with precast panels with exposed aggregate finish and hardwood-framed windows. Internal timber partitions are arranged on the 3 ft 4 in module. The lifts and stairs are expressed on the east elevation by a glazed hardwood screen running the full height of the building. A wall of brown-grey Bedford bricks, independent of the frame and its columns, encloses the social club's two rooms on the ground floor together with the service rooms behind; the large plate-glass windows are framed in timber. The timber-faced roof of the club continues as a canopy over the main entrance.

Comment.   This is an important building, easily missed. H. H. Powell's excellent stations at Harlow, Bishop's Stortford and Broxbourne are perhaps more familiar to Cambridge people. The Intergrid building system used here was first evolved for schools. Significantly, it has been introduced into Cambridge in an office block, rather than by the university or colleges. The qualities of this building are in fact universal: commonsense layout, with the service rooms overlooking the rail yards at the rear; speedy and efficient construction, taking only ten months in all; and exposed concrete of such fine quality that it needed no internal plastering. The

Great Eastern House

unadorned structure, crisply regular like a Georgian terrace, has an individuality lacking in speculative office blocks such as Kett House nearby. It is the conventionally built ground floor that now looks drab: messy weathering on the first floor slab beneath a ragged flashing, and blotchy woodwork at odds with the Miesian clarity of the club structure with its Baccardi-derived entrance pillar. Even less adequate is the lift and water tower, heavily patterned behind and appearing awkwardly over the roofline at the front. The modular construction throughout, which makes future expansion or modification easier, has already had a crucial test, for the Regional Traffic Manager moved in 1964 to Norwich and much of Great Eastern House is now commercially let.

Kett House   M

Station Road

Date.   1961–2

Architects.   Trehearne & Norman, Preston & Partners

Contractor.   Rattee & Kett Ltd.

Requirement.   Offices for letting.

Description.   Kett House occupies the site of Rattee & Kett's old headquarters, no longer needed when they moved to the other side of the railway. So a picturesque group of Gothic Revival sheds and villa has been replaced by this conventional concrete-framed office block, which provides four floors of offices along Station Road and two floors in a secondary block enclosing a forecourt towards Hills Road. Infill panels are of brick, with some curtain walling on the ground floor. The lower block has covered parking space at ground level.

Comment. Treherne & Norman, Preston & Partners are among the better of London's commercial architects and some of their works (State House, Holborn) transcend the monotony of most spec office building by showing a sensitivity to town planning considerations. Kett House is not one of these. Its awkward, thrusting use of this important corner site shows up every banality, down to the patterned brickwork on one blank end wall and the curious bas-relief of Kett's tree, by Willi Soukop, on the other.

Station Road Redevelopment N

1 Offices **2** Housing **3** Kett House

Proposed. 1966

Architect. Brett & Pollen (Viscount Esher)

Description. The site is on the south side of Station Road and is bounded by the line of the proposed inner by-pass and Hills Road. The sketch design shows four long office blocks at right-angles to Station Road and identical in height and bay width to the adjoining Kett House. They differ only in that the ground floor is partially open. On the Hills Road side are shown 49 houses in terraces, some straight, some staggered, grouped picturesquely around little courts. Whether the architects will be able to use the same proportions as Kett House and yet avoid its banalities, time alone will tell. Whether the two halves of the scheme will cohere, is a moot point. If they succeed on both counts, this will be a valuable addition to Cambridge, particularly as the part-owners of the site, St. John's College, have had a poor record previously of comprehensive redevelopment (see Barton Road page 186).

Magnet Bowl O

Mill Road

Date. 1964–5

Architect. G. M. Vickers

Contractor. J. M. Hill & Sons Ltd. (Ampthill)

Cost. £100,000

Description. This 24-lane tenpin bowling centre lies at the other end of Mill Road from Parker's Piece. The plot of previously derelict land has a 140 ft frontage—unusually wide for an otherwise built-up street, but exceptionally narrow for a bowling centre, which has to conform to the precise measurements of standardized equipment. The lanes, each 60 ft by 3 ft 6 in, are placed parallel with the road, in a single space laid out in a series of strips: the pin decks with a maintenance passageway behind, the lanes themselves, the players' approach area (16 ft wide), spectators' and players' seating (14 ft), the foyer (14 ft) and the snack bar, changing rooms and lavatories. Next to the snack bar is the central control desk. Apart from two rows of columns defining the snack bar and service rooms, the structure is a single span of castellated steelwork supported on loadbearing brick walls, with brown facings. The main space is artificially lit and ventilated. At the rear of the building is another row of service and plant rooms in brick, including the club bar and league room. The street façade has a broad windowless wall (with illuminated lettering) set back behind a lawn with a transplanted tree; the porch, which has a projecting timber canopy on steel columns, has thick wooden mullions and a copper fascia, as have the large windows to the two bars. The rear doors lead out to parking space for 74 cars. Internal finishes are largely in plastic and asbestos tiling, with myriad spotlights in the foyer contrasting with the uniform brightness of the playing area.

Comment. Bowling is liturgically one of the most dogmatic of modern religions: so fantastically expensive is the equipment—about £3,000 a lane, making approximately half the cost of each building —that the game's rapid promotion in Britain (over 200 centres opened since January 1960) can be traced almost entirely to the slump which menaced the principal equipment manufacturers, A.M.F. Inc., after they had flooded the American market. According to A.M.F. tenpin is 'a scientifically captivating sport played regularly and seriously in an atmosphere of friendly competition'—i.e. there is virtually nothing to it, except the magic of its mechanical aids and the attraction of its club atmosphere. Undoubtedly the reaction of most bourgeois stylefanciers to the Magnet Bowl will be gratitude that it is all in such good taste, particularly in Mill Road of the plebs. G. M. Vickers has indeed done a capable layout on a difficult site even though the snack bar is cramped; and he has used the approved emblems of enlightenment—sensitive expanses of brickwork, dignified timber mullions, a Jacobsen-style portecochère, a transplanted tree with tiles and pebbles at its base. The lettering is civilized and only the glittering copper fascias are a little brash at present. All this is thoroughly decent and bravely done. But it is not really relevant. If the inside is visually stunning—one of the finest modern interiors in Cambridge—it is just because it is 'scientifically captivating'—the only piece of architecture locally that *is*, apart from the Radio Telescope (see page 184). The equipment, which the architect had to accept willy-nilly, is not, thank heavens, in good taste. It whizzes and pops and shimmers: the lanes in polished hardwood, the seats in bright red plastic, the lit-up score panels, the Freudian pins and balls. Fortunately Vickers has entered into the act himself with his swooping folds of suspended ceiling dropping downwards across the lanes and exaggerating the curiously infinite distance to the pins.

The Magnet Bowl, entrance

Housing

Eastern Cambridge has large areas of sprawling council housing at Cherry Hinton and at Meadowlands, following the line of the abortive outer bypass. The 'Racehorse' pub at Meadowlands is a pleasant building by a local architect G. M. Vickers, who has also done a nearby block of middle-class flats, Quainton Close (1961–2). Off Cherry Hinton Road, there is an estate of 80 terrace houses called Derwent Close designed by Herbert Cox & Gear of St. Albans. Built in 1961–3, Derwent Close shows the more urban, compact layout first introduced in the area by David Roberts and Eric Lyons (see below). Lyons's first span housing in Cambridge consists of a small terrace of brick cross-wall houses in Crozier Road (1956). Lyster and Grillet have done two residential schemes in the area: a surgery at 620 Newmarket Road (1963), a well-detailed flat-roofed house; and flats at 150 Cherry Hinton Road (1965), which show a pleasant sense of scale. Compactness and human scale can be seen in the old people's flats in Napier Street, designed by the

East Road development: maisonettes

City Surveyor's department. Lilac Court, Cherry Hinton Road, built in 1961–2, is another terraced layout providing 30 flats. As yet these estates have not made much impact on the general planning (or lack of planning) of eastern Cambridge, but they do show encouraging signs of changing middle class taste.

In Cherry Hinton there are three schemes by the City Architect's department which stand out against the poor quality of the rest of the housing there. In the High Street, is the branch library with maisonettes on two floors cantilevered slightly over it. The upper floors are in dark, loadbearing brick; the walls are supported by reinforced concrete beams and columns on the ground floor to permit extensive glazing for the library. A single-storey foyer is added in front and built in white brick. Further north, opposite the church, is a row of 14 flats and maisonettes in two short terraces called Langdale Close. The flats are on the ground floor and the maisonettes are reached from a first-floor deck. They are built in re-used stock brick cross-walls with tiling used on the infill panels. This is a very well-behaved group which fits well into the wooded surroundings, but unfortunately is too small to have more than a local effect on the disorder of Cherry Hinton. The most curious of the three is the group of bungalows known as Teversham Drift built in pink brick which is just north of Langdale on the road to Teversham. There is one further development by the department, off Mill Road, consisting of 50 flatlets, 17 houses and 12 bungalows, partly for elderly people, called Brookfields. This is in bright red brick, with an almost deliberate chunkiness: unfortunately, poor grouping along a meandering road has partly destroyed the effect of an otherwise promising scheme. Hinton House (1963) is an inoffensive old people's home on the same side by the county architect.

East Road Redevelopment P

East Road, Norfolk Street

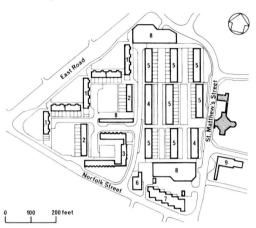

0   100   200 feet

1 Four-storey maisonettes **2** Three-storey houses **3** Two-storey old people's houses **4** Two-storey old people's flats **5** Two- and three-bedroom houses **6** 'Man in the Moon' pub **7** Shops **8** Garages **9** Cherry Tree Club

Date.   1959–68 (Stages I–III)

Architects.   David Roberts & Geoffrey Clarke

Contractors.   Johnson & Bailey Ltd.;
                   Coulson & Son Ltd.

Cost.   £148,650 (Stage I)
                   £136,474 (Stage II)

Requirement.   Comprehensive redevelopment, including 17 terrace houses, 90 maisonettes, shops and 24 old people's homes.

Description.   This is the first major slum redevelopment in the centre of Cambridge. The flats and maisonettes of stages I–II occupy a triangular site between East Road and Norfolk Street.
Stages I and II are axially related to the side streets, not to the widened East Road, towards which zigzags a continuous four-storey block of 72 two-bedroom maisonettes. Behind these, there are three courtyards, two closed and one open. They are formed from straight terraces, three-storey three-bedroom houses of two different types. The ground level drops sharply from East Road, so that access

to the zigzag block is direct to the second floor gallery, serving the upper maisonettes. This black timbered gallery crosses the block at each corner, being always on the north or east side. This leaves south and west aspects free for the bay windows of the living rooms. At the corners there are stairs down, communal waste-disposal chutes and clothes-drying areas. Half the ground-floor maisonettes and houses have their own walled yards. There is a block of 15 garages along the service road (a cruciform cul-de-sac) and 17 car ports built into houses. In the communal areas are a number of transplanted trees (one given by the Civic Trust) in addition to two large existing trees. The structure is of repetitive loadbearing brick cross-walls throughout, with exposed concrete floor slabs and yellow stock facing bricks. There are standardized aluminium floor-to-ceiling windows.
Stage III, between Staffordshire Street and St. Matthew's Street is developed differently with three blocks of housing running north/south, each divided into three. At the southern end, on Norfolk Street, are shops and 'The Man in the Moon' pub. Parking is arranged in two blocks, one just south of the houses and one to the north by East Road providing 192 car spaces. On the other side of St. Matthew's Street, which is retained as a main distributor road, is the Cherry Trees old people's club, also designed by David Roberts. Stage III is also of brick cross-walls, yellow-faced, and the shops form an echelon carrying on the axis the houses form. At each of the projecting corners of the shops is a large free-standing brick column.

Comment.   David Roberts's low cost housing is quite as excellent as his college and school buildings. His clear lines of quiet brickwork have an underlying sensitivity to the austere, windswept climate of East Anglia. The façades are quite free, the windows not necessarily corresponding on all levels. While the continuous concrete floor slabs keep the layers clearly apart horizontally, the vertical division between houses is perhaps unfortunately disguised. The heavy timber planks protecting the galleries, placed flat to the façades, are an unusual and effective detail, preventing the feeling of insecurity usual in access galleries. Throughout there is a subtle play of diagonals, customary in Mr. Roberts's work. This is put to good effect in the shops, which face both ways down the street. Although the three-storey houses are a trifle narrow, all these buildings

East Road redevelopment: shops in Norfolk Street

are pleasant to live in, spacious, light and warm in winter. The simple courtyard layout provides enclosed playgrounds and meeting places, without infringing privacy.

There is one unfortunate aspect of the design, and of the site: the relationship to the widened East Road and to the probable redevelopments beyond (see page 12). Although the buildings get away from the busy main road, the triangular patches of grass between are an unhappy hinterland. Nor, too, has Stage III developed any strong relationship with St. Matthew's church or the Cherry Trees club, which is particularly to be regretted. Two aspects of the brief are also unfortunate: the unimaginative retention of existing streets and the inadequate provision of garages (one per four families). As a result the service roads are used for open-air parking, spoiling

the courtyards. This pre-Buchanan parsimony is largely rectified in Stage III which overcomes the parking problem by concentrating it in two blocks rather than relying on culs-de-sac.

Highsett

Q

Hills Road and Tenison Avenue

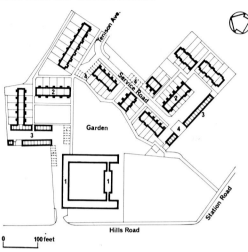

0   100 feet

1 Flats **2** Houses **3** Garages **4** Car parks

Date.	1958–60, 1962, 1963–4
Architects.	Eric Lyons & Partners
Contractors.	Wates Ltd. (Stage I). Rattee & Kett Ltd. (Stages II and III)

Requirement. 85 flats, maisonettes and houses for Span Developments Ltd.

Description. When first published in 1957, this project aroused some controversy because Mr. Lyons proposed a 15-storey block of bachelor flats, set well back from the road in centre of an open court flanked by lower terraces. The strongly modelled concrete tower (which has probably influenced recent work by the G.L.C.) was reluctantly accepted by the planning authorities but is not now to be erected. In its place, salvaged from the previous Victorian villas, is a triangular garden with luxuriant trees, banks and grottoes. The first building, on a deceptively short frontage to Hills Road, is a three-storey closed courtyard forming an atrium to the rest of the site. From the walled gateway to the street, a paved way leads axially through the courtyard, penetrating the east and west wings at ground level through a cloister of slim concrete columns and beams painted white. Glazed staircases lead to 31 flats of various types in three wings. In the fourth (north), a cloister on the court side supports six 'studio maisonettes', which are entered on the other side from an external gallery at first-floor level over 12 garages. The service road leads further back to a compound of 25 garages; these are on one side of an informal Stage II courtyard of two-storey houses, 17 in all stretching to the site's back entrance in Tenison Avenue. From there a second service cul-de-sac gives access beyond the central garden to Stage III: 31 more houses, mainly three-storey, plus 17 more garages and a walled pathway to Station Road.

The basic structure throughout is of 9 in brick crosswalls, with concrete slabs and underfloor heating. In Stage I, apart from the concrete-columned cloisters, facings are primarily in dark blue tile-hanging—the arrowhead shape specially designed by the architects—with asbestos panels to the ground floor, aluminium windows and end walls of pale buff bricks. Stage II by contrast has yellow stock bricks, white weatherboarding and glazed porches; the crosswalls, projecting slightly into the fascia, alternate with broader strips of walling separating the through living-rooms from a parallel strip of kitchen, staircase and study. In the taller houses of Stage III, hard golden bricks with raked joints largely disguise the crosswalls and floors. Panels of white boarding vertically connect the big windows of ground floor dining room, first floor living room and second floor master bedroom. The stack of service rooms alongside, with a high boarded water tank, is recessed behind a projecting cloakroom and porch—and the dustbin enclosure extends still further to wall in a forecourt.

Comment. Highsett displays all the best Span qualities and is uncommonly interesting in showing three different phases of Eric Lyons's development. One of the few post-war architects to specialize in housing, he has achieved an uncanny sense of place partly because of his long experience in combating the by-laws which tend to chop up enclosure into sausage lengths (with windy grass verges). Half-naked children gambol in the gardens of Highsett, fully protected from the East Anglian blast of wind. But also, like Lutyens or Nash, Lyons succeeds in unashamedly embracing his clients' aspirations. Span can be sneered at for being 'middle class utopia', a Colour Supplement heaven—but that is

Highsett Stage I, view back to Hills Road from the court

Highsett, Stage III

Highsett, Stage II

what it *is*. Instead of the crumbling whiteness of the Pioneers or the neo-slummy textures of the Brutalists, Lyons provides a permissive Arcadia of natural surfaces, descended from Blaise Hamlet and Bedford Park. Those who want the spacious and the natural (including most architects) will no doubt purchase old houses instead; but Span-dwellers prefer compactness and artificiality with plenty of built-in furniture, spotless kitchenettes and a garnishing of instant landscape.

Highsett's special attraction is kinetic: vistas constantly dissolve and re-assemble, as the pedestrian passes from enclosed court and formal paving, through an exotic garden to the grander walled avenues of Stage III, and then obliquely out to Station Road through a miniature alleyway. Separation of vehicles from pedestrians is handled effortlessly without losing the car or confusing the postman. The irritations start, however, as soon as one stops to look—in Stage I, for example, at the arty forecourt to Hills Road and at the sweet-toothed Surrey tile-hanging. Stage II, if rather bald, is more East Anglian in its yellow walling and white fencing Stage III is the most dubious part, with its sudden change to hard golden bricks and an intense vertical emphasis, carried to excessive heights in the narrow-paled gates and in the silly outside light (with house number on it). The *piano nobile* living room and the high-walled garden are an acceptable response to the demand for 'town houses' with a certain swank; but too much of the detailing seems like an attempt by Lyons to get back at his brutalist critics. The drawing board *tour-de-force* of projections and recessions includes an over-emphatic mullion in the big windows, which looks more like a crosswall than the crosswall itself, and an absurd precast concrete gutter over the cloakroom window, which implies an overflow from the cistern. Much neater and wittier mannerism appears in the butterfly gable walls, where an insubstantial shiny pipe appears to 'support' the whole roof through another oversized concrete spouthead.

Northern Area

Chesterton, Arbury, King's Hedges, Huntingdon Road

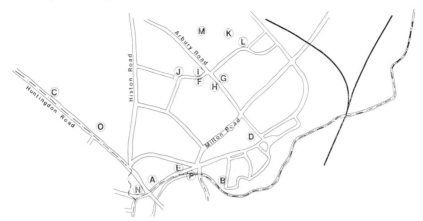

A slightly separate world, with a continuous river barrier between it and the centre, this northern part of Cambridge has a traditional aloofness from the city. The royal castle overlooked it from Castle Hill, where the mound still survives next to Shire Hall. Pleasant cottage housing in the Victoria Road area expanded quickly in the 1860's because the area was outside the borough and had lower rates. Indeed the urban district of Chesterton was only united with Cambridge in 1911. Between the wars, ribbon development along Milton Road together with Pye's works succeeded in throttling the old village of Chesterton. The post-war Arbury Estate (page 119), despite its shortcomings of layout and design, has tried to create a northern centre, with communal buildings grouped close together. The real trouble is its very low density. Although the ugliness of urban life is missing from its cottagey wastes, the compensations of humanity and liveliness are missing too. It leapt the Histon Road and the city fathers then cast hungry eyes on the remaining 200 acres of open space north of Arbury Road which had first been refused by the Minister in 1954. This has now been developed as the King's Hedges Estate which shows considerable promise, despite a weak start.

On Castle Hill, Sir William Holford prepared designs in 1955–6 for new assize courts, together with office and library accommodation, on the site of the Victorian assize courts, demolished in 1954. The new two-storey building was to be in brick with simpli-fied-classical façades and a formal portico entrance set a little to one side. The scheme has been shelved, for the moment, because of financial restrictions. The site has meanwhile been laid out with lawns and a sunken car park by the late county architect, R. H. Crompton, who in 1959 added an extra storey to the Shire Hall itself.

University and College Buildings

In this segment of Cambridge, there is little obvious sign of the post-war university. There is one college outside the city boundaries (Girton), one large col-lege hostel (Clare's on Castle Hill) and one boat-house worth notice (Corpus–Sidney), to all of which David Roberts has contributed work of distinction. The playing fields have been given various pavilions of which the only notable one is Sir William Holford and Partners' design for the University Athletic Club.

Sir William's pavilion provides changing and exer-cise rooms and a two-storey club room. There is a balcony overlooking the track, reached by an open spiral staircase of steel. The building is steel-framed with brick walls and cedar cladding, and copper roofs sloping down from front and back towards the centre. The contractor is William Sindall and the cost £20,000. It was finished in 1965.

Other post-war university or academic buildings in-clude Professor Llewelyn-Davies's important re-search building for the Animal Research Laboratory (see below), and the extension of Morley Horder's National Institute of Agricultural Botany by J. B. F. Cowper and Poole. This is a straightforward con-crete-framed building forming three sides of a court. More interesting is the storage building and boiler house erected on a site to the north in 1963 to the designs of the same architects. This three-storey building, elegantly detailed, has red brick facings on the lower floors and an aluminium curtain wall above.

One of the most recent schemes is the extension to the Dunn Nutritional Laboratory by Lyons, Israel and Ellis (1966–7). It was built by the University in con-junction with the Medical Research Council, and constructed in red brick cross walls with exposed concrete floor slabs.

Following Mr. Ede's magnanimous gift of his art collection to the university, an appeal for the exten-sion of Kettle's Yard (see page 129) has been started and designs prepared by Sir Leslie Martin.

Clare Castle Hill Hostel   A

Chesterton Lane

Date.	1957–8
Architect.	David Roberts
Contractors.	Kerridge Ltd.
Cost.	£92,000
Requirement.	Rooms for 40 undergraduates, two caretaker's flats, two breakfast rooms, kitchen.

Description. The site, approached on foot by a winding path from Chesterton Lane, is a narrow up-hill strip along the east side of a garden, which contains two villas used as Clare lodgings.

The main block is four-storeyed and contains 10 bed-sitting rooms on each floor. It is divided in two sections vertically, with only emergency doors be-tween. At the end of each section is a side-wing set at an angle to the main block, containing a breakfast room and a caretaker's flat. In the triangular spaces between main wing and side wings are the two timber-framed staircases. The staircases lead on each floor to a corridor running along the back (east side) of the main block. Off the corridor open service rooms, grouped in towers, on the east side, and bed-sitters on the west side, facing the garden.

Each room is set at a diagonal to the corridor and parallel to its next-door neighbour, so that two ex-ternal walls (south and west) face with storey-height windows into the garden, and two internal walls form a triangular space for washing and storage units with the corridor on the third side. This results in a zigzag formation, the structure being of load-bearing brick with concrete floor slabs at each level faced with blue slate. Facing bricks are yellow throughout.

The side wings have exposed timber ceilings in the breakfast rooms and low-pitched roofs. In front of the upper breakfast room is a stepped area, paved formally in brick and stone; behind it is a group of garages, approached by the service road on the

114

Clare Castle Hill Hostel

eastern boundary of the site.

Comment. This is one of Cambridge's best post-war buildings. Its principal qualities are freedom and simplicity. There is freedom in layout and landscaping; freedom from the collegiate shibboleths of enclosed courts; and freedom from the gloom of academic introversion (colours are light and bright, with a Scandinavian tone in the staircases and breakfast rooms). There is simplicity in the structural expression of brick and concrete; and simplicity in the basic idea of diagonal zigzag formation, canting each room so as to gain the maximum light and air and leaving corridors and gyp rooms to the cheerless views to the north and east. Considering that this was Mr. Roberts's first departure along these lines, it was an extraordinary relaxed and unpretentious achievement. It blends perfectly with the hilly garden and with the two

existing villas, of which one is red brick and flint Gothic, and the other is white washed neo-Georgian. There are some questionable details. There is no expression of the division between the two parts of the hostel. There is insufficient clarity between loadbearing and non-loadbearing brickwork in the service towers and there is an unfortunate clash externally where the main wing meets the side-wings, which belong in manner to Mr. Roberts's earlier period. Other criticisms are perhaps accounted for by lack of finance: the furnishings are rather hard and utilitarian and the windows should be doubleglazed. The corridors are noisy.

Nevertheless, this is an outstanding building. It is interesting that Mr. Roberts was unaware, when he made his design, of a building with similar zigzag planning, Anders Tengbom's training college at Lidingö, Sweden (erected in 1958).

Corpus Christi and Sidney Sussex, Boathouse   B

off Victoria Avenue

Date. 1958–9

Architect. David Roberts

Contractors. William Sindall Ltd.

Cost. £13,000

Requirement. Boathouse for two colleges.

Description. This is the first post-war boat-house and is a two-storeyed structure. The two colleges' boats are stored in three bays which extend behind the main building in a structure of asbestos-cement sheeting on a light steel frame. Free-standing spiral staircases of pre-cast concrete lead up to the first-floor gallery which runs in front of the two clubrooms and changing-rooms. Infill panels are of yellow brick. Railings are of wrought iron, with handrails and staircase treads of teak.

Comment. This is a graceful little building, making the most of its small budget. The thin, angular lines are appropriate to a riverside setting. Unlike the Oxford boathouses, it does not overlook racing and thus the spartan club facilities are sufficient.

Girton College

307 undergraduates, 57 postgraduates, 35 fellows.

Girton has seen three generations of Waterhouse, all designing in some sort of institutional Tudor. In 1955 a new east window, by L. C. Evetts of Newcastle, was inserted into the 1901–2 chapel. Its depiction of Christ in Majesty and six scenes from the Passion is rich in colour, though its dependence on pre-cedent (Chartres) is far greater than Evett's later windows at Downing (see page 17).
A decisive break from neo-Tudor came in 1962, with David Roberts's flat for the Mistress. This occupies the first floor of the east wing of Eliza Baker Court, above the fellows' parlour and dining room. Mr. Roberts has boldly contrasted his flat-roofed,

wooden-framed structure with the red brick and terracotta of the surrounding buildings. It consists of a continuous 13-bay curtain wall, with short link-ing panels of brickwork at either end. The windows are given a random pattern by their Venetian blinds. In its Miesian proportions and beautiful clarity of expression, this building enhances the hard geo-metry of Waterhouse's buildings.

Animal Research Laboratory   C

Huntingdon Road

Date. 1959–60

Architects. Professor Lord Llewelyn-Davies and John Musgrove

Contractors. Johnson & Bailey Ltd.

Cost. £30,000

Requirement. Extension to laboratory for Agri-cultural Research Council.

Description. This building was the direct out-come of the programme of research on laboratory design proposed to the Nuffield Foundation by the Agricultural Research Council, and carried out from 1954 as the first project of the foundation's division of architectural studies. It consists of a small one-storey building, about 70 ft by 40 ft, connected with the existing laboratory by an enclosed corridor. The following accommodation was needed: five rooms for chromatography, tissue culture, instruments, low temperatures and centrifuge; a common room with kitchen and ancillary rooms (lavatories, clean-er's store). The building is divided by loadbearing brick cross-walls into six bays with 11 ft 6 in centres. On either side of the central corridors are the rooms: 24 ft deep laboratories and common room facing south and 12 ft deep special rooms facing north. In addition to large double-glazed windows fitted with a system of external louvres, the laboratories have a continuous louvred rooflight which also lights the corridor. The centrifuge room is specially surrounded by 9 in brick cross-walls with a 2 in cavity, which give a sound insulation value of over 55 dB.

Regional Hospital Board Headquarters: model

Comment. This little white-brick building, with its straightforward functional appearance and steeply pitched roof light, has the rational quality of the early nineteenth century industrial buildings. It is one of the most important new buildings in Cambridge, because this deceptive simplicity of appearance hides the immense volume of research that went into its design. Professor Llewelyn-Davies, who also did pioneering work on hospitals, has here tackled every problem that faces the laboratory designer: lighting, ventilation, insulation, fittings and so on. The research, of which a full account is available in 'The Design of Research Laboratories' (O.U.P. 1961), has recently been incorporated in other buildings, such as the Cancer Research Laboratories in Lincoln's Inn Fields. Study of its results must be strongly urged on all future designers of laboratories in Cambridge, so that we have no more semi Beaux Arts palaces of the Chemistry and Engineering variety. Labs have a straightforward industrial purpose for which only straightforward industrial buildings are suitable.

Regional Hospital D
Board Headquarters

Date. 1963–4

Architects. Johns, Slater & Haward, in association with Guy Aldis, architect to the Board.

Contractors. Johnson & Bailey Ltd.

Cost. £164,140

Requirement. Offices, board room, Hollerith plant room, boiler house.

Description. The East Anglian Hospital Board originally occupied a number of separate buildings. The new headquarters lie north of Chesterton Road and are entered from Union Lane, but eventually a new relief road will run east–west alongside them, so they had to be planned to be entered from both directions.

Other conditions were the large area of office space to be provided and the extremely narrow cost limits laid down. In addition, offices had to be as flexible as possible and capable of expansion.

The four-storey slab of offices has a single-storey entrance hall and boardroom wing stretching eastwards from the centre. The boardroom itself is distinguished by a timber joisted pyramid roof with a central roof light. Because of noise and fumes respectively, the Hollerith plant room and boiler house are separate buildings to the south of the multistorey block. The plant room is connected by a covered way, which will eventually be replaced by the extension of the office block. Construction throughout is of brick walls and piers, with silver-grey handmade facing bricks and precast concrete edge beams with a bush-hammered limestone aggregate. Owing to the cost limits, complete flexibility in the office areas was not possible, but standardized dimensions and the layout of services and partitions allow for considerable rearrangement.

Comment.   This office block is the first work in Cambridge of a well-known Ipswich firm of architects. The simplicity of structure has allowed high quality finishes, but these have not been allowed to swamp the direct expression of the concrete floors and brick columns, threaded together as in brick warehouses of Ipswich or Norwich. The sides away from the road of the office and board-room wings form part of an irregular courtyard with Guy Aldis's recent and proposed extensions to the adjoining hospital. One of the important features of this building is its remarkable value for money, the result of collaboration at an early stage in design between the architects, the engineers (Charles Weiss and Partners) and the quantity surveyors (Lewis and Marshall). It is high time that this sort of pre-planning entered into university design at Cambridge. The slit windows close to the centre of the office block *do* indicate lavatories, unlike those at the Local Examination Syndicate (page 91) or Spence's building at Queens' (page 41). It is a pity that the big car park in front of the buildings is not screened in any way (the members' lounge overlooks it with low-sill windows).

Cambridge Instruments   E

Chesterton Road

Date.	1957–8, 1960–1
Architects.	Edward D. Mills & Partners
Contractors.	J. Jarvis & Sons
Cost.	£200,000 (approx.)

Requirement. Laboratories and drawing office; instrument assembly rooms and administrative offices.

Description.   There are two clearly defined stages: first, the four-storey block facing Chesterton Road containing three floors of laboratories and a drawing office and covered balcony on the top floor; secondly, the three-storey wing facing Carlyle Road with covered parking and two floors of assembly rooms and offices. Both stages are linked to a common entrance at the S.W. corner and to the existing factory building behind. The concrete frame structure has long span beams for the labs. The facing materials are buff brick for the end walls, artificial stone and Westmorland slate panels for the façade. Special attention has been given to heating and air conditioning, with a lavish provision of service ducts to give complete flexibility of internal layout.

Comment.   Edward Mills has reached the front rank of English architects by designing in two widely separate fields: factories and Methodist churches. Cambridge Instruments is efficient and pleasantly detailed within. But because of its prominent site next to Jesus Lock, it is regrettable that functional clarity was not carried through consistently. The cellular grid gives little idea of the broad internal spaces and the fussiness of the stone and slate decor makes the whole building look more like a spec office block than an electronics laboratory. Mill's excellent laboratory for Fisons (1959–61) at Harston, five miles south of Cambridge, is worth a visit, as is his Great Ouse House (page 85).

Arbury Estate   F

Arbury and King's Hedges Estates
1 Arbury Court 2 'Snowcat' pub 3 St. Nicholas Ferrar

4 Manor Schools 5 Arbury Branch Library 6 Kingsway Flats 7 'Jenny Wren' pub 8 King's Hedges shops 9 Edgecombe Flats 10 Nun's Way housing 11 King's Hedges School

Site. Bounded by Arbury, Milton, Gilbert and Histon Roads.

Date. 1955–

Architects. T. V. Burrows, city surveyor (housing, schools, shops). Gordon Logie, city architect (Kingsway, Branch Library). S. E. Dykes Bower (St. Nicholas Ferrar). David Roberts ('The Snowcat')

Arbury Estate is an attempt to found a self-contained suburb of Cambridge—a mid-twentieth century village with its own church, pubs, shopping centre and schools. In intention it was an admirable attempt to get away from the straggling ribbon development of between the wars. Access from the main roads is limited to a small number of distributor roads. Off these in turn run minor roads and culs-de-sac, and there are a number of pedestrian alleyways and paths. The housing is laid out in a variety of forms: some detached, some semi-detached and a majority of terraced houses in groups of four to six. There are also blocks of six-storey flats in Roseford Road. All this is not very different in vital statistics from a neighbourhood area in a first generation new town. It shares the same general advantages—gardens for almost everyone, healthy open spaces for children, a humane scale—and the same crippling defects— an inadequate traffic system, far too few garages, a diffuse unneighbourly layout with great distances between groups of houses and a general lack of focus. At Arbury, things are made worse by the evident lack of the three-dimensional planning inherent in the new towns. Architecturally the housing

Arbury Estate centre, showing, left to right, St. Nicholas Ferrar's Church, Manor secondary schools, 'Snowcat' public house and the shopping centre

is extremely weak: prim brick terraces with utility steel or concrete doorways of modish design. The general plan of Arbury defies rational analysis. The roads curve in the relaxed manner of the garden city, but the layout totally lacks the disciplined formality that in fact lay behind the plans of Letchworth or Hampstead Garden Suburb. The result has been a squandering of Cambridge's short supply of housing land, not merely in unusable grass verges and planted street corners, but in large patches of coarse grass, signifying nothing.

Nowhere is this gap between humane intention and chaotic performance more evident than at the Alex Wood/Arbury Road junction. Here are the buildings which in theory should unite the community: a pedestrian shopping precinct, a pub, two secondary schools and a Church. The haphazard and unrelated effect is not the result of poor architectural detail: the public house, 'The Snowcat', is one of the best of its date in the country. Again, the Manor secondary school, designed in the city surveyor's department, uses an industrialized building system with intelligence and considerable flexibility. Admittedly the church of St. Nicholas Ferrar is an embarrassment, in the sort of gimcrack which has compromised the Church of England long after the great Victorians last designed in Gothic with passion and sincerity. This gloomy, dark brick building, built in 1957–8

(chancel) and 1963–4 (nave) seems weird compared with other new churches in Cambridge, let alone those on the Continent. It displays Romanesque in the nave arcade, seventeenth-century Gothic in the windows, and early twentieth-century Anglican good taste in the interior decor. The architect was Stephen Dykes Bower, surveyor to Westminster Abbey.

The pedestrian shopping centre (Arbury Court), a three-sided courtyard opening off the bend in Alex Wood Road, is placed so that it can only be seen from a few angles and does not link up with the nearby housing. Parked cars screen it from the road. This is a great pity, because the shopping centre is quite well designed in itself—and pedestrian precincts were by no means as widely accepted in 1957–8 as they are now. Above the shops are maisonettes and flats, making two four-storey sides joined by a three-storey wing. The structure is a simple reinforced concrete frame, expressed clearly in the ground floor colonnades and upper floor access balconies. Facings are in pale yellow bricks with precast panels on one end elevation. The mosaic covering of the colonnades is an unfortunate commercial cliché. The main design weakness is the failure to make anything of the courtyard space, which is an expanse of tarmac, inset with paving stones, litter baskets and free-standing advertisement displays. The space could still be made lively,

Arbury Estate, shopping centre

for example, by the erection of a café or tea bar in a light-hearted building of temporary construction. The city architect Gordon Logie has made two additions to the estate since his appointment in 1962: these are the Branch Library at the corner of Alex Wood and Arbury Roads and a block of flats, 'Kingsway', at the end of Roseford Road (see below). These both show a marked improvement of design that augurs well for future housing in the city. Other buildings on the Arbury Estate include the junior and infants schools in Carlton Way, earlier and less successful efforts by the city surveyor's department, and on Milton Road the R.C. church of St. Laurence (1958) by Barry Hastings, a Gothic design over which a veil is best drawn.

Manor Secondary School   G

Arbury Road

Date.	1958–9 (boys); 1959–60 (girls)
Architects.	W. Doig and M. R. Francis of the city surveyor's department.
Contractors.	Gilbert-Ash Ltd.
Cost.	£300,000

Description. Cambridge's third post-war secondary school stands on 19 acres of open land across the road from Arbury Court. The separate girls' and boys' departments, each for 450 pupils, are joined by shared dining-rooms. Each department is planned round a grassed courtyard. The girls' buildings are mainly two-storeyed, but the boys' buildings are dominated by a four-storey block. The school uses the Intergrid building system developed by the contractors for the Ministry of Education, using prestressed and precast columns and beams. The system was first used in Cambridge at Great Eastern House (see page 103). Large all-round windows are provided, with infill panels of concrete slabs of various aggregates and of dark blue glass

'Snowcat' public house, interior

in the four-storey block. The total floor space is 70,000 sq ft.

Comment. Built under the city's delegated powers in education, this is a well-designed school much superior to those recently built by the county. The buildings form a satisfactorily compact group, reflecting the trend in the mid-fifties away from the earlier spread-out finger plan for schools (as at Impington village college). The light elegant glass panels of the classroom block contrast well with the exposed concrete panels of the lower buildings which form a plinth when seen from a distance. An evident weakness is the inability of the Intergrid system to articulate clearly the main public rooms, such as the boys' assembly hall. The walnut tree in the girls' courtyard is a welcome relief among the standard rectilinear bays.

'Snowcat' Public House   H

Arbury Estate

Date.   1959–60

Architect.   David Roberts

Contractor.   Kidman & Son Ltd.

Cost.   £16,000

Description. This public house, situated next to Arbury Court, is clearly divided into three: a one-storey part containing men's and women's cloakrooms and a corridor connecting the bars; a two-storey part at the opposite end containing off-sales and a kitchen–dining-room below, and the publican's flat above; and, between these two parts, the public and private bars, which are placed parallel with each other so that they share a common servery and chimney stack. The two end parts have low-

'Snowcat' public house

Arbury Court branch library

pitched roofs, and the bars have a monopitch which rises so that it runs without a break into the roof-line of the two-storeyed part. The structure is of load-bearing brick walls and pillars, with golden facing bricks exposed internally in the bars. The public bar is over 40 ft long. Chairs, tables and stools were specially selected. The floor is of black Southwater paviors. The timber roof is exposed.

Comment.   This is a highly successful building, one of the few modern pubs that is neither antique nor 'with it' nor pretentiously 'sensitive to working-class culture'. It is just a thoroughly sensible, elegant and economical building. The simple facings externally are given distinction by the long projecting windows of the bars, the timber slatting above and the rising roof line, which has the gaiety of a cocked hat, besides being 'expressive of function'. Inside, the light timber furnishings (not too light) combine well with the exposed brick pillars, with raked joints, between which are set tables and chairs. The positioning of the tables in these bays next to the long windows means an openness to the outside world more common in cafés than pubs. The chimney stack is prominent externally. The building reflects credit on Greene King & Son, whose 'Rose and Crown' on Newmarket Road (1928), showed a similar awareness of contemporary taste (even if that neo-Georgian design looks dated now).

Arbury Court Branch Library   I

Date.	1965
Architect.	Gordon Logie, city architect
Contractor.	Henry J. Rodgers & Partners, Comberton.
Cost.	£15,061

Description.   Sited on the corner of this bleak intersection, the library was to serve as a physical and visual link between Arbury Road and Arbury Court. Its curving shape accentuates the importance of this link. It is single-storey, built in loadbearing brick with steel joists. Bush-hammered concrete lintels are placed over the openings and the windows are anodized aluminium. Internally, lowered ceilings have been used to create an intimate scale in the junior library and to emphasize the importance of the issue desk. An exhibition and browsing area has been introduced between the adult and junior sections.

Comment.   Not surprisingly, this pleasant little building has been quite overwhelmed by the task of uniting Arbury Court with the rest of the scheme. It has become just another incident in this peculiar assortment of architectural odds-and-ends. For itself, however, like the other buildings dealt with in the area, it is attractively detailed and well thought-out. The entrance is cleverly announced by the break in the curving brick wall; the interiors are appropriate to their function; and the lighting is good. It is an unassuming but successful product of a kind which one has begun to expect from the architect's department.

Kingsway Flats   J

At the junction of Roseford Road, Alex Wood Road and Carlton Way.

Date.   1966–8

Architect.   Gordon Logie, city architect

Contractor.   Kerridge Ltd.

Cost.   £480,000

Requirement. Flats, garages, children's play-spaces, and a health and dental clinic.

Description. The flats are arranged in five five-storey blocks which form a large open-sided court at the corner of Carlton Way and Topham Way, a smaller similar court to the north on Mere Way and a garage court on Butler Way and Roseford Road. In the large southern court are garages over which has been provided a substantial paved area for ball-games, linked by ramps and stairs to ground level. At its north-eastern corner the upper level is linked directly to the flats. The smaller court on Mere Way has an infants' play area with sand, water and climbing logs. The flats have an access gallery at third floor level reached by lifts at two points: from this gallery stairs go up and down to the second and fourth floors, while the first floor is reached by stairs from the ground. This means that no one need climb more than one flight of stairs.

The construction is brick cross-wall with precast concrete floor and roof slabs. Only the roof slab is expressed, where an exposed granite aggregate is used. The bricks are Dorking pressed facings dark red in colour.

Comment. This is a successful attempt at relating blocks of flats to an awkward space in the midst of existing housing. They provide a useful focal point at the end of Alex Wood Road and Carlton Way which both had badly lacked hitherto. Moreover, the spaces between the blocks seem to make good sense, too; although there seems to be a danger that the infants could easily stray off their playspace onto the road. But the large court over the garages provides a much needed hard area. Only the flats themselves are unsatisfactory. The large areas of dark brickwork present a massive and over-

Kingsway flats, seen across play area

bearing front that was not suggested in the original sketches. Perhaps a stronger expression of the cross walls and a subduing of the panels between would have created a less gloomy outlook.

King's Hedges Estate   K

Site.   Bounded by King's Hedges, Arbury, Milton and Histon Roads.

Date.   1962–

Architects.   T. V. Burrows, city surveyor (housing); Gordon Logie, city architect (housing, schools); David Roberts ('Jenny Wren'); Vickers & Undrill (Surgery).

Housing was started off King's Hedges Road before the war, as a continuation north from Chesterton; but this remained an isolated development until after the completion of the greater part of the Arbury Estate with which it is now linked.

The first half of the new estate was designed by the city surveyor's department and begun in 1962. Spreading south-westwards from King's Hedges Road along the spine of Campkin Road, which joins Arbury Road by the Manor Schools, the languid curves and suburban layout seem to be a depressing repetition of Arbury. All the same elements are there: the vacant greenswards, the coy terraces, the meaningless disposition of roads, and the evident lack of three-dimensional planning. And yet King's Hedges is not a total failure in the same way as Arbury. This is partly due to the fact that Campkin Road serves clearly as a spine to which the other roads are tributary; it is also due to the fact that the 'centre' of King's Hedges, unlike that at Arbury, is not a collection of disparate elements, but has a certain surprising unity. At a curve in Campkin Road, the housing steps back on either side to form what is effectively a village green. A small row of shops closes one end—to one side the terrace of houses is staggered back, and in the western corner is the 'Jenny Wren' pub by David Roberts. There is, too, an improvement in the detailing of the houses at this point with trim weather boarding replacing acres of brick. Only the 'Jenny Wren' is a curious disappointment in comparison with the 'Snowcat' at Arbury. Sited at the corner of Campkin Road and St. Kilda Avenue, it presents a strangely aggressive collection of deep, dark-stained fascias with an entrance on the corner.

When Gordon Logie was appointed city architect, King's Hedges was further developed and became an experimental breeding ground for new ideas.

One of the first developments was the use of Calder prefabricated houses in Nun's Way and Cameron Road; but these proved too inflexible and poorly finished, with a result that only some 30 houses were built. West of Nun's Way are the 'Edgecombe' flats—96 dwellings in six different-sized blocks—which are informally but successfully grouped around a cul-de-sac. They are three-storeyed and built of loadbearing brick with tower-like staircases projecting on the inside of the blocks. More successful than the flats is likely to be the housing on the north side of Nun's Way, described below.

There are two schools in the district, the Grove and King's Hedges Primary Schools. The Grove School is south of Campkin Road and L-shaped, facing south-west across its playground. The King's Hedges School is described in more detail on page 126. Also on the estate is a surgery by Vickers and Undrill beyond the Grove School. A long block parallel to the road is broken by two wings with mono-pitch roofs forming an open court. White-painted boarding and brickwork are used within the court but elsewhere the brickwork is left unpainted. The architects have succeeded in creating a simple, almost 'farmhouse' style which is highly appropriate.

King's Hedges   Stage IV   L

Nun's Way

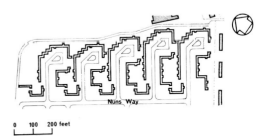

0   100   200 feet

Date.   1966–

Architect.   Gordon Logie, city architect

Cost.   £370,000 (approx.)

Requirement.   40 one-bedroom flats, 42 two-bedroom houses, 52 three-bedroom houses and four four-bedroom houses.

Nun's Way housing, model

Description. The configuration of the development is determined by the interlocking of pedestrian and vehicular access. Down the back of the area runs Nun's Way and parallel to it a footpath linking the scheme to the centre of the estate. From Nun's Way five short culs-de-sac run at right-angles between the culs-de-sac. The terraces are moulded around this pattern of routes with each house having a 'front' on the footpath or one of the courts, and a 'back' with a private walled patio and a hard-standing for car-port or garage. The basic units are the two-bedroom house, which has been slightly extended to provide the larger versions, and the one-bedroom flat. These have been designed to be linked in a wide variety of ways, thus providing the great flexibility of layout. A local gault brick is being used for the scheme with dark grey concrete roof tiles.

Comment. This is the first fully 'Radburnised' layout at King's Hedges and looks as though it will be the most successful scheme the architect's department have yet attempted. It seems to have achieved success on two counts which other Radburn layouts have failed to do. In the first instance, the relationship between the front and back entries is a clearly comprehensible one, since the form of the courts can be understood from Nun's Way as from the footpath. In the second instance, the use of rear patios should ensure that there is a private side to each house and that there are no garage yards which children will find more exciting to play in than the courts in front. And best of all, for the first time on either estate, the development has a truly urban scale of continuous enclosure.

King's Hedges Primary School

Date. 1966–8

Architect. Gordon Logie, city architect

Contractor. M. Wynn Ltd.

Cost. £57,000

Description. The first stage of the school is the infants department consisting of two groups of three classrooms placed around shared activity spaces, from which they are divided by sliding partitions. These groups are placed symmetrically about the playground entry: on this axis also lies the sunken assembly hall. The symmetry is broken by the staff wing and road entrance. Linking the infants and junior departments, which otherwise are physically separated, are the shared kitchen and boiler rooms. The organization of the juniors department will be similar, with a third group of classrooms on a first floor. The structure is timber framed with infill panels of blue flint-lime bricks, and the building is topped with a series of mono-pitch roofs giving east-facing clerestory windows.

Comment. This is likely to be a building of considerable merit when fully completed. It shows on plan the best of modern educational thinking, as pioneered by the Ministry of Education architects, and it also shares some of their weaknesses. The difficulty with school building is that the variety of spaces and the complexity of their inter-relationships all too often defies a coherent architectural solution, as the famous Evelyn Lowe school shows. A strong attempt has been made here to achieve a unity while giving proper expression to the individual parts; but the repetition of the mono-pitch roofs may yet prove over-articulated in the circumstances.

Churches in Northern Cambridge

Other than St. Nicholas Ferrar and St. Laurence R.C. churches already mentioned, two new churches have appeared in the area. The first is the Methodist Church designed by Douglas Harding, a former associate of Hughes & Bicknell, at the corner of Scotland and Green End Roads. It consists of an octagonal all-purpose hall/church linked by an entrance porch to a rectangular smaller hall with kitchens and cloakrooms beyond. At one side of the octagon is the sanctuary which can be screened off; at the far side is a stage. The roof is made of timber prefabricated sections surmounted by a cross. It was built by Kidman in 1965–6 and cost £12,500. It is an agreeable, undemanding building.

The other is the Arbury Baptist church in Arbury Road designed by Robert J. Wyatt and built by R. Slingsby Ltd. (1965–6). The fan shaped new building is linked to the existing church by a choir and organ gallery under which are sliding doors. At this point there is a porch linking the old schoolroom and the new entrance: this is reached across a courtyard divided by the new vestry and classroom from the road. The communion table is at the southern end, nearest the road, and over it the roof rises to an apex at a brick buttress, on top of which is a cross. At this southern end the wall is staggered to provide narrow vertical windows facing away from the road. The cost was £15,000. This is not a subtle building but it evidently works quite well. The pale brown brickwork seems to accentuate the flimsiness of design, although the creation of an internal courtyard is an agreeable feature. The buttress-spire is over contrived, but presents an acceptable face to Arbury Road.

Arbury Road Baptist Church

New Spring public lavatory

New Spring Public Lavatory   P

Mitcham's Corner

Date.   1966

Architect.   Gordon Logie, city architect

Contractor.   B. L. Osbourne

Cost.   £7,000

Requirement. New public lavatories to replace those under the Mitcham's Corner roundabout and stores for the permanent moorings on the river.

Description. The building sits well back from the road to form a paved forecourt in front, bounded by low brick walls. Steps lead down on each side to the riverside gardens and to the stores under the lavatories. At the upper forecourt level, the external wall breaks back to form a covered entry, defined by two slender steel columns. The structure is load-bearing brick with a timber-framed roof. There is a continuous clerestory below the roof.

Comment. Public lavatories are usually the object of derision or scorn: borough surveyors have long built them with a perfunctoriness which was considered fitting for their use. For this reason, the market-places of our towns are disfigured by little red-brick boxes nestling obtrusively among the cars. How refreshing it is, then, to find this well-designed building which has had considerable thought put into it. It not only adequately serves its purpose but enhances the immediate surroundings with its low, clean lines. It is an excellent sign that care is being lavished on buildings hitherto considered unworthy of it, in recognition that it is the smaller details that often make or mar the public environment.

Housing in the Northern Area

If it is carried through, Eric Lyons's scheme for the rebuilding of Castle Hill will be the largest consistently developed part of the area apart from the Arbury and King's Hedges Estates. The site is to the west of Castle Hill and north of Honey Hill and extends as far as Mount Pleasant. The initial sketches show a rather folksy layout of flats loosely grouped around irregularly placed courts; these are linked by a series of pedestrian ways. Traffic access would be around the periphery of the site. The joint clients are the city council, St. John's College and Storey's Charity.

Between Chesterton and Milton Roads low density housing sprawl has continued unchecked. Some of it is city surveyor's work, much of it is private development. Two blocks of flats are worth a glance: Mayfair Court, Milton Road (1962) by G. M. Vickers, and Ailsa Court, Chesterton Road (also 1962) by Royce, Stephenson & Tasker. Ailsa Court, with its elegant grey brick and white weather-boarded bay windows, has nine maisonettes, which, for reasons of property speculation, are supported on concrete

columns above Shell's Chesterton service station. Not even this clean and attractive design can survive such a harsh contrast as that.

Mr. Vickers' latest flats in the area are for Contemporary Homes Ltd., at Pentlands Close between Chesterton Road and the river. Pentlands Close consists of 36 flats in two four-storey blocks with staircase towers and brown brick facings reminiscent of Churchill College.

Between Milton Road and Leys Road, Trend Homes (see Sherlock Close, page 130) have laid out an estate of 65 houses in eight two-storey terraces, loosely grouped around a central landscaped space. As in other designs by James & Bywaters, an attractive layout is marred by an excess of modish colours and materials.

Another development by James & Bywaters consisting of flats identical to those in Sherlock Close has just been built at the corner of Hurst Park Avenue.

Pleasance & Read have designed 16 terrace houses at Birch Close, off Milton Road. There are 10 bungalows at Chesterton Hall Crescent by Ellis & Gardner: here, a pleasant design has been spoilt by poor landscaping details, not supervised by the architects.

16 Girton Road, close to the college, is a small bungalow, remodelled and extended soon after the war by Walter Bor, now in partnership with Lord Llewelyn-Davies. He added a studio and bathroom on one side and an entrance, kitchen and dining bay to the living room on the other.

Other recent houses in Chesterton include Nevil Shute's house in Thrifts Walk by C. J. Bourne, and 7 Hurst Park Avenue by G. M. Vickers. Also by Mr. Bourne are the St. Raphael Club hall in Hawthorn Way (1962) and the new wing at Langdon House old people's home in Scotland Road (1962–3). Cambanks, in Union Lane, is an estate of 45 two-bedroom flats by D. R. Hickman (1963–4), who has also designed two three-storey blocks of flats in Chapel Street called Chesterton Towers. Roger Scott has designed two houses, one a doctor's surgery at 2a Hurst Park Road (1963–4) and the other in Montague Road (1966–7). The Montague Road house is a modish piece of design with brick cross walls and glazed ends. Internally, the pedestrian planning belies the refined exterior.

Honey Hill, with the tower of St. Peter's Church and the house of Jim Ede (right)

Honey Hill   N

Northampton Street

Date.   1957–9

Architect.   C. J. Bourne of the city surveyor's department.

Contractor.   Johnson & Bailey Ltd.

Cost.   £28,000

Requirement.   Sixteen houses for old people.

Description.   Honey Hill is the result of slum clearance of the cottages to the north of Northampton Street. The old people's flats are set on a terrace above a broad grassed bank and are reached by two paved paths. There are two buildings, a single storey block and a larger L-shaped two-storey group, in which flats open off staircase halls. Communal clothes-drying space is provided at the rear, where the path leads through to St. Peter Street. St. Peter's Church (the spire was restored in 1963) forms the focal point of the group. The structure is of load-bearing brick, with buff and brown facings and special treatment of metal balconies and lamp standards.

Next door, completing the group to the east, is the house of Jim Ede in Kettle's Yard, a three-storey building converted from three old cottages in 1957 to designs by Rowland Aldridge and Mr. Ede himself. It consists of a flat on ground level with two open plan floors above devoted to Mr. Ede's collection of modern paintings. The walls are rough plastered inside and faced externally with the original bricks (a Georgian window was salvaged from the

Prudential site). A bay with a spiral staircase has been added.

Comment.   A successful piece of townscape, in which the buildings have been artfully manipulated to form a village centre, with church spire, green and cottages. The architecture is unpretentious and intimate in scale and the pedestrian system is good. The self-conscious traditionalism perhaps subordinates the old people's needs to aesthetic prettiness. In fact they complain of the coldness of the staircase halls and about their distance from the road, the bustle of which they tend to miss in their enforced seclusion.

Mr. Ede's house is an excellent piece of conversion, maximizing the space available by using the least possible number of partitions. The low ceilings, rounded corners and rough plaster give a feeling of spaciousness—somewhat in the Arts and Crafts tradition—more genuinely, because more personally, picturesque than the old people's flats.

Sherlock Close   O

off Huntingdon Road

Date.   1960

Architects.   James & Bywaters

Contractors.   Peploe & Partners Ltd.

Cost.   £120,000

Requirement.   Estate of 60 flats for Trend Homes.

Description.   This medium density estate, entered from Sherlock Road, consists of five three-storey terraces of 12 flats each, laid out round two open garden courtyards. The approach road leads to 30 garages at the rear of the site. Each block of flats has two entrances, leading to central circular stairs serving six flats each. Flats have a dining space off the living room and two bedrooms, together with hall, kitchen, bath and utility rooms. The structure is of loadbearing brick with a wide variety of finishes. Panels of black brick alternate with brickwork painted white; the upper walls facing the gardens are tile-hung.

Sherlock Close, repainting in progress

Comment.   Sherlock Close's developers deserve much praise for breaking away from the sterile pattern of most spec building and following the lead of Span. The planning of this development is simple and good; the approach road and garages are well related to the flats and pedestrian courtyards. The flats themselves are spacious and attractive, with a partially open plan. Doubts, however, are aroused by the detailing, in which the Span style is carried into extremes of mannerism. Red tiles, black tiles, blue tiles, black bricks, white-painted bricks, all add up to terrible confusion. The white-painted bricks have weathered badly (as at Churchill nearby). The pleasant green lawns of the courtyards have been arbitrarily cut up by flowering shrubs, flower beds and mounds. This lack of discipline damages a basically encouraging piece of design.

Western Area

Newnham, Madingley Road ; Grantchester, Coton, Barton, Comberton, Kingston and Caldecote Villages

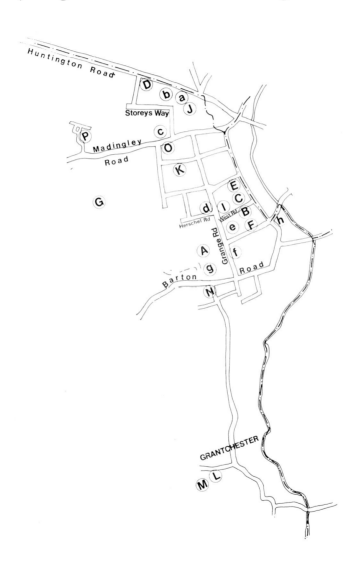

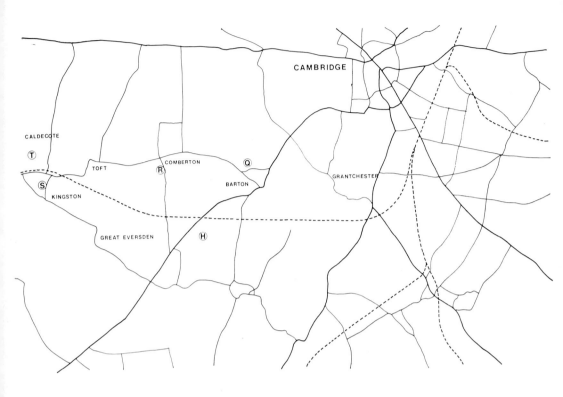

Until the building of Fen Causeway (1928), farmland survived continuously up to the walls of the colleges. But after the Act of 1870 permitted dons to marry, the Grange Road axis gradually became a garden suburb of posh villas and playing fields, developed by the colleges on their parallel strips of land beyond the Backs. In 1924 Clare took the momentous step of building what was in effect a twin college separated from First Court by the Backs, which were henceforth destined to change from their original status as back gardens into a central super-court or campus for the whole university. Clare's Memorial Court was given a quite elegant Ivy League trim by Sir Giles Gilbert Scott and although he followed this up in the University Library tower (financed by Rockefeller) with a more menacing American derivative, at least he sowed the seeds of town planning by means of university–college co-operation.

Sir William Holford in his 1950 Report stated optimistically that 'the university administration is aware of the need for a general plan for development and is trying to prepare one based on the needs of departments and on the grouping most likely to promote the efficient working of the university machine.' He instanced the university's acquisition of the Sidgwick Avenue site for the Arts Faculties and of science sites along Madingley Road.

The subsequent harvest has been of dragons' teeth, born of architecturally eminent dragons, no doubt, but almost untamed by thoughts of town planning. The attitude of successive Vice-Chancellors to the county's plans for Cambridge has been hypocritical: we will tell you how to plan the centre of your city, so long as you allow us to go west in our own sweet way. An urban quality which took eight hundred years to evolve on the east side of the Backs has exploded in barely eighty on the west, and urban quality has quickly surrendered to suburban sprawl. Can anyone believe that Sidgwick Avenue's colleges and faculties are the equal, as a total environment, of those of Senate House Passage? There has been an almost irreparable failure to co-ordinate the planning of the three new colleges (Churchill, Fitzwilliam, New Hall) and the adjoining Wychfield site of Trinity Hall. These four sites between Madingley and Huntingdon Roads were specifically designated by Holford in 1950 for college expansion; and in 1958 Peter Chamberlin, who was one of the competing architects for all three colleges, did have the wit to propose such a precinct, establishing a clear pedestrian route between Huntingdon Road and the University Library. But this part of his designs was ignored.

There is bound to be a flood of new buildings in West Cambridge in the next decade. The postgraduate 'bulge' is already in evidence (Leckhampton, Darwin, Clare Hall, University College). The older colleges have generally preferred to continue packing their undergraduates into their medieval precincts; this delay in moving west could be a blessing in disguise if the time was used to channel new development along planned lines. Are the garden suburb roads of 1870 sufficient? Where will cyclists and pedestrians go? The decision of the science faculties to move west, according to the Deer Report's recommendations, has resulted in a plan by Robert Matthew, Johnson-Marshall and Partners, which takes the line of Burrells Walk and the Coton footpath as an east–west axis. Between this new science area and the Backs, it is vitally important that the narrow strips of college land should not be allowed to hamstring urban redevelopment.

Churchill College   c

363 undergraduates, 243 postgraduates, 79 fellows.

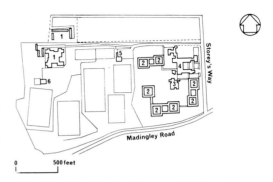

1 Graduate flats 2 Residential courts 3 Wolfson Hall and Bracken Room 4 Central buildings 5 Sports pavilion 6 Chapel

Sir Winston Churchill liked inventive people rather than nice people—Lloyd George or Beaverbrook in politics, Lord Cherwell in science. He came to realize that scientific skill in the future could give more influence to Britain than military power in the past. But lack of enthusiasm among prospective benefactors prevented the idea of an English M.I.T. or a postgraduate institute at Birmingham as memorials to him, after his retirement in 1955. A new Cambridge college by contrast proved irresistible, and the academic committee's outline scheme was rapidly approved by the Senate (13 February 1958). The scale was to be unusually large: 540 students and 60 fellows, two-thirds of them scientists, with as many as 500 students living-in (Trinity has only just over 400 residents). Also 20 family flats were to be provided for postgraduates—a welcome, if belated, recognition of the facts of life.

A two-stage competition was held in 1958–9, limited to the top twenty-one of those days. For posterity's amusement they were: Architects' Co-Partnership; Sir Hugh Casson, Neville Conder & Partners; H. T. Cadbury-Brown; Chamberlin, Powell & Son; Brett & Pollen; James Cubitt & Partners; David Aberdeen & Partners; Ernö Goldfinger; Howell, Killick & Partridge; Lyons, Israel & Ellis; Robert Matthew, Johnson-Marshall & Partners; Yorke, Rosenberg & Mardall; Norman & Dawbarn; Powell & Moya; David Roberts; Richard Sheppard, Robson & Partners; Alison & Peter Smithson; James Stirling & James Gowan; Frederick Gibberd & Partners; Fry, Drew,

Drake & Lasdun; and Tayler & Green. The assessors were Sir Basil Spence, Sir William Holford, Sir Leslie Martin, Noel Annan, chairman of the academic committee, and Sir John Cockcroft, the master-elect. They made five stipulations: a distinguished design, a clear collegiate identity, a suitable environment, a plan for growth in stages and a 'target cost' close to £1.1 million. The 42-acre sloping field between Madingley Road and Storeys Way formed part of the collegiate area suggested by Holford in 1950—apparently distant from the city centre but actually close to the new academic focus of the University Library—and closer still to the new science area of the Deer Report (see page 183). Its weakness was the distant threat of a by-pass for the city across it—now diverted to the western boundary. The competition was disappointing, as few of the competitors appreciated the scale required, let alone what the appropriate form of a science-based college might be—a question which perhaps the client could not answer either. Four designs were selected for development in more detail. Stirling & Gowan's had a single vast court of residences raised on a grass-ramped plinth, with four freestanding tower blocks containing public rooms and flats. The assessors liked the brutally modelled effects in concrete but criticized the monotony of the terraces and the 'closed form' of the court (visually impossible to phase).

Chamberlin, Powell & Bon courageously looked beyond the site boundaries and suggested moving New Hall, for which they had been commissioned, to the vacant field on the opposite side of Storeys Way, and then siting University flats to extend the new precinct as far as Lasdun's Fitzwilliam. Unfortunately the layout of this symbolic flirtation with co-education was rigid and formalistic, with a Byzantinising chapel; it was the only one of the four, however, which was within the target cost.

Howell, Killick & Partridge were acclaimed by the critics for their spectacular use of precast concrete units, with the projecting 'chocolate bar' windows which have since become their trade mark. Two huge polygonal courtyards opened towards the playing fields, with their brilliant white facetted façades reflected in a large lake. But the design was disqualified for its waste of space (25 per cent more than the most economic floor area) and waste of money (£1.32 million)—an ironic fate in view of what the selected scheme has actually cost.

Richard Sheppard, Robson & Partners were never-theless worthy winners—if 'worthy' is not a pejorative word. First they placed the research flats in a separate group, beyond the proposed by-pass, to form a 'base camp' for the college, undisturbed by building work on the main site. Then they began at the human end of the telescope with the individual living room; pushed out of it a bay window with a window seat; grouped it in fours round a three-storey toplit staircase with breakfast room, bathroom, shower and lavatories—a social unit of 12 which has since been adopted officially by the U.G.C.; and then grouped the staircases in fours round courts, the courts in fours as clusters of courts, and the clusters in fours round a 'campus' into a college. This may sound a mathematical diagram of a college, but even in the original design the hierarchy was relaxed almost haphazardly, to fit the site, with traditional romantic assumptions of collegiate permanence, built into the warmth and solidity of brick and concrete. There has been continuous revision of the design as each phase has proceeded.

Research Flats: Stage I

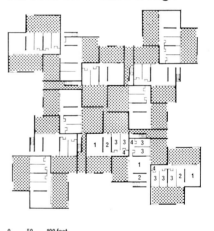

0   50   100 feet

Ground floor plan
1 Living room **2** Dining room **3** Bedroom **4** Bathroom
Dotted areas indicate enclosed open spaces

Date.   1959–60

Architects.   Richard   Sheppard,   Robson   &
                           Partners

Contractor. Bernard Sunley & Sons Ltd.

Cost. £120,000

Requirement. 20 two- and three-bedroom flats.

Description. The flats form a self-centred group, distinct from the rest of the college, from which they were originally to be separated by the city's western by-pass. (This now likely to run instead through the belt of trees behind.) There are 12 flats at ground level (see plan) in a symmetrical swastika layout. Each has a large living room, small dining–kitchen, two or three bedrooms and bathroom; and each has two outdoor terraces secluded by storey-height walls, which are (or were) painted white to be visually continuous with the white plaster internally. Large windows to the terraces are connected horizontally by an almost continuous clerestory strip beneath the upswept floor slab. The eight first-floor flats are similar, with a single roof terrace. Apart from fair-faced concrete floor slabs, materials are consistently soft and brown: walls of Stamfordstone brick, window frames of iroko, floors of cork tile, and a deep roof fascia of copper. Heating is by finned radiators with fans.

Comment. This cluster of long brown walls and apparently random slit windows sits securely on a wooded plateau, to which Churchill's open grassland rises in three graceful terraces (landscape architect, Sheila Haywood). The convincingly domestic silhouette succeeds at close quarters in keeping just this side of a 'hill village' cliché. The 'patio flat' is an attractive form, humanely scaled and well planted, and there is a delightful freshness and restraint in its detailing—in the outside stairways to the upper flats, for example. But the formalism of the symmetrical plan is disturbing: it looks pretty in two dimensions from directly overhead (as drawn here), but that is not how the sun shines, even if the continuous clerestory helps to let light in. The focal centrepoint of the courtyard is merely a 4 ft square gap where four patio walls fail to meet. This basic indecision is more worrying than the weaknesses of detailing: white-washed walls where cheap Fletton bricks are now pinkly and blotchily exposed; smooth concrete which is far from smooth; dining–kitchens which are poky for all but newly-weds.

Churchill flats from the south east

Main Buildings: Stages II–VII

Date. 1961–8

Architects. Richard Sheppard, Robson & Partners

Contractor. Rattee & Kett Ltd.

Cost. £2,508,000

Residential Courts

Requirement. Accommodation for a total of 453 students, 21 fellows and three tutors in a series of separate stages: 119 students and two fellows (Stage II), 117 students and five fellows (Stage IV), 153 students, seven fellows and two tutorial rooms (Stage VI) and 64 students and seven fellows (Stage VII).

Description. Successive revisions by Sheppard have reduced the number of residential courts from 20 to 10, with an increase in their respective size from 65 ft and 45 ft square to 75 ft and 55 ft square. Stages II and IV, on either side of the Central Buildings (see below), each consist of three courts: two large and grassed, with a sunken lawn, linked by one small and paved. One side of the smaller court is reduced from three storeys to two with a roof terrace opening from specially large sets of rooms for fellows. Otherwise the 12 staircases serve about 10 rooms each, with a mixture of sets and bedsitters for undergraduates and postgraduates. Stage VI (along Madingley Road) is externally similar, but a considerable increase in numbers (and hence economy) has been achieved by replacing groups of four two-room sets by six study–bedrooms and by reducing the staircases from 12 to 10. Sir Isaac Wolfson stipulated as donor that Stage VII should also be an independent unit, but it has been reduced to only a single court, with a two-storey link to Stage

Churchill College, detail of residential courts

VI; if the college decides eventually to admit women students, they could be accommodated in this court. The crosswall structure, opened in cloisters at ground level between the courts, is faced throughout in brown Stamfordstone brick with raked joints. The concrete floor slabs have been shuttered *in situ* in rough 'courses' (equal in height to the bricks) where they are exposed on 'gable ends'; otherwise they are clad with precast slabs of white Norwegian quartz aggregate. Fascias and flashings are of copper.

As the social pivots, the staircases punctuate the courts at irregular intervals as toplit towers of unbroken brickwork, inside and out. The cantilevered precast treads are covered with rubber sheeting; handrails and newel posts, forming a square helix round the open well, are of British Columbian pine, used also for doors and other joinery. Landings on each side, with continuous vertical glazing, lead to bathrooms, showers, lavatories and (on each stair) a 'breakfast room'—an enlarged kitchenette with a small bay window. Larger bay windows, teak framed and separately cantilevered, light the living rooms and study–bedrooms; each bay contains a wide terrazzo window seat with central heating unit beneath. The living rooms are on average just over 160 sq ft (17 ft 9 in between crosswalls but only 9 ft 6 in deep). Walls are generally plastered white, with a continuous pine picture rail; beds are from a range designed by Ahrends, Burton & Koralek.

Comment. Since the competition, Sheppard has continuously altered and elaborated his design, so that the cost has eventually escalated to Churchillian proportions; and he has then had to revise and reduce it. Throughout their evolution, the residential courts have retained an unobtrusive sense of place which is most satisfying. The rooms are sober, spacious and adaptable, with a wide variety of outlook, into or out from the courts. This has fully justified the expense of eliminating corridors. The broad bay windows with their heated seats would still be admirably generous, if individual cantilevers (and mini-roofs with chippings) were exchanged for a less extravagant expression of vertical stacking. The toplit staircase towers, with their luminous brickwork and robust joinery, are unmatched aesthetically by Cambridge's more contrived efforts. The consistent handling throughout of a few materials is matched by the consistently excellent craftsmanship of the contractors.

In the courts, however, the humane and appropriate articulation of individual windows and staircases has led inexorably, as the design has evolved, to unnecessary articulation of everything else. Pelion has been heaved upon Ossa. Who would now remember Sheppard's pristine enthusiasm for a 'flow of space' from court to court? Even after his enlargement of them from the original design, the courts remain rather claustrophobic on dull days and, punch-drunk with bay windows and raked-jointed brickwork (every single brick articulated), they have seemed to diminish again as each further phase has been completed. The space of 'cloisters' is chopped up remorselessly by barriers of brick crosswall, which carry groaning lengths of concrete chassis beam and decking. The sunk-paved-sunk arrangement of the courts makes two-thirds of the public ground inaccessible to the public.

Outside the courts, seen from the wider campus, the heaping up of residences in the landscape is much more successful. Not only has the programme of phasing proved admirably adaptable to the college's frequent changes of mind and budget, but the rhythm of projecting bays can be read in sufficient lengths for the generous scale of the wide-frontage rooms to tell. Confusing from every angle, however, is the apparently arbitrary introduction of precast concrete facing slabs; these are in fact logically related to an attempt by Sheppard to solve the eternal corner problem of the court, which is made more difficult in a case like this where two sets of crosswalls are bound to collide at right-angles. In each case Sheppard brings one set of crosswalls through to the out-of-court façade, and gives the floor slabs in the crosswall 'gable ends' an *in situ* rough-shuttered finish. In all other positions—'infill' positions between crosswalls— he gives the floor slabs the marginally less 'permanent' effect of precast cladding; yet this variety does not tell because the 'infill' walls are faced in Stamfordstone brick no less heavy than the 'structural' crosswalls. In any case, on the court side there is still a ragged pile-up, where a thin vertical slit is used to separate two rival sets of 'infill' walls.

Central Buildings

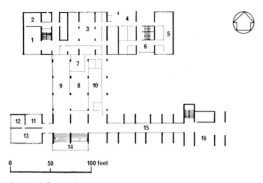

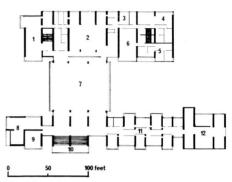

Ground floor plan

1 S.C.R. common room 2 S.C.R. quiet room 3 Furniture store 4 Loading bay 5 Linen rooms 6 Club room entrance 7 Wine store 8 Snack bar and buttery 9 Common room 10 Cloakrooms 11 Television room 12 Quiet room 13 Middle common room 14 Main staircase 15 Entrance cloister 16 Porter's lodge

First floor plan

1 S.C.R. dining room 2 Kitchens 3 Kitchen offices 4 Staff mess 5 Sick bay 6 Club room 7 Dining hall 8 Junior common room 9 Women's common room 10 Main staircase 11 Master and Tutor's offices 12 Bursary

Requirement. Master's Lodge (part of Stage II). Dining hall and kitchens, common rooms and buttery; clubroom, sickbays, college offices, boiler house, squash courts and main entrance (Stage III). Wolfson assembly hall, Bracken Library, Bevin reading rooms (Stage V). Sports pavilion (part of Stage VI). Chapel (separate commission by Chapel Society).

Description. From the start Sheppard has placed his main entrance just round the corner in Storeys Way (a town planning condition, as Madingley Road is to become a dual carriageway); and car parking is round yet another corner, off the service road which leads up the northern boundary of the site to the research flats. All else about the central buildings is utterly different from the 1959 design. A free-standing rectangular block of simple Cartesian geometry, with a number of free-wheeling satellites, has been transformed into a massively romantic 'hill city' of interconnected brick-paved spaces with a central axis which carries visually for more than four hundred yards to the top of the hill, where the long-awaited chapel thudded to earth in 1967.

Towards Storeys Way there is now a broad, paved forecourt with a concrete-balustraded bridge over a pool. This is aligned axially on a giant portico of brick formed by an extra two-storey crosswall which projects forward on either side of Geoffrey Clarke's

massive seven-barred pivoting gate of aluminium. The portico stands asymmetrically in the layout of the college. To the left, the residential courts of Stage IV extend a solid flank down to the Madingley Road corner, and between them and the portico the distant libraries block (Stage V) closes the gap. To the right, beyond a stretch of grass on which sits Henry Moore's craggy 'Three-piece Reclining Figure' of 1961–2, is the brick cube of the squash courts. Between it and the no less massive boiler house, the twin concrete stack of which forms the dominant accent of the college from a distance, is a cross-axial approach from the car park, through an elaborate sculptural link block of rough-shuttered concrete. This contains changing rooms on the two upper levels, with giant twin beams poking their ends through the clerestory windows; immediately next to it, a mighty exhaust vent of rough concrete is clipped to the side of the boiler house.

The portico itself leads into the left-hand stem of the main H-shaped complex of public rooms. From it a brick-paved, brick-walled cloister, 225 ft long stretches into the heart of the college, open on both sides for two-thirds of the way. Above its louvred timber ceiling is the college's lavish suite of administrative offices; these have a teak-framed window wall, alternately projecting and recessed, which is framed top and bottom by precast slabs spanning between rough concrete beams. A covered walkway,

138

of a standard design in fair-faced concrete used to connect all the residential courts with the central buildings, passes through from Stage IV on the left to the inner part of the right-hand court beyond the boiler house, where a concrete and teak staircase rises over offices to a balconied clubroom and sickbay wing. The windowless eastern gable of the dining hall—the crossbar of the H—forms an immense backcloth to the entrance courts at first floor level.

The main cloister eventually leads through glazed doors to an irregular entrance hall, also brick-walled and brick-paved, in which the centrepiece is the shuttered concrete foundation stone, lettered by Edward Wright. To the left, as another massive cross-axis, a 22 ft wide brick-paved staircase rises majestically, past a brooding bust of Churchill by Oscar Nemon[1], to a half-landing with a panoramic view of the campus; then it doubles back to an ante-hall landing (still brick-paved and brick-walled) from which the hall itself is entered. This massive room (72 ft by 38 ft), which seats 300, is roofed in three barrel vaults of shell concrete covered in copper sheeting; these stress the cross-axis of the entrance and of the kitchen on the opposite side. Natural light pours through big lunette windows under the vaults and is further diffused between projecting precast mullions in the walls beneath. The prominent light fittings are slung low over the tables in continuous copper troughs (this time on the main axis). The main end walls, which are windowless, are clad internally to their full height in elaborately modelled acoustic panelling of western red cedar (a gift from British Columbia). Both the public entrance and the kitchen entrance are screened at low level by acoustic walls of specially mounted bricks with foam rubber joints. The kitchen, which has a similar window wall to the administrative offices, overlooks the car park and service yard, in which there is an elaborately shuttered concrete sub-station. Below the kitchens are extensive stores and service areas. To the west of the hall, at the top of the H, are the two common room wings, overlooking another open court, in which stand Moore's 'Reclining Figure' of 1953–4 and Barbara Hepworth's superbly eloquent 'Squares With Two Circles' (1963). The three senior common rooms are to the north; a formal dining room on the first floor, seating 60 and richly panelled in black bean (given by New Zealand), is connected by a toplit staircase to the main combination room and the quiet room at ground level (Tasmanian oak

this time). On the south side are no less than five students' common rooms: on the first floor, the main junior combination room and the women's room; at ground level, the middle combination room, the television room and the quiet room. All these have panelling donated by other Commonwealth countries. The furniture throughout is by Robin Day; that for the dining hall, in teak, was specially designed. Fabrics are by Lucienne Day. Between the two common room wings at ground level is the communal heart of the college—the buttery, which has a combined bar, snack bar and shop raised four steps above a common meeting space. From here a fully glazed window wall provides a vista up the college's playing fields, past the covered walkway to Stage II, past the Hepworth sculpture and past the sports pavilion to the terminal 'pavilion' of the chapel at the top of the hill.

The library group can be reached under cover to the south. It is a free-standing block in the middle of the campus, with a long foyer paved in buff quarry tiles. The Wolfson hall has raked seating for 250, facing a proscenium stage, which is designed for music and drama as well as general assembly and has equipment for simultaneous translation into four languages. The Bracken library, open 24 hours a day for undergraduates, is a long tall room, lit continuously on the east side between closely set precast mullions similar to those of the dining hall; the reading tables have built-in strip lighting. At one end is a tapestry by Jean Lurçat, in his typical neo-Chinese vein; it was presented by de Gaulle. The open shelving on the west side is separated from the main reading room by a line of rough-shuttered concrete columns; the roof-lighting overhead has been installed for when an extra gallery has to be installed later. A further area of enclosed stacks helps to insulate library from assembly hall. Finally at the eastern end of the foyer a grand staircase rises slowly round a brick apse to the first floor, where the Bevin reading rooms for postgraduates (a main library and a smaller sitting room) are situated over the foyer, together with the librarians' offices.

From the senior common room wing there is direct access, via a guest wing, to the master's lodge, a large self-contained house with a separate private entrance from the service road under a massive canopy. This private entrance leads into the private wing of the T-shaped building: living room, study and secretary's office below; two main bedrooms

1. A second bust of Churchill, by Sir Jacob Epstein, was presented to the college in 1966 but has not yet been sited.

Churchill College, entrance with Henry Moore reclining figure, foreground

above. The ceremonial wing has the kitchen and dining-room at the service road end, followed by a library and a guest dining room, which can be thrown into one and face the private wing across a small formal garden. On the first floor are a main guest bedroom, three other bedrooms and a house-keeper's flat.

The sports pavilion contains yet another common room, a general social and games room, which runs the full length of the building, with a fully glazed view southward over the playing fields. On the north, behind the bar and servery, are the groundsman's office and the two toplit changing rooms. The timber framing and deep boarded fascia are dark stained, as in the rest of Stage VI; clerestory glazing emphasizes elsewhere the non-loadbearing character of the screen walls of Stamfordstone brick.

At last the chapel is reached. With the promise of £35,000 from the Rev. Timothy Beaumont, foundations were originally piled for it opposite the dining hall, in the traditionally focal position—wedged between the boiler house and the main entrance. After elaborate controversy and compromise, a Chapel Trust was formed, independently from the college, and it was decided to resite the building 'at a seemly distance'. Sheppard therefore found himself designing a hilltop temple close to the Observatory; be-

tween them may eventually run the western by-pass. The site is approached from the research flats by a winding path through a wooded glade. It is a centrally planned building on the Byzantine 'inscribed cross' plan used frequently by Wren. The altar is placed exactly on the central square of brick paving. It is framed by four massive concrete columns and lit from above by five skylights alternating with four blank timber panels in a three-by-three grid. Externally the skylights appear as a dominant cluster of monopitch-roofed boxes clad in copper. From the four columns, deep beams are cantilevered in all four directions, carrying a high ceiling which projects dramatically beyond the external walls to emphasize the central cross. The cantilevers are stressed by keeping the bounding wall of Stamfordstone brick down to the level of the underside of the beams (so that the infill corners have lower roofs) and then by cutting around and below each beam, a deep slit, which has been filled with blue-tinted glass. A low recess to the west encloses the baptistery and a shallower one of full height takes the organ.

Comment. A college of scientists built with medieval certainty to last a thousand years is not the inscrutable paradox it sounds; the predominance of

Churchill College: the Bracken Library with the Wolfson Hall and Bevin Rooms behind

undergraduate scientists in C.I.C.C.U. (the university's evangelical society) is a foretaste of their more mature conservatism as graduates. It was not a scientist but an historian who at Oxford commissioned Arne Jacobsen's machine aesthetic; and it was the history faculty who at Cambridge commissioned James Stirling's technological fantasy.

Richard Sheppard has gauged supremely well the emotional temper of his clients—solid, warm, slightly rustic. The master's lodge is the most romantic part of the precinct: rambling, rather withdrawn from the world, its eccentric details range from the challenging rough-concrete canopy of the private entrance, with its sheltered patio, to the quite slaphappy alternation of windows with mighty concrete lintels and windows with no lintels at all. Yet the domestic planning is done efficiently and cosily in the best English tradition. The trustees had specifically demanded 'the traditional Cambridge pattern of sets' and they had reminded competitors that Cambridge colleges are 'arranged round courts . . . the characteristic form . . . based on staircase access'.

Churchill's central buildings, with their broad brick-paved concourses and landings, their spacious timber-lined common rooms and their sophisticated service rooms, are deservedly regarded already as one of Cambridge's great works of architecture,

setting a new scale for collegiate life. But then, as Professor Pevsner points out, Cambridge has very few buildings that consciously set out to be great. Many critics have made the obvious comparison between the massive rough-hewn college and the massive rough-hewn hero it commemorates: 'in-, formal but grand', in Banham's words, 'not unlike the finest-hour image of the stout person in siren suit'. But is that a relevant comparison for a peacetime community of scientists? These heaving masses of mud-coloured brickwork and timber-patterned concrete tend indeed to be like a peacetime Churchill: *c'est magnifique, mais c'est toujours la guerre.* The central building in the competition design was a flat-roofed concrete block of a geometry as cool and agnostic as Sheppard's Walsall training college; but it was gradually transmuted (via spirelets of Canadian cedar) to the emotionally demanding and highly picturesque hill city which now we see. As Keith Scott has put it, 'Churchill College relies heavily on traditional handcraft techniques and . . . makes one feel that architects of quality are determined to have one last hell-bent fling to establish their design reputations before disappearing in a vast dead sea of industrialized anonymity. One can almost see them casting a baleful eye at the avidity of York and reaching with grim determination for an even blunter

Churchill College, chapel

Churchill College, sports pavilion

6B pencil.' But the brick and concrete were also chosen for their hard-wearing quality.

Churchill succeeds triumphantly in those less formal parts where traditional collegiate forms are still vital and appropriate—but, in the symbolic peaks of hall and chapel which once would have tied it together into a single image of community, it inevitably lacks conviction. For informal conviviality Sheppard has placed unerringly at the heart of his plan the buttery —a cleverly combined bar, snack bar and shop, which sits beneath the dining hall and faces out into the campus from the end of the main entrance gallery. The changes of level and the unobtrusive backcloth of mature timber create a space which has already proved indispensable, as a democratic forum for the different brands of common room grouped hierarchically about it. The common rooms themselves, with their sumptuous woodwork, achieve variety unpretentiously—Sheppard has not been tempted by the money available. The furniture by Robin Day, at his best in the handsome teak seats in the hall, is consistently adequate, even if the black leather armchairs and club chairs seem a little too familiar from the showrooms. Lucienne Day's curtains are curiously pale and indecisive. The library interiors are also excellent. As a public reading room, the Bracken library gives the student a soothing background atmosphere by its calm concrete structure and softly diffused lighting. The Bevin rooms upstairs are successfully articulated in a more intimate way with low ceilings and the familiar bay windows.

Churchill is a particularly exciting college to move around in the spotlit darkness which covers so much of the October–June academic 'year', particularly for scientists, who tend to be away at their labs from 9 to 5. Sheppard's romantic humanism is most attractively apparent in the covered meeting places of the central buildings. But in the daytime, with the crazily shuttered side entrance gesturing across to it from the squash courts, the pasted-on propylaeum of the main entrance seems rather stranded in a front court which has lost its chapel and most of its lake and gained instead only another admirable Moore. The concrete walkways which meander rather weakly along the slopes from cluster to cluster reveal the blemishes of poorly fair-faced concrete (not boarded) by day; whereas softly lit at night they immediately become pergolas of decisive routeing. The 225 ft all-brick entrance gallery, its paving slightly raised above the level of the grass courts, is magnificent, by day or by night. The fanatical consistency of the brickwork is particularly successful at the difficult junction where the hall steps rise majestically leftwards, past the bust of Churchill peering down from his craggy concrete bracket, to the panoramic window of the half-landing.

After that moment of hero-worship, there is anticlimax in the hall itself. Sheppard has provided the traditional grand room with an impressive post-Corbusian concrete vault; but the formality of it is broken down by the variety of wall surfaces and by the low-slung copper lighting troughs, so that the high table is insignificant—and inevitably, with less gowns and more women, formality will be dissolved. Le Corbusier, in his Dominican monastery at La Tourette, although himself an agnostic, was nevertholooc able to define in his architecture exactly what the beliefs of that community were; Sheppard by contrast was heard to say a year after winning the Churchill competition that 'No one seems to be able to tell me what a Cambridge college really is'. This central indecisiveness at Churchill was fully revealed in the seven-year mystery of the chapel—a saga worthy of C. P. Snow, who actually participated as mediator at one stage. Omitted by the original academic committee, proposed by Montefiore and offered by Beaumont, it was intended by Sheppard to have a traditionally prominent position marking the main entrance. After its foundations had been piled, it was rejected by Crick and other agnostic dons and changed into an inter-religious Hall of Meditation at the suggestion of Snow, but was then reaffirmed as Christian by the donor Beaumont. Transferred to a separate Chapel Trust by Cockcroft's compromise, it was finally swept away to a position at the far end of the playing fields, next to the heavenly speculations of the University Observatory.

The problem of the chapel as built is the design. Sheppard has attempted to give it a come-back on the college scene by grossly overscaling it as a kind of garden temple silhouetted against trees—the equivalent of a late eighteenth-century Doric eye-catcher. From the college, it groups happily with the other sculptures by Moore and Hepworth. But from close quarters the heavy-handed beams almost overwhelm the naively centralized plan: the younger liturgical architects years ago realized the simple fact that a priest occupies less space than the congregation he faces: so fan-shaped or elliptical plans are more suitable than circles (as at Liverpool Cathedral) or squares (as here).

The nearby sports pavilion shows by contrast how a straightforward expression of function, in well-chosen materials, can give a building the opportunity to develop its own character, from the identification with it of those who use it. Sheppard's later buildings have tended to be individually stamped with too heavy an 'image'. This is evident in the exterior of the Wolfson–Bracken group, with the undeniably powerful (but pointless) rooflit apse over the unimportant stair up to the Bevin rooms. Such a 'feature' smacks of imposing Art on the scientists. The college has cost more than twice its original target, yet architecturally it still cuts no clear overall image as a community—think of it and you think of its magnificent parts. From the Madingley Road approach, the heavy brown terraces are crowned, not by the chapel as intended by Sheppard, but by the campanile of the boiler house. What does *that* symbolize?

Graduate Flats

Date.	1965–7
Architects.	David Roberts & Partners
Contractor.	Rattee & Kett Ltd.
Requirement.	20 maisonettes and 20 flats

Description. Sited asymmetrically between Sheppard's Stage I Research Flats and the Storey's Way house of Whittingehame Lodge, this three-sided court faces across the college playing fields. Each pair of loadbearing brick crosswalls encloses a maisonette on the lower two floors, with a flat above. On the court side the ground floor of each maisonette has a small study and a private terrace alongside, with the living room recessed behind it; on the first floor the two bedrooms are both recessed, with a balcony over the study; but the flat on the top floor is brought forward again, with its L-shaped living room enclosing a study directly above that of the maisonette. Kitchens, bathrooms and stairs are kept to the rear of each wing and maisonettes are entered directly from the open parking area for 40 cars. Flats are reached from access galleries on corbelled out brickwork; these are reached by stairs at the outside ends of the blocks and at inside corners, where there are also stores on two levels and top floor launderettes. The same brick is used throughout for projecting crosswalls, infill panels and dwarf terrace walls; the flats have a concrete floor slab. Windows are aluminium sliders, and woodwork is painted black.

Comment. Churchill College behaved shabbily in discarding Richard Sheppard—and even more so in asking him to enter a limited competition with David Roberts (who had after all been among the runners-up in 1959). The excuse was that this second block of graduate flats was a new requirement; but basically this is another case of Cambridge dons playing Architectural Chairs. It is the more unfortunate that Roberts has here produced his least sensitive building in Cambridge. Round a grassed court which is neither particularly communal nor in the least private, the three blocks are inexplicably ill-related in scale and form to the Research Flats. The stiffly fractured corners are particularly weak in treatment. Roberts seems to have been absorbed in making a contribution to the Cambridge School of brickwork; the brick infill panels and piers which divide the windows have the same ambiguities as in his Master's Lodge for Magdalene and groundsmen's flats for St. John's—one is never sure what is structural and what is not. Admittedly the flats and maisonettes are well-planned internally and the elevation of each cross wall unit is clearly done. But the totality is joyless.

Clare Hall   d

Herschel Road

6 graduates, 32 fellows.

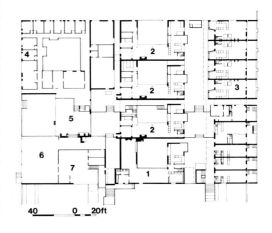

Ground floor plan

1 President's lodge 2 Fellow's patio house
3 Houses and flats for graduates 4 Studies
5 Common room 6 Dining room 7 Kitchens

Date.   1966–9

Architects.   Ralph Erskine; associates, Twist & Whitley

Contractor.   S. B. Thackeray Ltd.

Cost.   £300,000

Requirement. A graduate college, with 20 houses and flats, 10 studies for non-residents, dining, reading and common rooms.

Description. In 1965 Clare College, with the help of American benefactors, founded Cambridge's second graduate college—independent like Darwin, but not much larger than Corpus's dependent satellite, Leckhampton. The site of three acres lies just off Grange Road, in a road of Victorian villas; with a rear view southwards over the university football ground. Erskine has raised his buildings over a

144

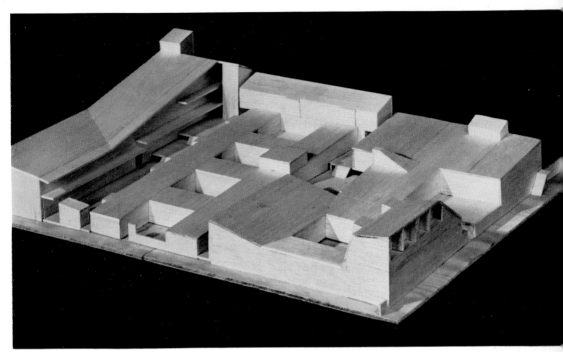

Clare Hall, model

covered semi-basement along the northern (Herschel Road) boundary, which contains parking for 37 cars, stores, boiler house and cloakrooms for common rooms. The site is clearly divided into three strips, for flats, houses and common rooms respectively. In the centre of the Herschel Road front lies the two-storey president's house, which has its upper floor cantilevered on each side as a porch over the pedestrian entrances to the site. Behind the president's house, in the central strip, are three four-bedroom courtyard houses. To the right, separated from the houses by the Family Walk, is an irregular block, starting at three storeys and diminishing to two: it has nine bed-sitters, three two-bedroom flats and a day nursery. It stays at two storeys for four four-bedroom terrace houses; the ground is meanwhile sloping down from the car park in two flights of steps. Erskine has unified the terrace by making the monopitch roof reflect the various slopes. On the other side of the president's house the Scholar's Walk, sloping similarly, separates the courtyard houses from the extensive common room block. This has a dining room and

kitchen at the Herschel Road end, then the common room itself with sliding windows to patio beyond and finally the reading room with a courtyard enclosed by ten separate studies and four other workrooms of various kinds. There is also a cross walk through the courtyard houses. From the common room patio, steps lead down to a wooded garden.

The buildings are all of loadbearing brick with some timber boarding. The floors and access decks are of concrete and the pantiled roofs of timber. The flats are reached by access decks from a projecting staircase next to the president's house; they and the terrace houses all have open-plan living areas with built-in seats and shelving as dividers. The courtyard houses have a big central living area, flanked by three bedrooms in one wing and the dining–kitchen with a fourth (housekeeper's) bedroom in the other. The five-bedroom president's house also has three wings; the ground floor contains a formal dining or meeting room in the centre, flanked by a big living area on one side and a family wing on the other.

Comment. As Cambridge's answer to Arne Jacobsen, Clare turned to the brilliant Swedish architect Ralph Erskine, English-born and English-trained, who is a leader of the post-Aalto generation of Scandinavian naturalists. Like Pietilä in Finland, he extends Aalto's sense of the organic—architecture in natural materials, built *in* rather than *on* the ground—to appeal to a younger generation who in a complicated urban society have an emotional need for an artificially simple life. Clare Hall should exhibit most of the advantages of this kind of domesticity. The site has been sub-divided with a logic and compactness which is truly urban, preserving the adjoining garden, while the tilt up-stage over the car park succeeds in bringing extra sunlight into the courtyards without infringing their privacy. The layout of the walkways and courtyards is handled delicately and flexibly. The internal planning, with its built-in dividers, should establish new standards for the academic family life that is so important in the new Cambridge society. The president's house is a fine centrepiece for those who can stomach the paternalism implied by entering the college under its arms.

But the college's success as a community will depend primarily on the communal wing. Reading room, dining room and common room exploit a series of intricate patios, terraces, halls and entrances which look delightful on the drawings—until it is remembered that this is not an aesthetic yachtsmen's pub in the Broads but an integral part of what must soon become a thickly urbanized area. In its context the arbitrarily picturesque quality of some of the detailing may jar; the walkways, for example, are to be dolled up as a kind of *Architectural Review* arcadia with cobbles, bollards, benches and flower-beds. The later drawings show a move away from some of the over-pretty and over-articulated forms: the long roof slope over the flats replaced a plethora of steps and fins, and two extra floors of workrooms have been cut off one side of the study court. Given a restraint on folksy details and a rigorous avoidance of hill-village analogies, the college should fit into its setting extremely successfully. In the straightforward peppering of little windows where functionally required, Erskine shows a lightness of touch which should be a profound relief from Cambridge's usual hammering of crosswalls.

Corpus Christi College   A
Leckhampton House

Off Grange Road, opposite Selwyn.

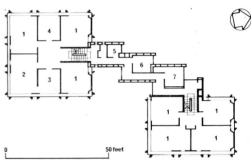

Typical floor plan
1 Research student's study-bedroom **2** and **3** Bachelor fellow's living room and bedroom **4** Married fellow's study **5** Fellow's bathroom **6** Kitchen **7** Washroom

Date.   1963–4

Architects and
Engineers.   Arup Associates

Contractor.   William Sindall Ltd.

Cost.   £77,139

Requirement. Bed-sitters for 24 research students, sets for four bachelor fellows and studies for three non-resident fellows.

Description. This graduate community has taken over a handsome Victorian villa (1880, by William Marshall) standing in eight acres of wooded garden. Total accommodation is for warden, five bachelor fellows and 30 research students, with studies for five non-resident married fellows. The new building is placed at the northern end of the site, as close as possible to the old house, both to preserve the gardens and to allow for possible extensions, should Leckhampton later become a graduate college. By splitting the accommodation into two staircase towers of four and five storeys, a southward view over the gardens is given to most of the rooms. The car park and rear entrance are screened from the garden by a long wall and by the stepped brick piers of an open concourse between

Leckhampton House: general view from garden with Henry Moore seated figure

the staircases. On this high link a staggered range of service rooms (gyprooms, bathrooms and lavatories), is raised so that they fall at two levels only and on half-landings of the staircases. The ground floor cloisters, on a continuous brick path 6 in high, encircle a large recreation room under one lower block and laundry, store and boiler house under the other. The 18 in brick crosswalls of the service wing, which contain ducts within their cavities, and the paving and back wall of the cloisters are all faced in multi-red brick to match the Victorian house. The staircases also have exposed brick walls, with concrete steps and carborundum inserts to the tread. The towers by contrast consist of a series of white pre-cast H-frames, with a lightly tooled limestone aggregate, which stand 2 ft 6 in forward from the full glazing of the rooms behind. Arup's claim three main advantages in this separation: the promotion of good weathering by preventing rain carrying dirt from glazing to concrete; the convenience of not having to dovetail windows and heating convectors into the main structure; above all, by extending floor

and ceiling slightly beyond the window, the achievement of full-height glazing without glare or excessive heat. The areas of infill panel, mainly on the north, are in a similar concrete, with a rougher texture. The five types of bed-sitter range from 184 to 234 sq ft. Walls and ceilings are white-painted plaster, windows are black-painted steel. Heating by convection from pipes within the afromosia window seats, is topped up by fans.

Comment. Leckhampton was a promising start to Cambridge's belated provision of community life for the Ph.D. industry—workers in which have often been used to greater freedom in other universities. The site has many advantages: it is just far enough away from the Backs for suburban arcadia still to be justifiable; it inherits a mature garden with magnificent trees, with a Tudor-style 'manor house' (built for P. W. H. Myers, the famous spiritualist) which from the start provided comfortable dining and common rooms (as well as more living space). The new buildings, twin pavilions, have a pleasingly

Leckhampton House; garden entrance

informal relationship with the existing house and with the Henry Moore 'Seated Figure' on the lawn. This is elegantly picturesque planning without the heavyweight hectoring and enforced togetherness of so many of the new college buildings. Only in the jagged multi-red teeth of the service wing, exposed inside as well, does the usual Cambridge *angst* appear—although for practicality and sociability the grouping of the service rooms at a split level has much to recommend it.

Designed by the architect–partner (Philip Dowson) in Britain's most famous firm of structural engineers, Leckhampton is one of three buildings experimenting with the same extreme separation of structure from infill, to the intended advantage of both (the others are at Bracknell New Town and Somerville College, Oxford). It is an all-too-rare example at Cambridge of the use of modern building techniques to improve the academic environment. The rooms are exceptionally spacious and flexible—clearly for adults and professionals; there is much variety in size and aspect without appearing to strain the structural system. The precast 'hanging frame' is similar in position to the 'peristylar grids' used by Skidmore, Owings & Merrill in their two recent

European works (Heinz and Banque Lambert). But S.O.M.'s concrete is in a grand palazzo manner, whereas Dowson's is entirely appropriate to the informality of the Leckhampton garden. Perhaps in detail it is a little too bright, a little too neat, a little finicky in its splays and offsets; and the crudity of the link block suggests a slight clash between a repetitive and rational system and the essentially picturesque and emotional siting. Would a single straight wing have been better? From within the building, however, there can be few such doubts. Their slenderness in section and beautifully tooled surfaces make the structures a constant background pleasure without intruding. There is a delightful involvement with the landscape through the fully glazed window walls; while the 'hanging frame' undoubtedly prevents the feelings of vertigo in Jacobsen's rooms at St. Catherine's, Oxford. The presidents can even use its gutter as a balcony, when sitting out on the window seat. There is throughout Leckhampton a stimulating connection and reaction between inside and outside, particularly in the beautifully detailed window walling in the focal recreation room, with its inclusive views of cloister, house and garden.

Darwin College   h

65 graduates, 25 fellows.

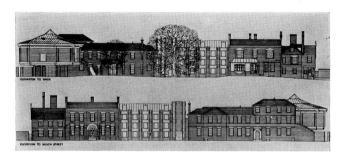

Newnham Grange

Silver Street

New Dining Hall   The Hermitage   New Residential Building

The Old Granary

Mill Pool

River Cam

Laundress Lane

SITE: PLANS AT FIRST FLOOR LEVEL

Little Island

Laundress Green

1:100

DARWIN COLLEGE   CAMBRIDGE

HOWELL KILLICK PARTRIDGE & AMIS ARCHITECTS

This is the first graduates college to be established in modern times and was founded by Gonville and Caius, St. John's and Trinity. It became an approved university foundation in 1965, and is housed in Newnham Grange in Silver Street, originally the first home of New Hall, together with the adjoining nineteenth-century house, The Hermitage and the Old Granary behind Newnham Grange. In 1966 Howell, Killick, Partridge & Amis were commissioned to design extra accommodation to meet the 80 graduates hoped for by October 1968.

New Building and Hall

Date.   1966–8

Architects.   Howell, Killick, Partridge & Amis

Contractor.   Kerridge Ltd.

Cost.   £205,140 (including conversion of The Hermitage).

Requirement.   34 student rooms, college offices and dining hall.

Description.   All the student accommodation has been placed in a small block linking The Hermitage and Newnham Grange. This is a three-storey building with a mansard, and is nearly the same height as both existing buildings. On the ground floor are some college offices; and The Hermitage has been converted into the college kitchen and staff block, with two members' common rooms. The study–bedrooms are designed to face both into the gardens and out onto Silver Street. A staircase block, with vertical slit-glazing, divides the block from The Hermitage, but there is no access to Newnham Grange. The dining-hall is an octagonal block between The Hermitage and Newnham Terrace, in Newnham Road. The hall, designed to seat 140, is supported on stilts, thus permitting access through to the garden beyond. A yellow-grey facing brick has been used, to match that of the existing buildings, and for the residential block is used in U-shaped piers, similar to the same architects' block for Sidney Sussex (see page 47). Aluminium windows are set in panels between the piers. The hall is set on a concrete structure, and here the similarity is with the architects' University Centre, just across the river. It has a complicated glazed roof structure.

Comment. The architects have shown considerable skill in matching the scale and the form of the Georgian buildings on either side. In a sense the task was made easy by the differing heights and the loose agglomeration of parts, especially in The Hermitage; but their own powerfully detailed block does not merely 'toe the line' but actually assists in creating a new cohesion. Less successful is the dining-room which has been placed in too small an opening to do it justice. An essentially idiosyncratic, isolated form such as this needs an open space to itself. Nevertheless, their buildings will make urban good sense of this corner of Cambridge.

Fitzwilliam College   b

420 undergraduates, 75 postgraduates, 40 fellows.

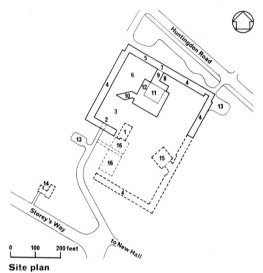

Site plan

1 Chapel 2 Main gate 3 Entrance court 4 Undergraduates
5 Fellows etc. 6 Fellows' garden 7 Servants 8
9 Kitchen 10 Parlour 11 Hall 12 Library 13 Car and
bicycle park 14 Master's lodge 15 Theatre 16 Lake

Fitzwilliam House was founded in 1889 as a receptacle for undergraduates unattached to any other college—some mature, some from abroad. With the Georgian house in Trumpington Street long outgrown, the University, to elevate Fitzwilliam to full collegiate status (in 1966), has acquired for it a new site, 7½ acres in Huntingdon Road—next to New Hall

and close to Churchill. Of architects invited in 1958 to submit preliminary designs, Chamberlin, Powell & Bon, who had just been appointed to design New Hall, urged that 'it would seem unimaginative not to make the most of this coincidence of three new colleges by designing a group of buildings which would match the majestic scale of the great periods of architecture'. In choosing Denys Lasdun & Partners, Fitzwilliam went to the post-war maestro most likely to succeed in doing this. But in briefing him they rejected the co-operation in planning suggested by Chamberlin, while playing up the so-called traditional demand for 'majestic scale'. The difficulty in doing this, however, has been the college's almost total lack of private endowment; and, as there was little incentive for yet another public appeal, there was no choice but to turn to the University Grants Committee, which lays down rigid standards of economy, particularly for residential buildings. Not only is lack of money likely to make Fitzwilliam's development slower than its neighbours, but a large part of the site, occupied by a large nineteenth-century villa (The Grove), is sterilized by the life interest of the present lessee.

Lasdun has therefore had to design a community which will grow; and in this respect his Fitzwilliam plan is perhaps the most important single piece of academic planning in post-war Cambridge. He has placed the central block of public rooms as near the centre of the site as possible—very close to the boundary fence of The Grove—and has then wrapped the residential buildings around it in a continuous spiral or 'snail-shell'. This means that the communal focus, firmly established at the start, will be able to change gradually from that of a commuter campus to that of a residential community while the college will environmentally be a complete entity around it at each stage.

Unfortunately this logical and architectural attractive plan has not fully succeeded in practice. This is, as Diana Rowntree has said, 'partly due to a steep rise in building costs, not matched by a rise in the U.G.C. grant; partly to an architectural exuberance that has refused to conform to the gradual tempo of the plan'. What is worse, the exuberance is only a superficial skin to bare bones within.

Stages I and II

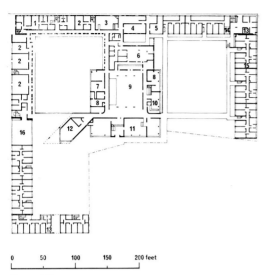

Fitzwilliam College: parlour and residential wing

Ground floor

1 Offices 2 Store 3 Boiler 4 Servants' hall 5 Laundry
6 Kitchen 7 Fellows 8 Cloakrooms 9 Hall 10 Bar 11 J.C.R.
12 Parlour 13 Porter 14 Shop 15 Fellows 16 Board room

Date.	1961–3, 1966–7
Architects.	Denys Lasdun & Partners
Contractor.	Johnson & Bailey Ltd.
Cost.	£317,000

Requirement. Hall and kitchen, common rooms, lecture room, music room and library. Rooms for 204 undergraduates and nine fellows: college offices and studies for 10 fellows; board room and guest rooms; rooms for 10 servants and nurse.

Description. With the completion of Stage II, the college's main entrance approach is from Storeys Way. To the left of the drive is the site of the Master's lodge and the car park; to the right is The Grove, behind its fence; ahead is the flat-topped entrance arch (with porter's lodge), which opens through two floors of the residential perimeter. Through it the far-spreading concrete canopy of the fellows' parlour announces the central buildings, which form a single square block free-standing

within the precinct, except for a low entrance and kitchen link to the north. The hall is placed centrally, and rises through two floors to its giant clerestory windows, forming an airy roof lantern, glazed all round. The precast concrete mullions support arches with spreading soffits, externally scalloped and internally forming a series of pendentives to an exposed diagrid ceiling of precast units. Inside the two deep perimeter beams at first and second floor level are exposed and rough shuttered, the ground level walls are recessed and panelled in pine; the first floor wall is rendered and is broken only by a recessed gallery.

The other public rooms, forming a solid base to this fantasy, are of loadbearing brick, with dark brownish purple facings and pine window frames. On the ground floor, which has windows deeply recessed above and below to form an almost continuous clerestory, the double senior combination room lies in the north-west corner, next to the entrance passage. Cloakrooms follow and then a short length of passage to the fellows' parlour which projects diagonally from the central building and ends in a point to form a separate ceremonial porch. On the south side are the middle combination room (for research students), the main stairs to the upper floor and the two-level J.C.R. on the corner nearest to The Grove. Above the S.C.R. and M.C.R. is the library, which has eight broad picture-frame windows projecting from a wall clad entirely in copper. Above the J.C.R. is the 210-seat lecture room which, with only narrow slit windows at the side, is largely top-lit, with louvres adjustable from below. On the east side of the hall are the buttery and bar and the main cloakrooms, with the undergraduate entertaining room and music room over. The kitchen lies

151

on the north side, and forms a single-storeyed L-shaped block with a pitched roof of copper, connecting by a passage to storage rooms, servants' hall and domestic quarters in the nearest part of the residential building.

The continuous residential block now forms the whole of the north and west side of the eventual precinct, with parts of the south and east, so there is a sense of complete enclosure in two complete courts, confirmed by the continuous three-storey roof line. The structure is of loadbearing brick cross-walls at irregular intervals corresponding to the varied spaces within, which are nevertheless confined by a uniform width of the block throughout, except for a recessed balcony on the second floor of staircases 'E' and 'F'. Concrete floor slabs are exposed in two continuous bands, within which the external wall panels of brownish purple brick are shuffled irregularly in a pattern of floor-to-ceiling slit windows of varying width. The roof, hidden behind a broken castellated parapet, is low-pitched.

The rooms are arranged on the staircase principle, with short lengths of central corridor and rooms single- or double-banked. At the south-west corner next to the entrance there are four residential staircases (A–D), each with 16–22 bedsitters and a big fellows' room. Staircase 'E' on the ground floor gives access to the board room, a square to the full width of the block; above are the master's and bursar's offices, with guest rooms and six bedsitters. Staircase 'F' has the two main college store rooms, with more offices and bedsitters. Staircases 'G', 'H' and 'J', beginning the Huntingdon Road wing, consist entirely of college offices and fellows' studies, with the ground floor boiler room on 'J'. Staircase 'K' is for the domestic staff. Staircases 'L', 'M', 'P', 'Q' and 'R' each contain 18–23 bedsitters and a fellows' room or set, with Staircase 'N' in the north-east corner containing the second porter's lodge and the college shop.

Eventually Stage II will be continued southward on the site of The Grove (the house can be kept if necessary) and will bend westwards, as far as the entrance drive, to form a third, southern court; this will provide another 150 bedsitters and eight fellows' rooms. Within it will be a theatre, a chapel and an ornamental lake.

Comment. Fitzwilliam is a worrying design, tossed off in a perverse moment by an architect who, at his best and with a big budget—in the Green Park

flats, the Royal College of Physicians, the proposed National Theatre—is equal to any of the world's grand masters. Fitzwilliam's snail-shell plan, as a diagram of collegiate growth, *is* Lasdun at his best; but its logic is largely obscured by its realisation. The U.G.C. budget is partly to blame, but elsewhere architects have succeeded within its discipline—Lasdun himself brilliantly at the University of East Anglia. A U.G.C. budget does emphasize the need for cool heads and a certain humility in preparing the brief for a new academic community. Fitzwilliam clearly wanted to be a proper Cambridge college of traditional type; the distressing Georgian-style furniture in the parlour and the beery-hearty leather armchairs in the J.C.R. are evidence of this. But, even in the eighteenth century, Cambridge colleges were not places for pomp. They were quiet and inexpensive sequences of courts and passageways, cumulative rather than intense in their environment, subconscious rather than self-conscious in their influence.

Fitzwilliam wanted pomp—and Lasdun has indulged his weakness (as in the Bethnal Green cluster flats) for enforcing intensity against the more strictly functional requirements of a brief. The hall undoubtedly is a splendid space, planned on a pure Renaissance system of proportion. But a close look shows the cheapness of the rendering on the upper walls; and the lantern itself, even from ground level, has a paperiness which does not convince (particularly in the triangular light fittings). Externally it is sheer pastry-cookery—an attempt at the kind of precast Gothic which Yamasaki builds in the States on unlimited budgets with superb finishes. Here, there it is perched instead on the massive dark brick plinth of the common rooms.

The interiors here are surprisingly sober, colours of blue, green and grey predominating, with dark wood floors and light wood furnishings. The public areas, with shuttered concrete beams and white-painted brickwork, are attractively lit by spotlights set into the ceilings. Externally however, the solidity of the common rooms as a plinth is dramatized by various sculptural effects: the scooped out copper-cladding of the library, the painfully narrow slits of the lecture hall and the aggressive splaying of the first floor cantilever where the brickwork is permanently stained with patches of white efflorescence caused by poor drainage of the massive brickwork. Apart from the arbitrary copper-knobbing of the library the upper walls everywhere are carried up to form

Fitzwilliam College: hall and library

Fitzwilliam College: residental accommodation from Huntingdon Road

intermittent bands of parapet, like battlements—a fashionable motif of about ten years ago. The fenestration of the residential block is self-consciously restless and ill-related, with the 'expressed floorslab' perversely carried across the staircase windows as a transom. At the north-east corner, by the porter's lodge, there is an untidy change in ground and floor levels. The gloomy brickwork is aggressively picked out with white mortar joints.

What is most curious is Lasdun's lack of regard for the residential environment. The rooms are inevitably small—120 sq ft is only 10 sq ft more than the U.G.C.'s minimum—but they need not have been so narrow and poky. There are three possible positions for the work-table and there is a deep terrazzo window ledge; but the window slits are neither pleasant to look at or to look out from. They exaggerate the feeling of being hedged in. The 9 in crosswalls give good sound insulation; some are plastered and some are just whitewashed. The staircases are almost undetailed, except for bull-nosed corners to

the walls, which are faced in common pink Flettons. The narrow cloister from staircase 'E' to the hall has heavy brick piers to confine and negate its space. Particularly unfortunate is the rigid maintenance of the width of the residential block. There is no attempt to pick out significant rooms or significant places. It should surely have been possible to work out a varied hierarchy within a quiet discipline of materials rather than a uniform perimeter block jazzed up with patterning, applied without regard to function.

Beneath all this, the basic layout remains excellent. The approach from Storeys Way, with the hall gradually revealed above and through the perimeter buildings, already shows a fine sense of enclosure, which mature landscaping can only enhance. On Huntingdon Road the uniform front lies back from the road in northern shadow at an angle; it will eventually clash violently with New Hall's Stage III chapel and entrance.

Gonville and Caius College

Harvey Court

West Road

B

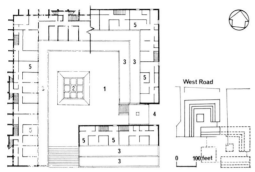

1 Court 2 Roof of breakfast room
3 Terrace 4 Entrance 5 Study-bedroom
Left hand side represents first floor level
Right hand side represents second floor level
Diagram on right shows possible future extension

Date.	1960–2
Architects.	Sir Leslie Martin & Colin St. John Wilson; assistant, Patrick Hodgkinson
Engineer.	Frank Newby of Felix J. Samuely & Partners
Contractors.	William Sindall Ltd.
Cost.	£232,000

Requirement. Hostel for about 100 undergraduates and a few fellows; storage and garage space; vacation use as a conference centre.

Description. With no further room for expansion on its city centre side, Caius decided to develop its property across the Backs, which immediately adjoins the Arts Faculties' precinct. Harvey Court was therefore designed as the prototype of a series of residential courts, each elevated to a condition of semi-privacy over a square storey-height plinth of public rooms. At Harvey Court nearly half the plinth is empty or filled with earth. On the west side are garages and stores, while on the east, a freestanding concrete canopy shelters the main entrance, with steps up to the courtyard and down to the breakfast room, kitchen and common room beneath it. The common room opens through French windows to the mature suburban garden on to the south, from which a second flight of steps, broad and open, rises steeply up to the formal, brick-paved courtyard. The three upper floors of bedsitting rooms and sets around it are stepped back in broad and continuous brick-paved terraces and are fully-glazed between the brick crosswalls, the ends of which are expressed as a series of structural piers. Three of the ranges are fully connected; but the fourth, isolated between the two flights of steps, is turned decisively back to front; this was done both to gain the southward view over the garden and to suggest a pivotal connecting point for future extensions of a consistent character, which could use the same canopied entrance on the east side for access to a second or third court (see plan).

The structural system of brick crosswalls is expressed on the outer 'street side' of the building—towards West Road, for instance—as a series of freestanding brick piers or 'fins', supporting the almost blank rear wall of the topmost terrace; through the intervening space behind the lower terraces are threaded the diagonal 'ducts' of the staircases. Internally these rise at five points from a broad perimeter ambulatory or 'long gallery' at first floor level, which is entered directly from the courtyard; paved in brick, it passes in a series of flat-topped brick arches through the crosswalls and the broad windows diffuse their light through close-set timber mullions. The nine small staircases lead steeply up to short lengths of landing, walled with whitewashed brick, and each containing a group of three to five rooms, with bath and service rooms. In the various groupings within the equal bays of the crosswalls, six basic types of individual room are developed; two types of study–bedroom; three types of study and bedroom; and divisible sets of two to three rooms, suitable for one fellow or two undergraduates.

Massive detailing in brown Stamfordstone brick is carried through consistently into every part of the building: flush jointing in mortar to make the walls appear monolithic; bull-nosed copings to emphasize the solidity and community of the terraces; a grid pattern of brick paving in two colours to pick up the

155

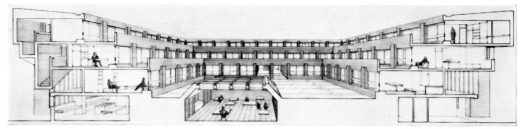

Harvey Court: perspective section

modular repetitiveness of the court and the cross-walls; slight recession of the timber window frames on the court side to emphasize the structural relationship of brick fins to glass infill and recession of the terrace parapets to make the gable walls distinct; deep splays for the tiny windows in the street side of the top terrace so as to make them appear punched or grooved into the solid mass. Off-centre in the court is a pyramidal brick plinth carrying a grid of 12 copper-clad roof-lights to the breakfast room. Floor slabs throughout are of reinforced concrete with a timber-joisted roof to the top floor. All window frames and internal joinery are in varnished Douglas fir, and all fascias and flashings are in lead-coated copper.

Comment.   Harvey Court is rare among English buildings of any period in being dominated by a consistent theoretical idea. Like Soane's Bank of England, Butterfield's Margaret Street church or the Smithsons' Hunstanton school, it defies the temptation to fit easily into its delightful surroundings. The puzzled tourist in West Road is faced with the blank walls and peripheral catwalks of an introverted fortress. If he penetrates the unobtrusive side entrance and mounts the sacrificial steps, his bafflement is compounded by the almost surrealist contrast of an excessively tight urban piazza, brown and brick-paved, with a wild English garden. Denied the picturesque pleasures of an informal 'Cambridge image', he searches for an appropriately alien epithet: Babylonian hanging garden, Grecian acropolis, Egyptian necropolis, Aztec temple, Chinese puzzle. Yet, even superficially, Harvey Court's brick geometry has an integrity, a puritanical singleness of mind, which is a deep relief from the frenetically varied surfaces of Sir Hugh Casson's nearby Arts faculties. Its impressive scale and its expressive forms contrast still more with the indecisive pink-

ness of King's Garden Hostel over the way. So what is the big idea? Sir Leslie Martin, since his days as Architect to the L.C.C. in the early fifties, has been obsessed with the invention of new forms of *residence*—forms which can ideally express the community life of a modern city. While his L.C.C. team were being acclaimed by the world's architectural press for their clever mingling of towers and terrace houses amid a verdant eighteenth-century landscape at Roehampton, he himself (with Colin Wilson, of the Roehampton team) had already rejected the fundamental assumption made there—an assumption rooted in the English tradition of Nash and of the Garden Cities that mass housing can be adequately 'composed' into a kind of built landscape painting. The real needs of an urban community—to meet, to park, to work and to play—had been betrayed by the manipulation of families in isolated towers. In schemes designed since his move to Cambridge as Professor in 1956, Sir Leslie and his colleagues have made one assumption: that the 'urbanity' of city life is intrinsically desirable—and in the case of student life, that residence itself should be the primary medium of higher education. In the context of Levittown or the University of California, this may be questionable, but not at Cambridge. Bathrooms, kitchens and bed-spaces—the functional components of residence—Sir Leslie sees not as ends in themselves, but only as a personal survival kit on a communal launching pad—hence their unobtrusive recession above and behind the dominant places of community life: outside places, such as piazza and terraces; inside places, such as 'long gallery' and common rooms. By means of the geometrical calculations which his new Institute of Built Form Studies is now refining, Sir Leslie has treated the whole site out to its full perimeter as though it were a single cube of building, in which an 'anti-form' or matrix of external space is then pared down and

Harvey Court: entrance canopy

Harvey Court: view from the garden

hollowed out as required for daylighting, access, circulation and sheer pleasure. By his single-building approach Martin can achieve very high densities without building high, while giving the residents generous external spaces for walking, meeting and playing, all elevated above the noise of motor traffic, which is buried in the plinth.

A single urban building, however, does not make a city. Harvey Court's problem is that in pioneering urbanity in the 'second city' beyond the Backs, it has been caught in a nexus of college property ownership which dictates separate plots, separate buildings and separate architects (like Martin)— each of them building his own disconnected fragment in suburbia. The stepped terrace of 'hanging garden' form was indeed first worked out for a central site in Cambridge (the abortive Market Court for King's—see page 28) where the organic cross-currents of city life would have made perfect sense of the features which re-appear in West Road: the

almost windowless barrier to the noise of street traffic; the public plinth giving a richness of multiple uses, here half-empty but at King's to be packed with shops; the hard-paved brick piazza, here a pretentiously elevated sanctuary but at King's an immediate extension of the market square; the spacious ambulatory for 'collecting' the staircases, conversationally under cover, here virtually unused, even when raining; the burrowing of the staircases themselves on the confined scale of urban tenements; the exposure of each room, by fully glazing it, to the passing crowd on the terraces and the piazza—at West Road only to an occasional party and a few easily embarrassed visitors. In West Road's English country garden (or its suburban–arcadian derivative), not one of these situations is yet applicable. The Court's introversion—its contemplation of its own piazza—excludes the residents from the north-easterly views in winter, across the Backs to King's Chapel. The architects have unwisely rationalized

Harvey Court: courtyard and terraces

this: 'the isolation of the site and its lack of prospect to north, east and west suggested a form as self-contained as possible'. Yet far from being isolated, it is in the heart of the new Western academic area. In refusing to be neighbourly and to suggest through routes from neighbouring properties, Harvey Court has ensured that its piazza will for long remain secluded and empty, without the enriching society of strangers passing by.

Without these umbilical connections necessary for urban life, Harvey Court ironically becomes just another stack of rooms—suburban, but without the privacy which at least suburbia normally gives. The rooms, although a variety of shapes and sizes is successfully contrived, are disappointing as, apart from the excellent built-in cupboards, the college rejected the furniture their architects suggested in favour of the commercial norm. This may have been justifiable economically, however; for the scheme as a whole, though intended by its architects as a

residential prototype of wide relevance, would be cripplingly expensive for all but Oxbridge—the cost per set was nearly twice the U.G.C. limits for publicly financed halls of residence.

This extravagance is partly the result of the beautifully sculptured finish, with its many special brick details which give delight to the connoisseur—the modular paving, the bull-nosed coping, the flush jointing. Wilson and Hodgkinson worked on these almost literally as sculptors, trying alternatives actually on the site. Professor Martin was in his youth associated with the English constructivist artists who adopted the philosophies of de Stijl; and he has a profound feeling for the basic geometry of block shapes. However, in constructing them, he has been as perverse as any of Cambridge's post-war 'grand masters' in rejecting the assistance of modern building techniques. In his attempt to build up an organic community, his design recalls Alvar Aalto's National Pensions Institute at Helsinki, with its

159

Harvey Court: long gallery

elevated garden, stepped offices and brick-and-copper detailing; but Aalto uses a concrete frame to enhance the free-flowing continuity of his public and private spaces. Similarly, Le Corbusier's concrete courtyard at La Tourette is plastic and flexibly moulded in its response to communal demands. Harvey Court by contrast is typically British in the rectilinear stiffness of its crosswall structure, with rigid corners which make the breakfast and common rooms awkwardly inaccessible from the rooms—everyone has to go outside and then in again. If the public rooms had been tied to the ambulatory, with continuous indoor circulation, the whole scheme might have come to life immediately. Another reason for its present moribund atmosphere is the architects' false 'consistency', motivated by that other British love, for texture, in bringing inside the ambulatory the romantically gloomy brownness of the brick; the difference between exterior and interior is nothing to be ashamed of in a cold climate, though British architects are reluctant to admit this. Aalto has always provided centrally heated public wombs which are warm and soft, with a plastered and panelled skin instead of the 'integrity' of continuous flesh. As an experiment, with the kind of intellectual struggle appropriate at a university, Harvey Court is Cambridge's most important post-war building; but because of its self-imposed isolation and stiffness, it remains for the moment unproven as a generator for community life.

King's College C
Garden Hostel

West Road

Date.	1948–50
Architect.	Geddes Hyslop
Contractor.	Rattee & Kett Ltd.
Cost.	£75,100
Requirement.	Hostel for 42 undergraduates.

Description. King's Garden Hostel is situated to the south of Clare Memorial Court, between the driveway to the University Library and the fellows' garden of King's. The hostel is planned on the corridor system, so that as many rooms as possible face south across the lawns towards West Road. The rooms are laid out in a block which is roughly cruciform in shape, with a long three-storey western arm. The main entrance faces south-east and has a Georgian-shaped doorway surmounted by a tall vertical staircase window of 'Swedish modern' derivation. All other windows are of a simple Georgian shape. The structure is of loadbearing brick, faced with pale pink bricks outside and generally plastered inside.
The main western arm has the living rooms along the south side of the corridor and the service rooms on the north side. On the ground floor of the short eastern arm is the breakfast room, with a curtain designed by Graham Sutherland. In the two staircases there are ornamental panels in ceramic tile designed by Quintin and Vanessa Bell and there is a small painting by Duncan Grant.

Comment. Garden Hostel, in view of its important and interesting site in the new western academic area, was one of the first and worst of post-war Cambridge's missed opportunities. Situated between the convinced traditionalism of Memorial Court and the convinced innovation of Harvey Court, it offers only suburban good taste, a hygienic arrangement of corridors and faint echoes of Georgian detail (such as the urns on the roof). The belated relics of the Bloomsbury Group compare unfavourably with the paintings preserved elsewhere in King's.

New Hall

a

183 undergraduates, 39 postgraduates, 19 fellows.

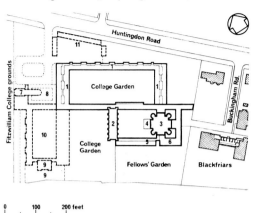

Site plan
1 Main residential block 2 Library 3 Dining hall 4 J.C.R.
5 S.C.R. 6 Fellows' drawing and dining rooms 7 Chapel
8 Pool 9 Principal's lodge & garden 10 Entrance court
11 Garages
Shaded areas indicate existing buildings

Cambridge's third college for women, founded in 1954, for its first ten years occupied an early nineteenth-century house in Silver Street (now part of Darwin College, page 149). The new Huntingdon Road site of 6.2 acres was presented by the Darwin family and Chamberlin, Powell & Bon were appointed architects in 1958. They rightly saw the opportunity to join up with the neighbouring colleges of Fitzwilliam and Churchill to form a coherent new precinct, aligned on the University Library tower beyond Madingley Road; but their comprehensive plan was ignored. A year later, after Lasdun's appointment for Fitzwilliam, they proposed in their finalist design in the Churchill competition to resite New Hall in the field opposite Churchill at the bottom of Storey's Way. Certainly the Huntingdon Road site is small; and phasing of work has been conditioned not only by the progress of the college's own appeal fund, but also by the survival of a life tenancy on part of The Grove (see Fitzwilliam), where entrance to the college from Storey's Way is to be provided.
Peter Chamberlin's design of 1960, intended to house 270 out of 280 undergraduates and 14 out of 30 fellows, is now two-thirds built. The mere glimpse of its snow-white dome and attendant minarets

lording it over academic suburbia has been enough for most CLASP-conscious critics to dismiss it out of hand as oriental buffoonery. The slick images of Rome and Byzantium, beautifully executed, inevitably recall the playboy monuments of recent American campuses. Yet underneath the funny hats is an entirely serious exercise in community planning carried through with masterly consistency. As at Butterfield's Keble, the planning of a modern college seems to have been conducted parallel to the aesthetic gymnastics without ever closely connecting with them.

Stages I and II

Date. 1962–6

Architects. Chamberlin, Powell & Bon

Contractor. W. & C. French Ltd.

Cost. £655,000

Requirement. Stage I, dining hall and kitchen, common rooms, library, offices, studies for fellows. Stage II, rooms for 180 undergraduates and 25 postgraduates.

Description. New Hall's central buildings were at first entered by everyone through the service door to Buckingham Road. But the essence of Chamberlin's plan is that they should eventually be only the climax to a broad public walkway which will run as a 'spine' from west to east (actually north-west to south-east), with the residential buildings encircling it in an irregular S-shape of open courts. The main entrance will be approached at right-angles from Huntingdon Road and also eventually from Storey's Way. It will consist of porters' lodge, lecture and newspaper rooms, with the chapel above, seating 30 for regular services in its apse and 120 more for major occasions in its ante-chapel, which is indirectly lit at clerestory level and suitable for use also as lecture room, concert hall or art gallery. The 'spine', as an open cloister, will first form the north side of a paved court (Stage III), set over an underground car park and flanked by two residential wings with the seven-bedroom President's lodge at the southern end. The farther of the two residential wings, with a largely open ground floor, will form a

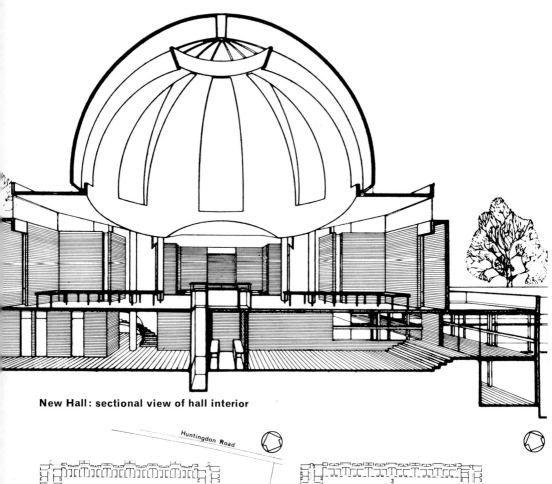

New Hall: sectional view of hall interior

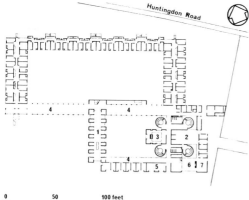

Huntingdon Road

Ground floor plan

1 Library **2** Kitchen **3** Junior combination room **4** Covered walkway **5** Senior combination room **6** Fellows' drawing room **7** Fellows' dining room

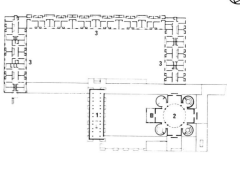

First floor plan

1 Library **2** Hall **3** Fellows' sets and undergraduates' rooms

162

New Hall: dining hall

direct continuation (bridging over the spine) of Stage II, a three-sided residential court which encloses the lawns of the college garden on the north side of the spine. Already the first bays of covered parking have been established in the lee of Stage II, with steps up from the excavated level to the truncated end of the 'spine'.

Stage II, financed mainly by the U.G.C. and the Nuffield Foundation, is built up from groups of 24 bed-sitters, eight on each floor, double-banked round service rooms and an open staircase well designed to accommodate a fork-lift truck serving all levels; the ground floor has a continuous corridor connecting all staircases. On the Huntingdon Road site, however, rooms face into the court only, with service rooms forming a barrier towards the traffic. On the first two floors there are four basic types of bed-sitter, alternating in pairs; the various positions for built-in wash basins, cupboards and beds (the latter a concrete shelf with a foam mattress) dictate the wall and window pattern externally and also the landing widths internally. On the first

floor of the Huntingdon Road wing there is a group of two-room fellows' sets; in the west wing there are some three-room fellows' sets; and next to the 'spine' in the east wing is the sick-bay. On the upper two floors, also alternating in pairs, there are unusual two-level rooms, each for two people, with a steep wooden stairway to the upper level; a private roof terrace is shared by each group of eight rooms (four on the Huntingdon Road side). The architects have advised throughout on the choice of new furniture and light fittings, and have designed the built-in joinery (of iroko).

The 'spine' finally reaches the college's central group of public rooms, which were aided by the Wolfson Foundation. The 'spine' cloister is here walled off from the college garden and overlooks instead the pools and fountain of a formal court, which is dramatically lowered a whole storey to provide a second 'ground floor'. On the eastern side, with doors opening at the sunken level onto the fountain terrace, projects the tall box of the Junior Combination Room, planned on two levels with a gallery. Behind and above it, at first-floor levels, is the domed dining hall, reached by spiral staircases at the four corners—two for undergraduates, one for fellows and one for service. The hall, cruciform in plan, with a central servery lift which rises entire from the ground-floor kitchen (below which, at sunken level, is the bulk store). It is designed to contain the whole college at one sitting, but to be equally convenient for small numbers to eat in the conoid-roofed side bays. South of the hall at ground level are the Senior Combination Room, fellows' drawing room and fellows' dining room, overlooking a semi-private garden. The south wing continues with a suite of dons' and college offices, some used temporarily as bed-sitters; there are eight at ground and 13 at sunken level, reached on the court side by cloisters which echo that of the 'spine' opposite. Below the 'spine', facing into the court, are six guest rooms, a graduates' common room and four supervision rooms. Finally, on the west side of the court, rises the library, which has 48 readers' seats and ultimate capacity for 80,000 books (the stack at the sunken level is used at present for bed-sitters). It is a long three-storey room flanked at ground level by bookstacks and reading bays alternately; the two levels of open shelving above are reached by galleries from the main staircase and are roofed by a clerestory-lit tunnel vault. From the lower gallery there is access to the extensive system of roof terraces over the north and south wings, reached also from the dining hall. At the end of the 'spine' past the present porters' lodge and the kitchen offices, is the back entrance (note the ramp down to the bulk store and other storage rooms at sunken level under the kitchen). Here a single-storey extension has been built (1966; contractors, Johnson & Bailey Ltd.), containing squash courts, games room, studio and music rooms; this encloses a small open court towards Huntingdon Road, where the landscaping is kept open, without fences or walls.

The structure throughout is of reinforced concrete framing or brick crosswalls, with brick infill panels, and it is generally exposed internally as well as externally. The bricks are Sevenoaks white facings. The concrete, which is polished for columns and rails (in walkways, stairways, galleries) and bush-hammered to a rough texture for beams and ceilings, is composed of Ballidon limestone and white cement. Columns, handrails and sills are precast, as are the roofs of the library, dining hall and (eventually) chapel. The hall dome, of *ferro cimento,* has

eight separate leaves, each of them 45 ft long, seven-eighths of an inch thick and weighing over five tons. External paving is precast concrete, with blue quarry tiles in the covered ways and continued through to internal circulation areas. The library and certain other rooms have cork-tile floors; the dining hall has wood blocks. All joinery, including door frames and veneers, is of iroko. Heating and cooling are by electricity with underfloor cables giving a background temperature, supplemented by local heaters as required. Signs and nameplates are designed by Herbert Spencer.

Comment.   New Hall's considerable virtues are most consistently apparent in the residential wings. In his 24-room staircase groups and continuous ground floor corridors, Chamberlin has achieved a successful compromise between the institutional corridors of Girton and Newnham and the monastic staircases of medieval males. In order to make the best use of space within the U.G.C. budget, beds, desks and washbasins have mostly been built in, with four different arrangements in the single bed-sitters—a variety which is admirably reflected both in the crisp and clear rhythm of solid and void externally, and in the swelling and narrowing of the ground floor corridor. Particularly successful are the two-level two-girl rooms at the top, with a rooftop patio over the central corridor; the wooden stair is diminished to an almost suicidal ladder without outer handrail, the treads alternating from right and left, but the use of space is otherwise excellent (the desk in the lower window next to the bed, the wash-basin and storage under the stair). A bed-sitter, however, needs rapidly to become a different individual's home each autumn term; and in spite of the inset metal picture railing, the fearsome purity of these white-walled rooms is a deterrent to any such conversion. If sticky tape marks white brick indelibly, then pin-board should be imported instead.

In the shapes of the rooms, as at Churchill, emerges the spatial vocabulary of the entire college—the punching out of square recesses from a rectangular central space, thus achieving a relationship between spaces for one girl alone, spaces for two sharing, spaces for entertaining three or four—and ultimately spaces where the individual can be related to the collegiate community.

The grey-white brick may not exactly match the Cambridge vernacular—it is significantly different from the local cream-white gault from Burwell which can be seen on David Roberts' Blackfriars next door (see page 186)—but it has a powdery domesticity which is much more suitable than the precast units originally suggested by the architects and rejected for financial reasons. Unfortunately it has weathered badly in places, with a greenish growth below the coping.

The theme of rectangle-plus-bays is used in the lower parts of the main public rooms. In the library the areas for browsing and working are decisively separated from themselves and from the central catalogue avenue, with natural sidelight to the study tables and artificial toplight to the windowless stack bays. In the dining hall the four 'transepts' enable small numbers to eat there as naturally and informally as when the entire college is gathered for formal dinner. The central hotplate rises on a lift from the kitchen as a canopied pavilion ('like a giant cornucopia', as Chamberlin puts it), thus making self-service and waiter service equally convenient; and the top of the canopy, when withdrawn, becomes part of a dance floor.

Most post-war common rooms in Cambridge are wide-open 'hotel lounges' in which the telly can kill social life within seconds of being switched on. Richard Sheppard could afford a series of separate boxes for different uses. Chamberlin, however, provides inexhaustible variety within a single enclosure: he divides it with a central chimney-stack and staircase, pushes out small reading and talking bays, cuts tall slit windows between them to give glimpses of pools and paving, inserts a broad gallery which feels its way round every upper corner, opens a sliding window door to the courtyard terrace, and tops it all with a seductive rooftop barbecue.

Best of all is the spinal articulation of the college with open courts enclosing landscape 'bays' off the spacious cloisters; here the structural vocabulary is at its most crisp, with concrete tails of blue quarry tiles, bush-hammered ceilings, and deep fascia which truthfully indicates broad sun terraces overhead. The immaculate finish—and, unlike Churchill's, a modern finish—makes smoothly yet economically related flowing spaces out of what is actually a very confined site.

If only Chamberlin had stopped everywhere at those superbly textured bush-hammered ceilings—as he fortunately has in the J.C.R. and in the three S.C.R. spaces. But the library and hall suffered extraordinary convulsions above eye level. The library's upper floors, which seem wasteful of space for the

New Hall: sunken court with library

amount of shelving provided, are reached via an incongruously grand staircase and mannered Venetian-window arcading, reminiscent of Philip Johnson in the *haute-vulgarisation* of Palladio into a precast harem world. The dining hall changes from cruciform to circle by means of an awkward clerestory zone in which the glazing bars seem visibly to groan as they try to reconcile Dr. Jekyll-Chamberlin of the sociable spaces with Mr. Hyde-Chamberlin of the cruel dome—an arbitrary aesthetic imposition, beautifully made but visually hideous. In the court itself the spatial fluidity of the cloisters, crushed by these overbearing helmets, is brought down to the sunken level with a thud in the absurd pomp of the central fountain. The college can afford only a single spray, and in its normal absence, the basin has a false baptismal aura. The sinking of the court is itself refreshing as a means of linking and emphasizing the community; but the water, even allowing for the growth of a more luxuriant ecology, makes a rather miserable dark green moat. British weather has also chastened the materials: drips off the concrete have stained the brickwork, with particular shabbiness on the Ronchamp-devised semi-domes of the hall staircases. The neo-classical game can only be played the proper repertoire of drip mouldings, particularly after an all-concrete finish was counted out financially (the staircase towers actually remained all-concrete until the tenders came in).

Why these minarets and domes? Most of the older Cambridge colleges survived without them, confident in their own communal ideals. With the disintegration of belief, there seems a need in University circles to bolster up 'traditional' values with a kind post-Christian pomp—even though New Hall may have a chapel placed more centrally than Churchill's. An emotional architecture is apparently needed to elevate the increasingly informal liturgy of eating and reading. New Hall's curvaceous white skin seems a rather cynically masculine view of what a women's college should symbolize.

Newnham College   f

332 undergraduates, 74 postgraduates, 32 fellows.

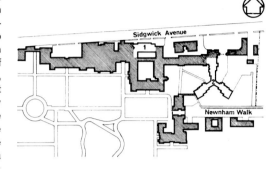

1 Library 2 New building

The evolution of Cambridge collegiate taste can be seen at its most typical at Newnham. In 1949 the college was at last opened up to Sidgwick Avenue and given an anaemic neo-Georgian porter's lodge and entrance gate in pale brick and white stone. The architects were Buckland & Heywood of Birmingham and the sculptor William Bloye. In 1957–8 a new Principal's Lodge was built on the original college drive, Newnham Walk, but on the axis of the new gate. Financed by a gift of £35,000 and a collection of antique furniture, Louis Osman's design is an eccentric attempt to combine the 'gracious living' of the past with the techniques and materials of today. A Pompeian villa in plan it externally displays a full-length portico with a dedicatory inscription and walls of handmade Dutch brick, which have rusticated quoins with added entasis. The courtyard, however, is entirely glass walled with enormous plate glass panels, each 19 ft high and 5 ft wide, to four of which are fixed abstract sculptures by Geoffrey Clarke of the Seasons, in cast aluminium and stained glass. The two staircases, oval spirals, have elegant open treads of ash and balusters of stainless steel. By contrast the main reception rooms, a double cube and two octagons, are dully sub-Georgian, decorated in pastel tints chosen by the architect's wife. In spite of some amusing details and the surprising luminosity of the central courtyard, the building remains an amalgam of phoney and eclectic detailing (the architect in fact is better known as a jewellery

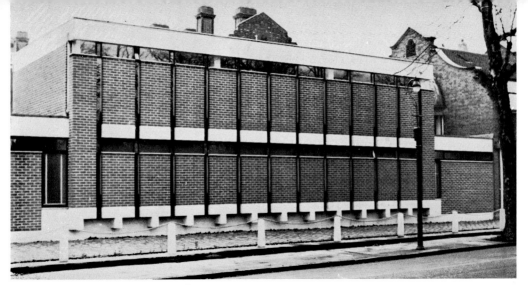

Newnham College: library extension

designer).

More recently Newnham has employed Christophe Grillet, a former associate of David Roberts. He made his début with an elegant extension of the old library along the Sidgwick Avenue frontage, and has now completed a major new residential building, ironically obstructing the carefully established axis between gateway and principal's lodge. Both buildings are described below.

Library Extension

Sidgwick Avenue

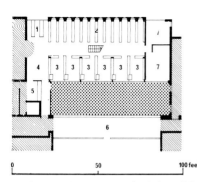

0   50   100 feet

1 Reference **2** Bookstacks **3** Study bays **4** Reference
5 Librarian **6** Corridor **7** Supervision rooms
Dotted areas indicate enclosed open spaces
Shaded areas indicate existing buildings

Date. 1961–2

Architects. Lyster & Grillet

Contractor. William Sindall Ltd.

Requirement. Extension to house 64,000 books and provide places for study.

Description. The site of about 80 ft by 35 ft lies parallel to Sidgwick Avenue and at right-angles to the old library of 1889, the enriched plaster-decorated apse of which had to be preserved. It now serves as the ceiling of the central concourse between the old and the new, which opens onto a small paved court, beyond which the existing central passageway of the college has been fully glazed. Most of the books are on open stacks on two floors to the north. The south side is one-storeyed to preserve daylighting of adjoining buildings, but it is kept fairly high to give more light and air to the six study places with individual desks, which are divided off by more stacks. There are 30 other seats, most of them under the slit windows facing Sidgwick Avenue. There is a book lift (desirable in a women's college), and a square-steel-framed staircase in the centre of the building (see plan).

Close to the entrance are the two librarians' top-lit rooms with a movable partition wall. The structure is a concrete frame, with red brick and hammered concrete facings on the street side and glazing towards

167

Newnham College new residential building: model

the court. The window wall to the study places has its concrete frame exposed, with black-painted steel windows. The floors are of p.v.c. sheet, most fittings and walls are painted white, the ceilings have acoustic tiles, and heating is underfloor, with local radiators for boosting.

Comment.   This little building possesses some of the appropriate femininity and minuteness of scale that distinguished Basil Champneys' original buildings for the college. It has details reminiscent of the Roberts office, in which Mr. Grillet worked on Benson Court and the Clare Hostel, particularly the Sidgwick Avenue façade with its brick facings articulated a little fussily as 'books ends' for the stacks. The building is logically turned to the south for its main natural lighting, and to avoid traffic noise. The incorporation of Champneys' apse ceiling is very successful. A few details seem excessively off-the-peg: the acoustic ceilings, for example, and the curious frosted glass floor panels between the stacks. The reglazing of the college's central corridor is an attempt to combine transparency with privacy within the library; there is a pleasant paved and planted patio between it and the study space windows, which are detailed much more directly than the street façade.

New Building

Date.   1966–8

Architects.   Lyster & Grillet

Contractor.   Kerridge Ltd.

Cost.   £300,000

Requirement.   Rooms for 65 undergraduates and two fellows, changing rooms, outstudents' common room, college offices, portress's and housekeeper's rooms, and laundry.

Description.   The northern wing of the new Y-shaped building connects at right-angles to the post-war porter's lodge and also to the pre-war Fawcett Building. From a central lift and duct shaft the two other wings radiate diagonally towards Newnham Walk, both of them cut off in mid-lawn, although a covered way links the western arm to Champneys' ornate Pfeiffer Building. Besides the lift, each wing has its own staircase to the undergraduate rooms on the upper three floors; these are arranged in a gradually swelling echelon arrangement around a central corridor, one of each room being splayed. Each wing has its own kitchens and bathrooms. The east and west wings have nine bed-sitters on each floor, except where there is a fellow's set, but the north wing also contains maid's rooms and stores and the number of bedsitters varies. The ground floor, which is recessed, contains under the east wing the changing rooms and outstudents' common room (divisible by sliding partitions into three square bays). Under the west wing are seven college offices and under the north wing are the entrance hall, two portress's rooms, a housekeeper's room and the laundry.

The structure is of loadbearing *in situ* concrete crosswalls and floor slabs. It is clad in precast concrete panels with projecting windows, faced with red tiles. At the end of each wing the exposed *in situ* walls are clad in lead sheathing, as is the pyramidal roof-light over the central core. Windows are aluminium, except on the ground floor where the glazing is storey-height and of steel. The Wolfson Foundation has given a third of the cost.

Comment. This is the kind of competent infill building one has come to expect from Lyster & Grillet. It has a good relationship with Basil Champneys' buildings, the facetting of the walls in short lengths helping to preserve the domestic scale. The red tiles made fashionable by James Stirling are here shown to be good neighbours to Pont Street Dutch. More important is the way the building's diagonal axis suggests new directions for the college's future expansion. The rooms are pleasantly irregular and varied in shape, and they are socially well-grouped. Yet in this relaxed adaptation to the *genius loci,* the layout perhaps becomes too inconsequential for a plan form which emphasises its central pivotal point. A Y-shape logically should either have three equal arms radiating from the centre (as this tries to do), or it should have two long arms reached through a short link (as is really the case here). There is an unresolved junction of the northern arm with the admittedly unhelpful Fawcett Building and porter's lodge. Again, the apparent centrality of the building denies its obvious possibilities of extension. The 'chocolate bar' window treatment is derived from the work of Howell, Killick, Partridge and Amis who first used such storey-height units in their runner-up Churchill design of 1959 (see page 134). It makes the non-loadbearing panels appear much stronger and more structural than they really are; the jointing needs more emphatic expression than it is given here.

Selwyn College   e

309 undergraduates, 52 postgraduates, 31 fellows.

Selwyn was poorly endowed, and shortage of money has hampered building. The east end of Blomfield's 1882 chapel was refloored in 1950, and stall canopies were added in 1951 and 1953. Then the east wall was cleaned in 1957, and some chunky bronze statuary by Karin Jonzen was added. Otherwise nothing was done after the war until 1959. In that year James Stirling & James Gowan were appointed to draw up a long-term development plan, capable of being executed in stages (below). This was rejected, partly for functional reasons, presumably the college was wary of the effect of so much glass; and partly because the site conflicted with the Economics and Politics building which had been designed essentially as part of the college precinct—an example of university–college co-operation for which both must be congratulated. In 1964 Robert Matthew, Johnson-Marshall & Partners, to whose design the common rooms (see below) had just been constructed, were to make plans for replacing three villas on the Grange Road–Cranmer Road corner. They proposed to house 88 undergraduates and 11 research fellows in two ten-storey towers and a three-storey block. Not only did this run into trouble with the planning authorities and the Royal Fine Art Commission for possible damage to the sky-line, but when a donor arrived on the scene—the same Mr. Cripps from Nottingham who gave the magnificent new building to St. John's—he suggested, and the college chose, a Nottingham firm, Cartwright, Woollatt & Partners; Robert Matthew, Johnson-Marshall & Partners retired. The large new block, now nearing completion, is a mealy-mouthed hulk of the kind one had hoped not to see again in Cambridge.

Selwyn College Development Plan

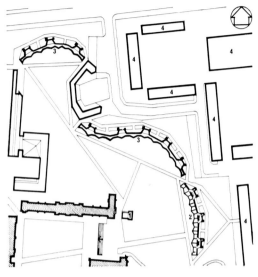

1 Junior common room **2** Residential Stage I **3** Residential, later stages **4** Proposed arts faculties buildings

Proposed. 1960–1

Architects. James Stirling & James Gowan

Description. Selwyn did well to commission one of the most brilliant younger firms (Ham Common flats, Leicester engineering labs) to prepare a full-scale development plan. Their solution was characteristically single-minded. Taking the privacy of the college garden as the overriding necessity, they placed their Stage I residential block at the far end, visually closing the gap between the chapel and north range and shutting off surrounding buildings at Casson's Sidgwick Avenue site. In a garden pavilion at the base of the chapel steps was to be the new J.C.R., around which all the other new buildings were pivoted, forming a series of informal courts stretching round to Grange Road (see plan). All three residential buildings, accommodating 180 undergraduates, were to be four-storeyed, raised on grassy mounds, and fully glazed towards the garden, with windows set at varying angles to catch the sun —an early version of the crystalline formations at Leicester.

Mainly bedsitters, the rooms were to be of a remarkable variety of sizes and shapes, lit also by clerestory strip windows above the built-in washing and storage units at the back. Service rooms were to be in the staircase towers projecting at the rear.

Besides its considerable cost, the scheme had the strong drawback of disregarding its surroundings, particularly the Arts Faculties, towards which was to be merely a confined alleyway. Ironically, Stirling himself has now secured an important commission there (see page 179) which shows the same enervating brutality of detail and absolute 'take it or leave it' quality.

Senior and Junior Combination Rooms

Date. 1963–4

Architects. Robert Matthew, Johnson-Marshall & Partners; Stirrat Johnson-Marshall, partner-in-charge

Contractors. Johnson & Bailey Ltd.

Cost. £37,300

Requirement. S.C.R., J.C.R., two fellows' sets.

Description. This three-storey building closes the south-west corner of Blomfield's quadrangle, next to Grayson & Ould's Hall. The J.C.R. on the ground floor is entered from the court through a short cloister and lobby. In the existing annexe between it and the hall is the newly converted television room. The upper floor of this annexe is the old S.C.R., which is connected by a landing and pantry with the new S.C.R., which measures 45 ft by 30 ft and overlaps the J.C.R. on either side. On the floor above, the two fellows' sets are reached by a bridge from a staircase in Blomfield's entrance block.

The structure is a concrete frame, forming a cloister below but embedded in the upper walls, which are faced in red brick matching the Victorian buildings. The J.C.R. is lit from clerestory level and also by large windows to the court and to Grange Road. The S.C.R. is lit by clerestory windows towards Sidgwick Avenue, to which it will be exposed when Selwyn Close, a small house, is eventually demolished, and

170

by a large bay window towards the court. It is panelled on three walls, with a hand-woven textile by Peter Collingwood on the fourth. The fellows' sets are lit by dormer-windows.

Comment. This is a sophisticated infill building, fitting in easily with its surroundings, except on the court side, where the bay window, decorated with shields, is a distressing solecism, neither Tudor nor modern. It was clearly decided that the S.C.R. mattered most, so it takes pride of place—a broad brick box, with dormer-windowed rooms recessed above. The set-back J.C.R. below is so much smaller that it may well prove inadequate as an undergraduate concourse. It is an uninteresting boxy room, with no private alcoves of any kind; and the furnishings are not distinguished. The S.C.R. by contrast is a fine tall space, though it could have been allowed a little more natural light; as in the same architects' L.E.S. building (page 91), windows are reduced to monastic slits except for the north-facing bay.

Selwyn College, Cranmer Road site: model

Cranmer Road site

Date.   1966–8

Architects.   Cartwright, Woollatt & Partners

Contractor.   John Laing Construction Ltd.

Cost.   £584,000

Requirement. Rooms for 130 undergraduates, 31 graduates and 8 fellows, with breakfast room.

Description. The four-storey buildings form an open court, with Cranmer Road on the fourth (south) side. The eastern block is cut short to leave an opening for the entrance pathway from the Victorian college opposite; this runs straight up to the breakfast room which forms an isolated pavilion off-centre in the court; this is connected to the symmetrical northern wing by a covered way to a foyer entered also from the parking area at the rear of the building. The post-graduates occupy the centre of the northern wing, mostly in two-room sets, and they have their own common room on the ground floor. The undergraduate rooms, almost all bedsitters, are in the ends of the northern wing and in the two other wings. The eight fellows' sets, only two of them for residents, are distributed throughout the buildings. The rooms are in groups of about 25 round seven staircases, each marked by a continuous vertical slit and a roof canopy. The cross-wall structure is faced partly in red brick and partly in precast flint faced panels, with reconstructed stone piers. Flint-faced panels are also being used for the breakfast-room; this is planned as a diamond-shaped pavilion with movable partitions which can isolate a square toplit room set on the diagonal axis. In the remaining triangles are anterooms, a kitchen and cloakrooms.

Comment. If anyone doubts the architectural renaissance in recent Cambridge (whatever the continuing confusions over planning), he should visit this building, which is a nasty throwback to the pre-1958 sort of trite hostel. The sub-Tudor cloisters, carried right round the back as a blank-arched dado, and the crematorium-modern monumentality of the breakfast room, have the kind of obvious collegiate images that one would expect in a 'B' film set in modern Cambridge. 'Traditional forms used in an up-to-date manner' is the usual cant description. It could have been worse: the court is well-treed and pleasantly open (though a horrid traceried fence of the precast-Gothic Ed Stone kind is to hem it in), and the rooms are large. The planning authority managed to persuade the architects to improve the original version as the donor was understandably becoming restive.

Trinity Hall   D

Wychfield, Huntingdon Road

Date.	1967
Architects.	Arup Associates
Contractors.	Johnson & Bailey Ltd.
Cost.	£835,000

Requirement. 32 undergraduate rooms, two fellows' sets, common room, kitchen and lawn for Trinity Hall.

Description. Sited in front of the existing Wychfield House,[1] which itself lies immediately west of Fitzwilliam, this is the latest building to go up in Cambridge to the design of Arup's architect–engineer team under Philip Dowson. The clients, Trinity Hall, having seen Leckhampton House (see page 146), decided they wanted something similar. It is no coincidence, then, that the same system of precast H-frames should appear here too. But there are considerable differences which are worth noting. Wychfield is to be four-storeyed: on the ground floor there are the common room, laundry and kitchen which are built in brick and recessed well behind the frame. On the upper floors are the undergraduates' rooms grouped around the centrally-placed toplit stairshaft. From this, there is access to either end of the building; there are five rooms to the north and five with a fellow's set to the south (or seven rooms on the first floor). The two halves do not intercommunicate, except through this enclosed stair-shaft and the communal bathroom at the west side, and each half has its own gyproom. Unlike Leckhampton, the frame does not stand so far forward of the building and between each bay, a window projects forward. The planning of this block is composed, and there is no weak service corridor link such as detracts from Leckhampton; though it is disturbing to note that the centralized staircase is not quite central and that the disposition of the rooms is not equal. However excellent in isolation this building turns out to be, it is to Trinity Hall's discredit that it in no way relates to Fitzwilliam (although its relationship to the old house is good); it is therefore just one more chapter in the story of the north-western academic precinct that never was.

1. Another former Darwin house—Uncle Horace's in Gwen Raverat's book

University College   g

34 graduates, 70 fellows.

The third graduate college in three years, after Darwin and Clare Hall, was founded by the university itself in 1965 and was given the site of Bredon House in Barton Road, previously a hostel for New Hall. For this site Stillman & Eastwick-Field had already designed a scheme of graduate flats as long ago as 1960, but, like those by Tayler & Green (see page 87), it was inadequately briefed, as the university could not decide what it wanted. Desultory discussion of the design, for five years, officially kept alive even after University College took over the house, has now been quietly dropped. It seems a pity that the university could not have reappointed the same distinguished architects to design the new college's buildings; designs are awaited instead from a little-known firm of church architects at York, Ferrey & Mennim.

University Library Extensions   E

Burrells Walk

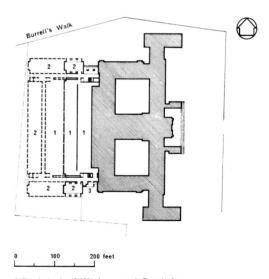

0   100   200 feet

1 Bookstacks **2** Work space **3** Goods bay

Proposed.   1966

Architects.   Gollins, Melvin, Ward & Partners

Description.   In 1951 the university decided to extend Sir Giles Gilbert Scott's monumental library of 1931–4 and a scheme estimated to cost about £1 million was prepared in Sir Giles's office. No money was forthcoming either privately or from the U.G.C., however, and in order to attract the latter, priority was given instead in 1959 to a proposed central science library. It then became clear that the university library would have to be extended in any case, and in 1962 Gollins, Melvin, Ward & Partners, famous for their Sheffield University Library, were commissioned to prepare a general plan for extending to the rear (the west) between Scott's reading room and Clare sports field.

The basic problem is that, in the palmy days of Rockefeller, Scott designed his library with a very high proportion of open shelving; although attractive to readers, this provides under 250,000 ft of shelving in the enormous building. The 1962 brief therefore calls for no less than 600,000 ft of compact reserve book shelving in closed stacks. There is also a shortage of reading rooms and of space for specialized work by the library staff; so the 1962 brief also asks for six large 100-seat reading rooms, 8 specialized 20-seat reading rooms and 10,000 sq ft of staff workrooms.

The architects' first proposal, in 1964, was for a vast square block of 13 tightly packed storeys, placed centrally, and flanked by two three-storey wings of reading rooms. The planning authorities rightly objected to the bulk of this on the skyline. The revised scheme (1966) is quite different. It accepts the main cornice level and the side walls of Scott's building as an absolute limitation of height and width on the perimeter; and it also recognizes that air conditioning makes it possible to 'bury' stacks out of sight more compactly than before. In view of doubts as to where the money will come from, the job is divided into two phases.

Stage I, costing just over £500,000, will perform the emergency task of removing rare books from Scott's building to 135,000 ft of closed shelving. This is arranged in a continuous wing on six levels across the back of Scott's building, with a narrow light well between them over two floors of workrooms and archives plus more stacks. Across each end of the new stack there is a workroom on the ground floor and two large reading rooms above that; there are five smaller workrooms on each side in a recession marking the break between Scott and Gollins. The new stack is windowless except for very narrow slits separating its back wall into bays; but this wall will itself be swallowed by the much larger extensions of Stage II. These will provide 465,000 sq ft of shelving, 34,000 sq ft of reading room and 10,800 sq ft of workroom space (making 19,300 sq ft of workroom altogether, compared with 10,000 in the 1962 brief)—a sign that requirements are increasing while Stage II is inevitably pushed into the distant future.

In this second phase an even bigger windowless stack, placed next to the first one, will be surrounded on the west side, as well as the north and south, by two floors of reading rooms over one of the workrooms. This establishes a unified external rhythm: the concrete frame is faced in a series of brick piers with full glazing to the workrooms and lower reading rooms; the upper reading rooms are then expressed as a series of closed toplit window bays. The brick will be dark in tone, but not necessarily the same as Scott's.

Comment.   This is a tactful treatment of what is basically a warehouse added to a monument. The transition is smoothed over by burying the stacks, and carrying the workrooms and reading rooms in a 'racetrack plan' round the perimeter. There they are expressed in a series of narrow bays, which are really only an exercise in pleasing façadism. Concrete floor slabs are more or less expressed, but the rhythm of brick piers bears little relation to that of the concrete spine walls within. The 'plinth' of workrooms and the double height reading rooms above establish a classical system of proportion similar to Scott's—although in the reading rooms the alternation between a floor of full glazing and a floor of toplighting seems unnecessarily arbitrary even in such an exercise.

Sidgwick Avenue site   F
Arts Faculties buildings

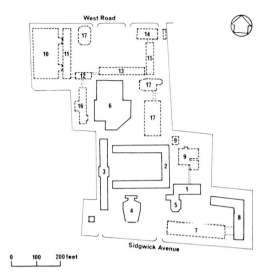

West Road

Sidgwick Avenue

| 0 | 100 | 200 feet |

Already built
1 Lecture halls **2** Faculties of English, Moral Sciences,
Modern and Medieval Languages **3** Faculty of Economics
and Politics **4** Lady Mitchell Hall **5** Little Hall **6** Faculty of
History (James Stirling) **7** Faculty of Oriental Studies,
to become, with **8** Faculty of Archaeology and Museum of
Archaeology and Ethnology
Designed but not built
9 Lecture halls (Casson, Conder & Partners)
Not designed
10 Museum of Classical Archaeology **11** Faculty of
Classics **12, 13, 14, 15** Faculties of Divinity, Oriental
Studies, Department of Aerial Photography and spare
accommodation **16** Institute of Criminology and canteen
17 Other lecture halls

Soon after the war, in 1950, the Arts Faculties decided to site their new precinct on the west side of
the Backs, on just over 13 acres, between Sidgwick
Avenue and West Road. A limited competition was
organized in May 1952, between Sir Hugh Casson,
the co-ordinating architect of the Festival of Britain,
and Robert Atkinson, who died later that year. The
designs of Sir Hugh and his partner, Neville Conder,
were approved in February 1954. Sidgwick Avenue
was the first of the post-war comprehensive university plans, predating Gollins, Melvin & Ward's
Sheffield by a year, and its chequered history is an
education in itself.
Work started in 1956 on laying out the former Corpus
Christi playing fields on the Sidgwick Avenue side

of the precinct. In 1960, after the first lecture block
had provoked both conservatives and radicals, the
Regent House voted out Casson, Conder & Partners'
first design for Lady Mitchell Hall, but paradoxically
approved the revised version a year later. More
serious was the university administration's 'discovery' that the Caius land along West Road had
not actually been bought; for, having built Harvey
Court nearby, the college decided to retain the land
for its own further expansion. Eventually it was
agreed that the university should still be allowed to
buy most of the West Road frontage, but hand over
to Caius, in compensation, a large area, square in
shape, close to the centre of the site. The total area
was thus reduced to 10½ acres. This has meant a
radical reorganization of the plans, apart from those
of the five buildings erected in 1958–64 on the Sidgwick Avenue front: the Faculty of Economics and
Politics; the raised faculty building for Modern
Languages, English and Moral Sciences; the Lady
Mitchell and Little Halls; and the first block of
lecture halls. They are all described below. Archaeology, Anthropology and Ethnology will still stand
next to the lecture halls, but on a more confined site
than originally; the faculty wing has now gone up,
but is being used temporarily for Oriental Studies.
In the plans approved in May 1963, the History
Faculty and Seeley Library are placed in the centre,
with the four-storey Criminology block and central
canteen next to them. Along the reduced eastern
side of the site will be a lecture hall for 300–500 and
two two-storey blocks of lecture rooms for 30–50
people. Towards West Road will be a large open
court, with a freestanding lecture hall surrounded
by the Classics building and the one-storey Classical Archaeology Museum to the west, and the buildings for Divinity and Oriental Studies and Aerial
Photography on the east. In the centre is a substantial block left free for 'overspill' from any of
these departments. This is an attempt to keep a
'political' flexibility no less tortuous than that of the
1956–64 buildings, in which only 10 per cent space
was allowed in excess of 1956 requirements. As will
be argued more fully below, the picturesque planning and the academic diplomacy of Casson–Conder
and their clients are no substitute for that *architectural* flexibility of genuinely modern structures
which has not yet reached Cambridge. The casualty
list from the earlier plan of buildings 'missing, be-
lieved killed', includes a 1,000-seat lecture hall, an
ornamental water court, the Architecture and Fine

Sidgwick Avenue site: Economics and Politics building seen from under raised faculty building

Arts Faculty (to stay at Scroope Terrace), and the Music School. Criminology, however, is an addition (may it be designed by Mr. Crook?). To satisfy the greatly increased need for parking, underground space for 300 cars will be provided.

Within this development plan, other architects will be employed besides Casson, Conder & Partners, who have been commissioned for the detailed design only of the Archaeology, Anthropology and Ethnology buildings and of the next block of lecture halls. The History Faculty and Seeley Library have already gone up to a strikingly original design by James Stirling (see below). Casson & Conder remain overall consultants.

Sidgwick Avenue: Stages I–IV

Date. 1956–68

Architects. Casson, Conder & Partners

Contractors. Johnson & Bailey Ltd. Economics and Politics, Kerridge Ltd.

Cost.

Lodge and Site Works £24,000
Lecture Halls £117,000
Raised Faculty Building £305,500
Economics and Politics £341,000
Lady Mitchell and Little Halls
£152,250
Oriental Studies £231,200
Total £1,170,950

Requirement. Lecture Halls (Stage I), Modern Languages, English and Moral Sciences (Stage II), Economics and Politics (Stage III), Lady Mitchell Hall and Little Hall (Stage IV) and Oriental Studies, later to become Archaeology and Anthropology Faculty wing (Stage V).

Description. Since 1964, the Sidgwick Avenue buildings have at last been visible coherently as a group, set back from the road behind a large open

175

Sidgwick Avenue site, showing Lady Mitchell Hall (left) and Economics and Politics building

car park (89 spaces) and dominated by the stone-faced buildings of Stage II, raised on a plinth and on a continuous cloister. The Stage II buildings form a three-sided court, the fourth side of which is formed by the brick-faced Economics and Politics building. The Lady Mitchell and Little Halls stand forward from the plinth towards Sidgwick Avenue. Next to the Little Hall is a concrete canopied porch, leading into the first lecture hall block, which projects to the east. Farther in that direction, with a street frontage to Sidgwick Avenue, is the Faculty of Oriental Studies. The lecture hall block (1958–9) will always be the tallest building on the site and its skyline was considered particularly important. It is built round two staircases, between which there is a fireproof spine wall which runs the length of the building. There are ten lecture theatres, seating a total of 950 people— the largest 150 and the smallest 25. A lift tower was added early in 1964 on the north side. The structure is of loadbearing brickwork on reinforced concrete columns and beams for the ground floor. Facings are brown Crowborough stocks, rough in texture, with strong concrete lintels to most windows; the lift tower by contrast is a white-painted concrete shaft. The steel roof-structure has timber purlins and boarding, and aluminium flashings. The fixed seating in the larger lecture halls was specially designed by the architects in association with T. M. Lupton. In front of the building there is a cobbled cycle park, with stands alternately of precast concrete and metal arranged radially around five trees. The Raised Faculty Building (1959–61) has a cloister of concrete *pilotis,* in which are three staircase halls,

rising to the libraries of modern and medieval languages in the north wing, the libraries of English and Moral Sciences to the south, and seminar rooms and studies to the east, which will eventually be 'overspill' space for the libraries. In the main libraries, all three floors are unified, with central open wells, and lit by four different varieties of window; the largest of these are two storeys high, with tripartite division by mullions. The top floor has a continuous clerestory window, which on the north and west sides is lowered to take up the entire wall space. The structure consists of reinforced concrete piers at ground level, supporting a first-floor slab of shot-blasted concrete in a black basalt aggregate. This in turn supports two rows of internal concrete columns, which support the aluminium-clad steel trussed roof, the fascia of which is anodized black. The reinforced concrete floors are also supported by the external walls of loadbearing Portland stone. In front of the south-east corner it was intended to erect a tall freestanding sculpture, but there will now be trees instead. The five-storey Economics and Politics building (1958–61) has a different structure, also concrete-framed, but clothed with reddish brick and provided with several steel-framed bay windows, painted black and white. By agreement with Selwyn College, the building was designed consciously as part of the college's precinct too. The central entrance arch is therefore open on that side as well as to the faculties' court; next to it on the ground floor is the temporary canteen for the site. The building is divided into two halves on either side of the entrance. The southern half has offices and studies on each of the upper floors, disposed regularly along a central corridor; beneath the canteen is the boiler, sufficient for a district heating scheme, the aluminium covered chimney of which is visible above the roofline. The northern half, with the Marshall Library of Economics occupying the space of the three middle floors, has lecture rooms on the top floor and storage space, used at present by the university library, in the basement. Within the Library, the galleries are linked physically by a spiral staircase at one end and visually by the scaffold-like light fittings which illuminate the ceiling. The rooms for African Studies on the top floor have since been taken over for Economics—the partitions in this part of the building were designed to be easily demountable. Close to the southern end of the faculty is the site's caretaker's lodge of white brick, with a central chimney, erected in 1956.

Lady Mitchell and Little Halls were finally completed in 1963–4. Both of them have loadbearing perimeter walls, polygonal in shape and faced in brown Crowborough stocks, and both have prominent roofs clad in ribbed aluminium sheet, designed to be seen from the overlooking faculties. The square Little Hall shares with the lecture hall block a massive concrete-columned porch, with an underside of white-painted timber. Seating 150, the interior is lit from a continuous clerestory and a giant 'candle-snuffer' rooflight with louvres. The steel and timber roof structure has a suspended timber ceiling which follows the slopes of the roof. The Lady Mitchell Hall is an irregular octagon seating 450. Besides lectures, it is intended to use its open stage for chamber music, films and drama. Entered through a black-painted steel and glass porch, it has its entrance foyer on a half level, with steps going down to cloakrooms, lavatories and green-rooms, and up to the rear of the stepped and raked seating in black leather. Internally as well as externally, the building is dominated by the two deep precast and post-stressed box beams which span 80 ft, longitudinally. Between them is a suspended ceiling of slatted timber; but the side slopes have exposed precast beams. The extensive side windows have anti-glare glass and adjustable vertical sunblinds; in front of them are galleries which lead to steps down to the stage. Among the facilities are a public address system, automatic projection, blackout curtains and variable lighting, with a duplicate control panel for the lecturer. The hall is fully air-conditioned, with blown air heating plus perimeter radiators. Floors are of cork tile, apart from the stage of timber strip.

Oriental Studies eventually will move to a site next to History, and then the present building will have a Museum wing added along Sidgwick Avenue (in front of Little Hall) when it is taken over by Archaeology, Anthropology and Ethnology. The rectangular block so far built (1966–8) has a full basement for storage, a ground floor containing common rooms, seminar rooms and stores and a first floor wholly occupied by a library. The top two floors of individual studies form a V-shaped court, within which the Library is rooflit. The reinforced concrete frame is exposed in bush-hammered columns on the two sides where the ground floor is recessed; otherwise, apart from storey height windows to the library on the west side, the upper walls consist of alternate bands of glazing and Crowborough stock brick. The roof has a deep aluminium fascia.

Comment.   Few people would deny the many successes of Casson & Conder's original plan and even of their revised version in creating a stage-set of picturesque townscape. The sequence of cloister and pathway, solid and void, grass and paving, has been thought out with all the co-ordinating care that the Festival of Britain received. Many of the detailed touches are extremely well done: the brilliantly conceived radiating cycle park, the neat concrete bollards incorporating light fittings, the comfortable seating in the lecture halls, the elegant steel bay windows in the Economics wing, the generous afrormosia door handles, the Little Hall as a whole. The box-beamed interior of Lady Mitchell Hall is genuinely impressive as a space, even if compromised without by the crinkly flimsiness of the aluminium sheeting and the wilful concealment of the four main columns supporting the beams. The rejected exterior of 1958–9 was in some ways better; in its ridge-backed concrete the architects abortively 'discovered' a fashionable image three years before Paul Rudolph at Yale actually exploited it.

But all these elegant details are only 'visual aids' to an overall picture of academic life which does not carry conviction. Even in picturesque terms, the playing off of separate masses is unsuccessful on a large scale: the Sidgwick Avenue car park is endless and scaleless, and although the two projecting halls are on the whole formally strong, their rough brown Crowborough brick walls read against only one building in background (the Raised Faculty court) which is contrastingly white-and-black and smooth.

The high lecture hall block overwhelms the Little Hall with a much more arbitrary roughness in the same brick, self-consciously 'early industrial warehouse' in its detailing; while the Economics and Politics wing, no less a teaching-cum-library building than the Raised Faculty, is disturbingly faced in a slightly different reddish brick. The new Oriental Studies block, however, while much more orderly and regular (clearly the product of a different hand in the firm), uses Crowborough brick again for its repetitive bands of infill.

More serious, however, is the environmental failure of the scheme, even in the very traditional terms which the architects set themselves. The Raised Faculty Building, with its extraordinarily arbitrary and illogical fenestration—particularly painful in libraries, which demand even lighting—was intended as a great collegiate courtyard where, in Sir Hugh's beautiful drawings of 1952, spikily gowned students could be seen wistfully dreaming together under the grand arcades. In fact, there is usually a half-gale blowing through these menacing black piers and few people hang around to enjoy the bracing atmosphere.

To have a collegiate ideal is not necessarily wrongheaded. Although superficially in stylistic terms the Casson–Conder drawings of 1952 must have appeared startlingly modern, the policy of dressing up university faculties to resemble colleges goes back to Sir T. G. Jackson's efforts on the Downing Site in 1907, in which there was an attempt to express the formal and public teaching of the university faculties in the same environmental forms as the informal and private teaching of the ancient colleges. It will in fact be possible to develop in the faculties only some of these intimacies of social contact if the students and lecturers feel encouraged to 'live' where they work, at least from 9 until 1. This is in fact beginning to happen at Sidgwick Avenue, because the site is so distant from the city centre; with cars (rightly) disallowed, the temporary canteen is crammed with customers—but it cannot be moved until the Criminology block is built, beneath which the 'permanent' canteen is planned to go.

The basic difference, however, between colleges and faculties as architecture is that one grows and changes so much faster and so much less predictably than the other. The Downing Site's plan petered out miserably. In the Arts Faculties the pressure is not so great, but even so there is abundant evidence, not only against the architects but against the

Senate committee which briefed them, that the Sidgwick Avenue buildings fail to meet the evolving requirements of a university. They are simply not flexible enough. The structure may use modern materials in places but its aesthetic assumptions are academically traditional, not standardized, not prefabricated, not extendible. The architects were faced with adding a lift tower (which should have been in his original brief) to one side of the lecture hall block, because it was too difficult to insert it inside the building; it was needed because at a late hour the university had demanded larger lecture halls, and some galleries were added which made the block much higher. The Economics Faculty is now devouring the 20 per cent 'overspill' it was allowed, and here at least in the top floor there is movable partitioning, which has already received a major reshuffle only three years after the completion of the building; but the Faculty cannot expand further until the canteen is removed from the ground floor and the library store from the basement (that in turn depends on when the University Library extensions are built). The most far-sighted feature of the whole site is the boiler house, which now heats the whole 'Left Bank' of the university, including the university library. Also praiseworthy, and directly the result of the collegiate ideals of Casson & Conder, is the way in which the Economics and Politics building has been planned as part of the enclosure of the garden of Selwyn College, with a pedestrian walkway and entrance; it is an all-too-rare case of university–college harmony, let alone architect–architect—and in fact it led directly to Selwyn dropping the Stirling & Gowan scheme for the college which was brutally back-turning in its relationship with Sidgwick Avenue. The irony of this is that Stirling has now completed a major job within the Arts precinct—and whether this will be equally destructive (survival of the reddest) remains to be seen. The problem is that university grants at Cambridge will probably go mainly to science in the next few years. How will Sidgwick Avenue cater for such exploding faculties as Economics and Politics? It may have to put up temporary huts; and the irony is that, visually bleak as Terrapin and Medway sheds can be in the mass, they are almost certainly better suited, even to the more static Arts Faculties, than Casson & Conder's picturesque, one-off, freestanding monuments. Their type of 'contemporary' is in many ways quite as traditional as 'traditional'.

Sidgwick Avenue: History Faculty

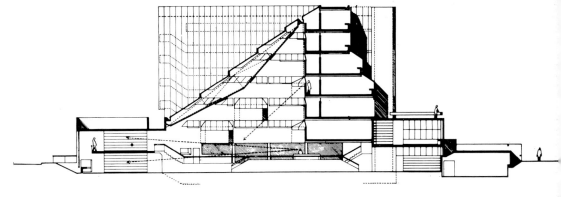

History faculty: section

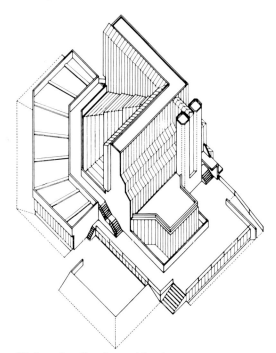

History faculty: isometric view

Date. 1964–8

Architect. James Stirling

Contractor. William Sindall Ltd.

Cost. £336,785

Requirement. 45 studies for staff; 14 seminar rooms of various sizes; faculty offices; Seeley Library; common rooms.

Description. For the first building at the northern end of the Arts Faculties Precinct, the Sidgwick Site Committee considered 15 British and foreign architects, saw buildings of six, commissioned sketches from three and finally chose James Stirling (then of Stirling & Cowan). His visually striking design of a glass-roofed tent-shaped library, enclosed as a quadrant by the two wings of an L-shaped faculty block, was chosen largely for two practical reasons: that it gives total suspension of library reading room radially from a raised control desk and that it integrates the library closely with the rest of the faculty (in the other sketch schemes, invited from Architects' Co-Partnership and David Roberts, they were divided into two separate blocks).

The building has a radial, multi-directional quality externally as well as internally, as it pivots on the narrow neck of land between the Casson–Conder courts and the future West Road court. The main entrance corridor lies at the back of the building on the west side (next to a single-storey extension of faculty offices). Undergraduates will mainly enter it from the south, where their cloakrooms are immediately below (in the basement) and their waiting rooms and common rooms immediately above. Senior members entering on the north side can conveniently ascend to their seminar rooms and offices by means of the main lift or stair, which are expressed prominently as twin towers on the corner of the building, or they can climb steps to the broad northern terrace, where a private entrance at first floor level leads past cloakrooms and lavatories as a prelude to the senior common room on the next floor.

Between the two main entrances is the dominating catalogue and control area of the library, raised 4 ft above the floor area in the luminous and lofty 'well' of the room. From this platform a gallery leads directly, without disturbing readers, to the two main levels of open shelving (10,300 ft); these are on and under an arc-shaped deck of concrete, freestanding as a mezzanine within a low perimeter extension of the polygonal quadrant. Because the spaces between the stacks fan out from 3 ft 1 in to 4 ft 2 in at the edge, they can easily be spied on from the control desk. The main library room is arranged flexibly for 300–360 readers, who can sit either at tables under the main soaring roof or at the 32 semi-private carrels attached to the window wall of the stacks extension or in any of six large reading bays on the north side; these are also in a single-storey extension, this time with clerestory lighting over the remaining 2,300 sq ft of shelving (containing folios). Beyond the reading bays on the north side is a single-storey wing, under a paved terrace, containing seminar rooms of 1,250 and 430 sq ft, with deep clerestory lighting; the larger one can be made available in the future for library expansion up to 428 readers in all. Also from the main library can be reached a typewriting room, with acoustically treated surfaces, and, on the first floor over the reading bays, the prominently projecting Research Room, with a continuous worktop and windows on three sides; close to it are rooms for microfilm reading and photo-copying, as well as the research students' common room. The roof of the Research Room forms a terrace to the senior common room.

The seven-storey faculty block contains studies and seminar rooms, ranging from 100 to 600 sq ft, with the smallest on the top two floors, reached by the lift, and the largest at the bottom. The two outer faces of the building therefore progressively widen by means of studio windows which throw light to the back of the larger rooms. There are continuous worktops at sill level. The two inner faces by contrast are vertical and have continuous corridors running directly round the library as a series of double-glazed balconies; these have corbelled out 'lay-bys' from which dramatic views down can be had. The double glazing is tilted so that the readers looking upwards can see only broken reflections. The balcony fronts are of fibrous plaster with acoustic patterns of fibreglass slots.

The structure is a concrete frame, with diagonal beams under the studio windows. Partition walls in the L-shaped block are of thermal concrete block, plastered and painted, and can be removed easily; floor finishes are of heavy linoleum, with sheet rubber in the library. Each floor slab has an upstand which stops 9 in short of the continuous glazing, the gap being used for Venetian blinds. The windows have mechanically operated glass louvres at floor and ceiling level for controlled draught-proof ventilation, and continuous heating pipes are situated at upstand and ceiling levels. Sliding aluminium ladders are built in, so that window cleaning can be done without scaffolding. The lantern roof of the library is of tubular steel with two levels of glazing, between which a 6 ft gap will contain crawlways for cleaning and maintenance; besides heating and ventilating plant, the gap also houses powerful lights with an electric eye to provide controlled dimming as a 'natural' transition from daylight to artificial light. The upper glazing is of opal glass (diffusing plyglass) which will prevent direct sun rays from penetrating to the interior. Externally, the end walls of the faculty contain 'escape stairs' in regular use by undergraduates, with a short-cut roofwalk connecting them across the top of the stacks extension and by steps down to the ground. The lower and end walls are faced with red engineering bricks; and there are matching red tiles to the terraces, lift and staircase towers, parapets and upstands, including the ramped enclosure to the cycle park at the northeast corner.

Comment. Hardly a stone's throw from Martin's built ideal of Residence at Harvey Court stands the glasshouse of Stirling's built ideal of Research. Both architects have attempted to create true environments for today's academic community, while

History Faculty, with Economics and Politics building (left)

over on Huntingdon Road the traditional images of formal dinner and official chapel are still being juggled with. In the liturgy of the specialized library, Stirling has come as near as anyone to finding a physical expression of the 'why' as well as the 'how' of a modern university. In spite of its fist-shaking angularity, its virulent red surfaces and its complicated crystalline glazing, it has, internally at least, the inexplicable obviousness of a great work of architecture, which results from the architect penetrating to the heart of the requirements in the brief. To the clients, a faculty not renowned for flights of fancy, the integrity of Stirling's structure was immediately convincing: visible integration of the whole faculty with its books was indicated at once in the grip of the quadrant-shaped tent in the L-shaped teaching block. The eager acceptance of an undivided radiating library was admittedly in one respect a spur-of-the-moment response: a massive theft of illustrations from rare books in several different college libraries was uncovered in 1963 and had made the history dons unusually security-conscious. Hence their warm approval of Stirling's positioning of the

control desk as an all-seeing eye, as in Bentham's panopticon prisons—a nightmare brought nearer by the one-way mirror effect of the slanted glazing on the corridor-balconies round the library well.
But in fact one of the best things about this library internally is the extent to which Stirling has been able to push out private study bays away from the all-dominant central space—carrels beyond the stacks, folio-lined reading bays and separately equipped research room are all visible as distinct volumes on the exterior of the building. The circulation space of the library entrance is sensitively distributed so as not to disturb, with a separate gallery to the stacks and a separate staircase to the research room. It is too early to say how successful the central space will be, as much depends on the environmental controls—heating and ventilating diffusion of the sun through plyglass and the maintenance of perpetual daylight by means of dimmers (a technique used by Aalto in his Rautatalo piazza). Still less proven at the time of writing were the seminar and study rooms, with their crucial window louvres at floor and ceiling. Stirling's praise of glass in our

members and the clumsiness of their connections. It is the space which counts.

Outside, however, the detailing gives less reality to the slogans of pure space; the outside skin of plexiglass is so opaque that it has to be looked at rather than looked through. In a building drawn and conceived almost entirely in terms of the sectional drawing (which can indeed be seen in that central space) and the axonometric drawing (which can only be seen from a helicopter), it is often disturbing to have to look, as the public is bound to look, at a flat-on elevation. On approaching the faculty from Casson & Conder's finicky 'townscape', it appears an unexpectedly big building, a bigness emphasized by the immediate impact of the quadrant form, with its emphatic diagonal axis. The convex tent is of a similar scale to Aalto's concave auditorium at Otaniemi, and the comparison is not to Stirling's advantage; for Aalto plants his building decisively in the ground at every point. Not only does Stirling go out of his way to be ill-mannered to Casson and to anyone else in sight, but he also (with the kind of English insouciance familiar from St. Martin-in-the-Fields' spire) lets his major forms sit like ornaments on an out-spreading plinth of single-storey wings. The tent is just propped up on the stacks; the twin lift-and-stair towers on the other side (much less tall and slim than in the axonometric) are sliced off by the terrace over the seminar rooms. This may become worse if future expansion increase the radial spread. Furthermore, Stirling has not been able to leave well alone: if from a distance the red tile skin seems perversely similar to the loadbearing red brick, from close quarters it seems perversely different when the two textures are slapped up against each other (where the entrance canopy wall touches the terrace, for example). The brickwork around the dons' entrance on the north side has been hacked about with plinths, ramps, steps, moats (one can only hope the blotching of efflorescence is temporary); and the twin towers, like the quadrant, suggest an emphatic axis which does not happen; for the twin entrances slip away to the side, with a rather silly double canopy. All this detracts from the directness of the glass walling above, which also turns out much stiffer than in the drawings—the diagonals of studios not being visible close to, leaving a series of vertical planes stepped back like a steamboat; the diagonal beams of the concrete are almost invisible.

climate sounds too simple, yet 'Hardwick Hall, more window than wall' is a well-established experiment. The thrill of the building lies, as at Leicester, in its dramatization of catwalks and terraces, not only the balconies inside, but the short-cut roofwalk over the stacks at the base of the lantern outside. Stirling's technology is modern, but in the romantically 'heroic' sense of the 'twenties; he has prayed at the relics of Sant' Elia and the Futurists; and he has thumbed those books of constructivist 'projects' by El Lissitsky and the Tatlin brothers in which it is never quite clear what was actually supposed to be built. The tubular steel structure of the library roof appears with a wonderful unexpectedness on the corridors; and so captivated are we by the whole view through the whole building that perhaps we are not too worried by the massive girth of the tubular steel

New physics building, from the west

Planning for Science

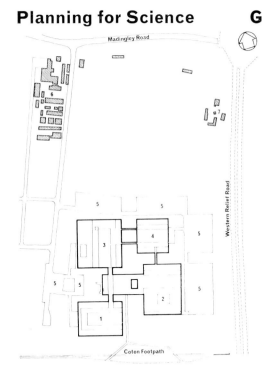

1 Research **2** Undergraduate teaching **3** Research **4** Long term needs **5** Parking **6** Merton Hall Farm **7** Vicars Farm

During 1965 a committee, headed by Professor Deer, began to investigate the probable needs of the science faculties during the coming 20 years. Their conclusions, published in a report to Senate early in 1966, were that although the site of the old Adden-brooke's Hospital would provide some space, the central area was now virtually saturated and a move to the western edge of the city had become imperative. The most pressing need they found was for Biochemistry (see page 51) which could be accommodated on the Addenbrooke's site and for the Cavendish Laboratory. On the strength of this report, Robert Matthew, Johnson-Marshall & Partners were commissioned to prepare a development plan for some 300 acres to the south of Madingley Road straddling the Coton footpath. Although the press hailed the scheme as a 'Science City', the design includes space for some of the other faculties as well as residential accommodation and a large area for communal facilities near the centre. The Coton footpath is used as a pedestrian and cyclists' spine and link with the centre of Cambridge, and road access is from the Madingley Road. The plan also shows the route of the western relief road which the architects thought should be given high priority to serve the increased traffic. One area only is planned east of this road, and this will be used for research in the humanities and social science.

After their first report, Robert Matthew, Johnson-Marshall & Partners prepared a more detailed study for the Cavendish Laboratory building. For this, they chose the site to the north of the footpath at the eastern edge of the area. They envisage that development will take place in four stages with the first stage for research, the second for undergraduate teaching, libraries, lecture rooms, catering and common rooms, the third for more research, and the fourth for long-term needs. These stages will be expressed as separate blocks, with circulation and service links. Circulation and service routes generally are to be placed on a regularly spaced grid. The initial sketches show a three-storey stepped building, clad evidently in precast concrete panels. The overall report came in for criticism from Sir Leslie Martin who maintained that the use of land was wasteful and that the effect of the scheme on the Backs and traffic had not been fully considered. His own view was that science should remain near the city centre and that the Newtown area would be a possible site for further expansion. But the desirability of a further erosion of the city by university buildings is surely questionable, and the western site provides splendid opportunities for the flexible layout that the science laboratories need. Unfortunately the preliminary designs for the Cavendish Laboratory still show the tendency to develop by blocks which characterizes the Sidgwick Avenue site, in spite of the service and pedestrian route grid. It would be an unmitigated disaster if this area were developed in a similar fashion, as it would jeopardize the University's scientific expansion.

One other disturbing feature has been the hurrying ahead of two buildings independently of the report. The first was the Institute of Theoretical Astronomy which was set up in 1965 with Professor Hoyle as director. Grants from the Nuffield Foundation, the Wolfson Foundation and the Science Research Council were to cover running and building costs. It was designed and built by Mowlem Ltd., through their subsidiary Rattee & Kett, on a site beside the Observatories. The building for Astronomy, completed in 1967, is a long single-storey block with another higher block at its southern end. It is of crosswall construction with the brown walls exaggeratedly expressed and full-height glazing between, under a deep ribbed aluminium fascia. It blends fairly successfully into the wooded site. Much less satisfactory is the other building to the north, for Geodesy and Geophysics, also financed by the Wolfson Foundation and also the result (1967–8) of a design-and-build 'package deal' by Mowlem Ltd. and Rattee & Kett. It is a pedestrian brick box, with a jazzy entrance canopy.

Poor as these buildings are, the greater tragedy is that Sir Edward Bullard and Professor Fred Hoyle should have deliberately opted out of the first co-ordinated plan for science the university has ever had, and have thus added (unscientifically) to the unrelated jungle of buildings in Western Cambridge.

Mullard Radio Astronomy Laboratory

Mullard Radio Telescope   H

Lord's Bridge, Barton

Date.   1964

Cost.   £75,000

Description.   This is the third and most refined telescope that the Mullard Radio Astronomy Laboratory have built. It was designed by Professor Martin Ryle himself. It consists of three reflectors each 60 feet in diameter of which two can move along a mile-long track and the third, central, one is fixed. Each dish can rotate on two axes simultaneously and the arrangement can apparently give a resolving power equivalent to that of a paraboloid reflector, one mile in diameter.

Comment.   The three great dishes dominate this area of countryside and give it an almost lunar scale. But although they make a significant contribution to the landscape, their real beauty lies in their structure and the implications it could have for architecture. As James Gowan wrote in the *Architect's Journal*: 'With the scanner in its extreme position, the structure becomes very eccentrically balanced and the result is so splendid that one doubts the necessity of framing up all our buildings like four-poster beds.' At all events, this grandeur of scale and the elemental nature of their form serve as a salutary reminder of the untapped possibilities that engineering has offered to architects since the viaducts and glass-houses of a century ago.

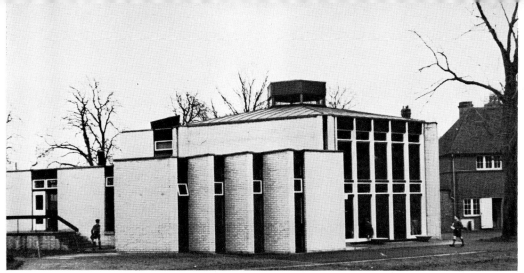

King's College School assembly hall

King's College School Assembly Hall

Grange Road

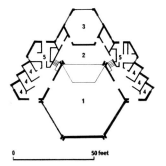

0 ——————— 50 feet

1 Assembly hall **2** Stage **3** Staff room
4 Practice rooms **5** Lavatories

Date.	1962-3
Architects.	Robert Matthew, Johnson-Marshall & Partners. Maurice Lee, partner-in-charge
Contractor.	Kerridge Ltd.
Cost.	£23,650

Requirement. A multi-purpose hall, staff room, changing rooms and music practice rooms.

Description. The King's College School occupies a red-brick Gothic building of 1880 (by W. M. Fawcett) and a second Victorian building facing Grange Road. The site for the new assembly hall lies between them and is intended to act as a focus and pivot. The hall is designed for daily purposes of assembly and 'prep' and has a small stage which can be extended with demountable units for orchestral concerts and plays. It will later also be used as a gymnasium.

The hall is hexagonal in shape and the other rooms are disposed symmetrically around its three northern sides. The south-west wall is entirely glazed, and the pitched roof is surmounted by a pyramid-topped lantern. Behind the stage is a second, smaller hexagonal room which will serve normally as the staff common room and occasionally as a green room for the stage. Set back from this in echelon are, first, the boiler room and store, then a group of lavatories on each side and finally three music practice rooms on each side. The staggered planning of the practice rooms is intended to reflect the sound from each room off the blank walls of its neighbours. Construction is of loadbearing brick, faced with local Burwell primrose gault facing bricks, unplastered internally. The six panel walls of the hall are returned at their ends to form buttresses in pairs, containing the rainwater pipes between them. Roof construction is of prefabricated beams of Douglas fir forming a saucer shaped cap.

Comment. This is a pleasant, well-disciplined

little building: uncompromisingly austere in its finishes and making the most of an awkward site and a complicated brief in a highly formal plan. Access to the stage from the staff-cum-green room and from the lateral corridors is well managed, and the splitting up of the practice rooms into two staggered groups is sensible. However, the symmetry comes to grief in the complicated sub-division of the two groups of lavatories, off which there are some awkwardly shaped cupboards and shower rooms. The off-centre lighting of the hall shows the difficulty in relating the building to both site and light.

Blackfriars   J

Buckingham Road, Huntingdon Road

Date.   1961–2

Architect.   David Roberts

Contractor.   Kerridge Ltd.

Requirement.   Lecture hall, convertible as a chapel; library, instruction rooms and main entrance.

Description.   This three-storey building links the two villas previously occupied by the Dominican friary. It closes the group symmetrically, with a central entrance flanked by two clerestory-lit instruction rooms on the west and the porter's room and staircase on the east. Behind these, running at right-angles to the front, is the visitors' corridor, originally to have been separated by a glazed timber screen from the canonical enclosure, which overlooks the garden. The first floor is occupied by the lecture room, which occupies four bays and is cantilevered out to form a narrow aisle either side, overhanging the ground floor. It is lit by tall side windows and is converted into a chapel at the weekends, with a movable altar. On the second floor, which returns to the size of the ground floor, is the library. It is clerestory-lit and also has a west window.
Massive brick columns and concrete beams at ground level support the loadbearing brickwalls above, in which the concrete floors are emphasized. The smooth yellowish Burwell gault facing bricks are exposed internally. Floor coverings include brick paving (ground), concrete tiles (first floor) and cork tiles (second floor).

Comment.   This is an exceedingly formal design. It is therefore a shock to find that, apart from the entrance itself, the axis of the building is at right-angles to the massive and beamy façade. Again, a staircase is hidden behind one blank end bay but not the other. The symmetry is visually related to the closure of the cul-de-sac. In other ways this is an admirably direct and straightforward building, worthy of the pioneering scholarship of the Dominicans. They have commissioned the first high quality modern religious building in Cambridge, following the example of their Order in France and Spain. The chapel–lecture hall is a beautiful room, austere, flexible and worshipful, allowing wide freedom in liturgical experiment. The exposed brickwork is fresh and simple (and local in origin). Above all, the linking of old and new is as direct and attractive as Mr. Roberts's work at Magdalene. The villas have been pleasingly redecorated inside and out, the yellow brick and pink washing contrasting with the new white brick.

Homes, Housing and Other Development

Like North Oxford, Western Cambridge is an area of dons' houses. A number of interesting houses have been built, not only in Cambridge itself, but in the outlying villages. These make a welcome break to the very low quality of suburban 'infill' and 'rounding off', to which all the villages have been subjected. These are reviewed on pages 190–200. Other houses in the area include that for Lord Adrian (1963–4), in Burrells Field off Grange Road. Designed by Patrick Hodgkinson, it has an interesting split-level plan. Its tall living room overlooks a raised garden terrace and connects at each end by steps to the first-floor master rooms, arranged en suite. Entrance hall, guest and staff rooms occupy the ground floor. The structure is mainly of brown Stamfordstone brick, with small deepset windows and south and west façades of cedar wood. Johnson & Bailey were the contractors.
Lord Rothschild's large house at the end of Herschel Road was designed, not (as at first intended) by Llewelyn-Davies & Weeks, the architects of his excellent village at Rushbrooke in Suffolk, but by an Oxford firm, Beecher & Stamford. They have used an anonymous cottage style of whitewashed brick.

Blackfriars

In Wilberforce Road, apart from the Youngman House (see page 193), there are No. 3 by Peter Boston (1965) of Saunders, Boston & Brock, formerly known as James & Bywaters, and No. 11 by David Roberts for himself (1955, enlarged 1957). David Roberts & Geoffrey Clarke have built a house over garages for the St. John's groundsman at the eastern end of Grange Road which exhibits more use of the brick panels and piers of their Magdalene Master's Lodge and Churchill Graduate Flats. It has a clean-limbed simplicity, but suffers from the same ambiguities of structure in the brickwork as do the larger buildings. In Conduit Head Road, 'Daylesford' was built by E. R. Collister in 1954 and enlarged by D. E. Pugh; its mannerisms compare unfavourably with the pioneer white-walled houses of the thirties nearby. In Lansdowne Road, there is a house for Dr. P. A. Merton, designed in the first instance by Justin Blanco White in 1962 who passed it on to her associate David Croghan. In the event, Dr. Merton, who built almost the entire house with his own hands, terminated the employment of both architects and with the help of a surveyor and consulting engineer re-detailed the house, altering its ground plan and putting in a steel frame. Thanks to its siting and timber cladding, the result is still pleasing. 13 Adams Road is an early work by Christophe Grillet (1956). 16 Bulstrode Gardens is a spec-built house extended in c. 1950 by Walter Bor. Vickers, Undrill & Partners have designed a small conventional bungalow in Huntingdon Road (No. 263); and they are responsible for an extension to the Plough & Harrow pub in Madingley Road and three small blocks of flats at 'Pinehurst' off Grange Road, for Contemporary Homes Ltd (next to the 'early modern' flats of T. P. Bennett). Speculative housing by T. F. Morris & Partners has appeared at Lansdowne Road, off Madingley Road (1959) and at Gough Way, off Barton Road (1963-4). In Gough Way is an isolated terrace of 12 flats designed by James and Bywaters for Trend Homes (see Sherlock Close, page 130), with a particularly successful layout of garages around a white-washed courtyard. They have also designed a block of flats, Croft Lodge, in Barton Road, and like Sherlock Close, it shows an improvement in the general standard of speculative building. Gough Way, however, leads to a deplorable area of suburban sprawl (landlord, St. John's College).

In Sidgwick Avenue, Dashwood House, for the vice-principal of Ridley Hall, is an eccentric brick villa by C. J. Bourne (1962)[1]; Ridley Hall's chapel, incidentally, has a reredos and neo-Georgian decoration by Sir Albert Richardson (1949). In Grange Road, Lady Margaret House has a utilitarian wing by S. C. Kerr-Bate and an appalling chapel in a Romano-Tudor style by J. Sebastian Comper (1955-6). Tyndale House, in Selwyn Gardens, has a warden's house, by William Ryder, and library (1955-6). Sir Giles Gilbert Scott's addition of 1953-5 to Clare's Memorial Court, known as Thirkhill Court, has clumsy neo-Georgian details. These are exaggerated by contrast with Henry Moore's 'Falling Warrior', erected at Clare's expense in 1961—a most praiseworthy piece of patronage. Off the Barton Road, the King's and Selwyn sports pavilion of 1959-60 is an elegant minor work, timber-clad, with concrete outside staircases, by W. E. Tatton Brown, chief architect to the Ministry of Health. Ian Forbes's School of Veterinary Studies in Madingley Road, with its rusticated quoins, round-headed windows and minimal pediments, is a decidedly unpleasant semi-traditional design of 1954-5. It consists of a farm (two Georgian pavilions), a veterinary hospital (rotunda with wings) and the school itself, a three-storey porticoed block.

Off Barton Road in Kings Road, there is a showroom for Tolliday's designed by David Croghan of Lyster & Grillet. This is a timber-framed building, with a steep pitched roof over the shop and offices placed at right-angles to the flat-roofed showroom. It makes a successful unobtrusive envelope for the agricultural machinery displayed. Farther afield, in Coton High Street, there is a very pleasant infant and junior school by the County Architect, P. R. Arthur. The hall and the four classrooms are grouped round a paved court across which lies a covered way linking the staff rooms to the hall. It is built of low-pitched steel roof beams supported on re-used Cambridgeshire facing brickwork, with boarded infill panels. It is a pleasant addition to a village which can boast no other post-war building of comparable quality.

---

1. Who also designed a new wing (1960) for the other Anglican theological college, Westcott House, in Jesus Lane (central area).

Laslett House K

3 Clarkson Road

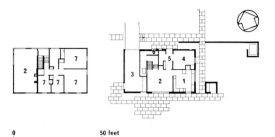

0 |————————————————| 50 feet

First and ground floor plans
1 Kitchen **2** Living and dining areas **3** Garage
4 Playroom **5** Lobby **6** Store **7** Bedroom

Date.	1959
Architect.	Trevor Dannatt
Contractor.	G. B. Brudenell of Godmanchester
Cost.	£5,750

Description.   Designed in 1957 for Peter Laslett, then a fellow of St. John's, No. 3 stands on college land near two other (less interesting) houses, for Professor Fred Hoyle and Mr. Rhoden.[1] The site is on open fields serrated by remains of medieval cultivation. No. 3 is set down a slope from the road. Mr. Laslett wanted the main living space to be on the first floor, with his two children on the ground floor, and Trevor Dannatt therefore adopted a split-level system. The low garage and laundry on one side of the house are surmounted by a tall and spacious living room, which has wide views in all directions. It opens off a landing half-way up the stairs to the bedrooms, which form the rest of the upper floor. Under the bedrooms are two distinct ground floor areas: the children's playroom, which is largely enclosed by solid wall; and the dining and kitchen areas, which are highly transparent with windows overlooking the garden and which are open towards the staircase and the glazed screen of the living room.

The structure is in two parts: the ground floor is of Holco lightweight concrete blocks, made in Sweden and painted black. The upper floor is faced with untreated cedar boarding, mellowing to a silver-grey.

Laslett House

The interior walls are of brick, mostly painted white, with certain areas tinted, being lit by semi-concealed floodlights. All services are in a central core, and the roof slopes down to it, thus avoiding external drainpipes. Central heating is oil-fired, but the living room also has an open fireplace with an ornamental brick chimney-piece.

Comment.   Trevor Dannatt is one of the most painstaking of architects and meticulously details everything down to the door-knobs, in a tradition which perhaps owes more to William Morris than to Scandinavia. No. 3's eccentric stylishness—the living room's brick fireplace and upper-level panelling, for example—is indeed different from the cool perfection of the Kennard house (page 86). Considering that it was a thoroughly one-off job, it was surprisingly cheap. The split-level planning is neatly carried out round the spacious central staircase, which visually connects the main living areas; while the children are enclosed in an acoustically well-sealed playroom with plenty of bare walls to withstand their energy. But unfortunately such differences of function have not been left aesthetically to speak for themselves. The external divisions into black plinth and grey *piano nobile* completely masks the internal change of levels and the artful arrangement of the windows only adds to the confusion. Secondly, the use of white-painted blockwork inside, although aesthetically delightful, pre-supposes a pretty stringent standard of maintenance for a family with children.

---

1. The former has been extended (**1966**) by John Young-man.

189

Salt Hill, Bridle Way, Grantchester

King's Cottages   L

Coton Road, Grantchester

Date.   1958

Architects.   Architects' Co-partnership.
Kenneth Capon, partner-in-charge

Contractor.   Rattee & Kett Ltd.

Cost.   £2,500 each

Requirement. Two semi-detached cottages for workers on the nearby King's Farm.

Description. In plan, these cottages are U-shaped, each enclosing a small courtyard facing the road, while on the opposite side they look across open fields. A glazed corridor, facing the courtyard, links the three bedrooms in one half of the U with the living rooms in the other half. The structure is of brick, painted white externally. The roof is covered with aluminium sheeting and pitched towards the courtyard.

Comment. Like the King's house (see below), these cottages fit extremely well into a bleak landscape, with their long low forms. The entrance courtyards are pleasantly sheltered and intimate in scale. However, they lack complete privacy and there is a preciousness about the windows, for example, which might delight a don more than a farmworker. The cottages are commendably cheap.

Salt Hill   M

Bridle Way, Grantchester

Date.   1959

Architects.   Architects' Co-partnership.
Kenneth Capon, partner-in-charge

Contractor. Rattee & Kett Ltd.

Cost. £8,000

Requirement. House for a married fellow of King's.

Description. This single-storey house is on an exposed site in open fields close to Grantchester village. It consists of two parts, the parents' wing, with living room, study and bedroom, and the children's wing, with playroom and two bedrooms. Between the two is the core, containing entrance hall, service and storage rooms, surmounted by roof tank, and, facing south onto the lawn, the kitchen and a covered loggia with continuous swivel-opening French windows extending from floor to roof. The two side wings are built of loadbearing brick, white plastered, extending above roof level and broken towards the road only by the central entrance and one vertical slit window for the cloakroom. The loggia has varnished timber columns and beams. There is underfloor central heating and a fireplace in the living room.

Comment. With its glazed central loggia, this house tries to achieve the same sort of unity between the two wings and between interior and garden that the Eric Sørensen house (above) achieves so effortlessly. The unfortunate difference is one of siting: Sørensen's is well-wooded and surrounded by walls, Kenneth Capon's is exposed to all the winds of East Anglia. It is not surprising therefore that the house is difficult to heat. Externally, cracks have appeared in the plaster (a curiously naive 'thirtyish' touch, this all-white rendering) and the varnish has been obliterated in patches. The present tenants have also found sound-proofing to be inadequate and have inserted some doors at the expense of the spatial relationships intended by the architect.

In spite of these drawbacks, mainly attributable to the site (which is delightful in summer), this is an elegant and sophisticated house. It is beautifully scaled in its parts and presents a fine 'desert fort' appearance to the village. The raising of the walls above the roofline, with the windows cutting into them as though they were battlements, is an interesting but irrational device. The house fits excellently into the landscape.

Two houses N

Nos. 2 & 2A Grantchester Road

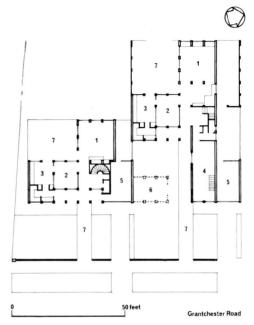

1 Living room 2 Dining room 3 Kitchen 4 Study
5 Garage 6 Studio 7 Paved area

Date. 1963–4

Architect. Colin St. J. Wilson

Contractor. Johnson & Bailey Ltd.

Requirement. Two houses, one for a university lecturer and the other for the architect.

Description. On the site of a Victorian villa, these two houses occupy two long narrow plots of land, and have gravel paths and lawns towards the road. To prevent overlooking, the houses are staggered in layout, although largely similar in their detailed plans. No. 2A is entered directly through a four-bay loggia. Mr. Wilson's house, No. 2, is set back beyond a paved court, closed on the other three sides by his studio, his study, beyond which is his garage, and by the other garage. The two houses are basically L-shaped, with kitchen, dining room and the long living room facing south and

2 and 2A Grantchester Road: entrance front

west to the garden across an enclosed and paved patio. Bedrooms are on the upper floor. Mr. Wilson's living room is two storeys high.

Structure is of concrete blocks forming high walls and columns, cast in Abergele limestone and white cement, both inside and outside the house, contrasting with the hardwood windows. The modular rhythm is emphasized by the repetitive columns at 5 ft centres. It is repeated in the patterned paving of the patio.

Comment. Looking like a fragment from an unbuilt city, these two columnar houses are clearly a most interesting design. The 4 in module (now widely adopted as the equivalent of the continental 10 cm. module) is employed to achieve an overall unity between the houses, while the structure allows considerable flexibility of spaces. The staggered layout, giving both privacy and pleasant enclosed spaces, is excellently managed, the ground floor plans having some similarity to that of the single-storey Kennard House. Mr. Wilson's double-height living room is very imposing.

The special distinction of these houses lies in the use of concrete blockwork as a luxury material. The brilliant whiteness of the largely blank upper walls and of the square columns below has a rough texture, which harmonizes with the local tradition of white brickwork, in contrast to the alien smoothness of Market Hostel (see page 29).

192

Youngman House   O

1 Wilberforce Road

0   10   20 feet

1 Living room 2 Dining room 3 Kitchen
4 Bedroom 5 Studio 6 Study

Date.	1965
Architect.	John Youngman
Contractor.	Prime, Cambridge
Cost.	£15,000

Description. The plan evolved from Dr. and Mrs. Youngman's desire for a courtyard house; the argument being that this would afford privacy if and when a field to the south was developed. Mr. Youngman based the plan on a 14 ft 3 in module, which is emphasized by the use of brick piers.

Entry is by a long drive along the side of the house, but what looks like a 'porte cochère' does in fact stop short of the front door. The module is broken only by the long hall passage which is only half a bay width. To the left of the front door is a guest suite, at the end of the hall are the principal rooms of the house along the north side, which are, from west to east, Mrs. Youngman's studio, a study, the two-bay-long sitting room and dining room. These rooms are divided by Japanese-style sliding screens, which mean that a variety of spaces are possible. To the west is the kitchen and beyond it the main bedroom.

The columns, of Staffordshire primrose hand-made bricks, are supported on short-bore piles, and are connected by ground and roof beams. This was to overcome the instability of the clay soil. The walls are of concrete blocks unplastered inside and out, and painted white. Just below the ceiling is a stained timber 'clerestory' panel which runs throughout the building, provided with openable vents. Glazed areas are full-height below the panel. Quarry tiles are used internally on the floors.

Youngman House, living room

Comment. From the road this is an excessively retiring bungalow, hardly visible amidst the vegetation. Even at close range, it is unprepossessing, with its stocky brick columns and concrete block walls. But by its very nature it is an inward-looking building and only inside do the virtues of its planning appear. Like the Meunier House (page 200) it relies on a very simple plan achieved with great economy of means. Unlike the Meunier House, this does not seem to be reflected in the cost. Certainly the appearance of the brick does not really appear to have justified the expense.

On the other hand, the flexibility in the northern wing of the building and the variety of spaces that can be

Cornford House: garden side

achieved with the sliding doors is admirable, and the south-facing patio becomes a viable proposition as an outdoor room. It is evidently much used as such. Owing to the extreme inward-looking nature of the design not much attempt has been made to incorporate the garden into the system. Only the guest rooms to the west, and the dining-room to the east, have any view of it, and it has not influenced the design at all. It is also surprising that the three bays which serve as carport and store for gardening tools should not have been extended to embrace the front door as well.

Cornford House P

Conduit Head Road

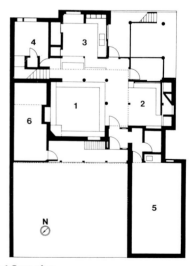

Ground floor plan
1 Living room 2 Dining room 3 Kitchen
4 Bedroom 5 Studio 6 Garage

Date. 1966–7

Architect. Colin St. J. Wilson

Contractor. Johnson & Bailey Ltd.

Description. The design was evolved from Mr. Cornford's desire for a dialectic between interior, inward-looking space and outward-looking exterior space, organized along a north/south diagonal axis. This is achieved by two squares overlapping on the diagonal: a main double-height living square protrudes onto the covered patio square which is reached through glazed doors. Within the internal square, a further division is made, between circulation and sitting space by a drop of two steps—a requirement of the brief—and a peristyle of three Columbian pine columns. Around this basic configuration are balanced two more single-height squares, kitchen and dining-room respectively, open to the main space. Beyond these in either direction lie a single bedroom and the studio for Mr. Cornford. The south-eastern arm of the circulation space is divided: half serves the staircase and the gallery access to the first floor, while the other half, under the gallery, serves the kitchen and bedrooms. Off the gallery are another bedroom, a study, and at the end, the main bedroom. From the gallery there is access to an external balcony with steps down onto the patio.

The entrance to the house is across a gravelled forecourt open to Conduit Head Road and bounded by a continuation of the north-east wall of the house and the studio. The front door opens off a brick paved porch.

The structure is part loadbearing brick, which forms an external shell, part timber post-and-lintel, and part timber stud walling. Timber structure occurs externally only at the patio, where three columns echo those inside; and at the front, in the porch.

The roof is the most complicated part of the structure. It reaches two apexes, over the patio and at the opposing corner, in a turret light over the hearth. The roof slopes down in two directions to an L-shaped valley over the line of columns around the sitting area. A further complication is added by the clerestory lighting over the gallery. Over the two-storey area the roof is supported by made-up half trusses, one of which is placed along the diagonal axis, spanning between columns. The other trusses rest on the brickwork and the space between the

Cornford House, perspective section

room and the wall is glazed. In the double-height area the roof is supported on joists, one of which similarly follows the diagonal axis. Materials used throughout are white-painted brick-work and stained horizontal boarding, while two of the bedrooms are plastered. Some of the windows are bronze-painted aluminium, but in the bedrooms, opening lights are replaced by plywood shutters, emphasizing the ventilating as opposed to the lighting function of the window.

Comment. Colin Wilson has shown, in his design for the School of Architecture's lecture-room block, considerable skill in handling mathematical relationships as an expressive medium. But where in the lecture room there was an antithesis between visual romanticism of the crude materials and the intellectual use of the golden section, here in the Cornford House the different materials reinforce and define the basic organization. The relationship of parts is not here in the nature of an architectural game but of the very essence, and it is perceptible as such. The strict adherence to a hierarchy of materials—square posts to support single height spaces, round columns to support double-height spaces, brick for external walls—is crucial to the

Wendon House: family room

development of the scheme. At the same time, the geometric complications are even more sophisticated than those at the School of Architecture. There are, too, poignant contrasts between materials, particularly where the 'soft' timber structure of the interior breaks out of the 'hard' brick shell at the patio and thus emphasizes the inherent principle of the design. It is a pity in this respect that at the nexus of the whole house where internal space protrudes upon external, heavy joinery sections should upset the nice balance between inside and outside too strongly in favour of the internal space. The major criticism of the building rests on the conflict between the diagonal axis and the frontal entrance. Various attempts are made at resolution, for example by the protraction of the studio, but particularly as that the wing is divorced from the rest of the building, these are by and large ineffectual. In the terms that the architect invites, the problem is strictly insoluble.

The external appearance of the house is far weaker than the sympathetic treatment of the interior. Materials, particularly the roof pantiles, seem overscaled and clumsy; but the chief weakness lies in the tortured complexities of the roof, which tend to mask the essential geometry of the design. It is in strong contrast to Colin Wilson's own house in Grantchester Road where expression of the façade is deliberately low-key.

Wendon House

39 New Road, Barton

Q

Date. 1965

Architects. Barry Gasson and John Meunier

Contractor. Rattee & Kett

Cost. £13,000

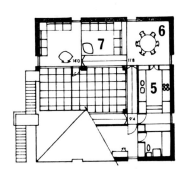

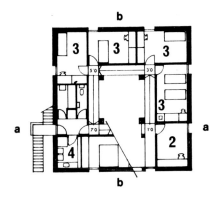

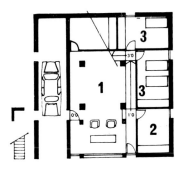

Top: roof plan. Bottom: ground floor. 2 intermediate levels

1 Family room **2** Study **3** Bedroom **4** Laundry
5 Kitchen **6** Dining room **7** Sitting room

Description. The house is set in $\frac{1}{3}$ of an acre a few minutes from the old centre of Barton village, but in fact the situation is more a suburban than a rural one. Mr. Wendon had clear ideas about the relationship of various spaces, and as a method of linking them the architects suggested a ramp. The organization is thus based on the vertical ramp which leads from a large family room in the well of the building to the living room at the top. Onto this ramp open all the subsidiary spaces, including five bedrooms, study, kitchen, cloakrooms and bathrooms, and a laundry. The central well is defined by four free-standing blockwork piers, around which the ramp winds. At the upper level, the living room opens onto a patio over the well. The front door is not at ground level but is halfway up: it is reached by a flight of steps which carries on up to the patio. The glazing consists of vertical lights the width of the ramp, except in the family room, which is extended southwards, which has a large sliding window giving onto the garden. The structure is loadbearing block, fair-faced inside and out. The boarded ceilings and joinery are treated with a clear preservative. All the rooms have electric ceiling heating. The choice of furniture and colour scheme was done largely by the architects.

Comment. A suburban site of the type which the Wendon House is built on clearly imposes a difficult problem on the architects. The nature of the internal organization added to the Wendons' lack of interest in the garden, has resulted in a fortress-like building, almost forbidding from the outside, exemplifying the principle that the Englishman's home is his castle. Having once slipped in through the narrow front door opening, the analogy still seems reasonable: as with the medieval hall, the family room dominates and the private rooms have a visibly subordinate relationship to it. The sequence of rooms was the outcome of considerable research into the needs of this family and was divided, in effect, into the parents' half from the entrance level upwards and the children's half, from the entrance level downwards. The concept may seem highly intellectualized from an analytical description, and indeed it is: but it has achieved a remarkable success in making this concept consciously apparent both to the family and the outsider. What has not really been achieved is the second set of relationships of the house to the village, and although the house dominates its bend in the road, it has avoided the possibility of integration, as the Taylor House (below) has tried not to. There are, of course, minor criticisms: unfortunately the module size which determined the width of the ramp had to be reduced for economy and in its turn the width of the windows was narrowed. This has resulted in certain areas receiving too little natural light, particularly the kitchen and some of the bedrooms. It is, nevertheless, a major achievement that so formalized a plan should have been so successful in providing for the needs of a family.

Taylor House R

3 South Lane, Comberton

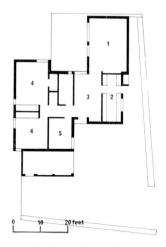

1 Living room 2 Kitchen 3 Dining 4 Bedroom 5 Study

Date.	1965–6
Architect.	J. R. B. Taylor
Contractor.	J. Gage, Bourn
Cost.	£4,400

Description. This is a two-bedroom bungalow built by Mr. Taylor for himself and his wife in the old part of Comberton. Because it is seen in relation to the older white-painted brick cottages, one of the important criteria was that it should help to consolidate the existing pattern of development, and possibly establish a norm for low-cost village housing. In plan it is Z-shaped: a spine corridor unites a bedroom block to the dining and living rooms placed at right angles. Externally this forms an entrance court in front and a paved terrace accessible from the living-room, at the rear, facing west.

Like the Meunier House, this building was an experiment in low-cost design using simple materials. As with White Walls, it was specially designed to be within the capabilities of a local builder. In direct contrast to the Meunier House there is no attempt to create a philosophy of natural materials, and the floor and ceiling finishes are all plastered and painted white. The windows which were taken straight from a catalogue, and tied together to form full-height units, are painted black. A mono-pitch roof slopes down from a high ridge at the eastern side; in the narrower living-room wing, this permits a higher ceiling.

Comment. Because of the similarity of intention, this house invites direct comparison with the others recently built. Certainly, the white painting of all the surfaces shows a single-mindedness of purpose which only the Meunier House matches. But the Meunier House was specifically designed as a one-off building: it did not try to establish a possible norm for village development. In that sense, it is comparable with any spec-builders' bungalow. The Taylor House, with its less involved logic, clearly does provide a solution; and as it stands does fulfil the aim of fitting into, and adding cohesion to, the village. The planning of the house seems weaker than with the others, partly because of the greater articulation of the various parts, rather than any inherent weakness in the basic divisions. One poor feature is the abrupt entry at right angles into the spine corridor: its position seems to have no great significance internally, and allows too little room for acclimatizing to the house and for the more mundane operation of taking off coats. Nevertheless, as an attempt at a new village vernacular, it is certainly a success, and is cheaper than any other of the houses described.

Meunier House, garden side

Taylor House, from the garden

Meunier House   S

Opposite the church, Caldecote

1 Living room 2 Kitchen 3 Bedroom 4 Study

Date.   1964

Architect.   John Meunier

Cost.   £5,000

Description.   The house is a single-storey building designed by John Meunier for himself. It stands in an orchard in a remote hamlet some seven miles from Cambridge. The building is designed as two overlapping squares, one ten foot high containing the living room and kitchen, the other, smaller, square 7 ft 6 in high containing the bathroom, two bedrooms and a study. These are placed on a raised square podium. The remaining space on the podium forms an entry patio and terrace reached through a glazed screen from the living-room. A service core is placed at the junction of the two volumes.

The structure consists of loadbearing brickwork, fair-faced both in and out: the joints are bucket-handled for greater precision. All exposed timber is of Columbian Pine treated internally with Cuprinol and externally with a single coat of clear preservative. Buff quarry tiles are used for the floors, but rush-matting and sisal carpeting cover the sitting area and bedrooms. Where washing occurs, that is in the kitchen and bathroom, white glazed tiles and formica are used as a foil to the more textured timber and brick. The house was built by direct labour.

Comment.   Although this is a building well-hidden from the public eye, it deserves to be seen. Mr. Meunier's aim was to build economically and simply, and create out of the most ordinary materials available an aesthetic that would enhance life. Certainly the casual eye will find none of the coyness which mars most 'vernacular', and will be struck instead with the austerity which the house possesses. But this is precisely its virtue: the totally uncluttered nature of both the interior and the exterior (there is a minimum of furniture and objets d'art—even paperbacks seem to have the texture of a building material) allow the lucid rationality of the plan to become a reality. The main spaces are simple but satisfying; the division into 'day' and 'night' quarters, practical. It is perhaps a little surprising then, that what surely is the nexus of the project, the overlap of the squares, contains nothing more eloquent than the bathroom and lavatory. The question that this house inevitably poses, as the

Wendon House does, is, to what extent can an architect ignore the cry for pretty fabrics and china dogs on the mantelpiece? Can 'holy poverty' be regarded as anything more than a personal philosophy? At least in the architect's own house there can be no such conflict. The natural materials are themselves used decoratively, so that there is an absolute unity in means and ends which singles out this building.

White Walls   T

opposite the church, Kingston

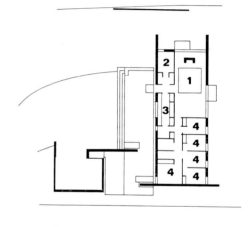

0   10   20 feet

1 Living room **2** Study **3** Kitchen **4** Bedroom

Date.   1965

Architect.   Darnton Holister

Contractor.   Rayner and Bullen Ltd, Barton

Description.   This is a long low house built by the architect for himself in a village seven miles from Cambridge. It was specifically designed to harmonize with the traditional white painted vernacular architecture, but set back as it is from the road, it is not seen in direct relation to any of the existing cottages.

It is designed on an 8 ft module, being three bays wide and eight long. It is divided into two halves with living rooms at one end and the sleeping area

White Walls: entrance front

at the other. Only the kitchen breaks this division, extending one bay beyond into the sleeping area. Longitudinally, it is divided so that the eastern bay is occupied by the kitchen, bathroom, utilities room and study, with the master bedroom at the northern end. The other two bays contain the remaining bedrooms and living room which look out to the south-west. To the south, the side walls are extended by a bay to form a sheltered terrace. In front of the house, the garage and garden store which form an L-shaped entrance court. The construction was kept deliberately simple to remain within the abilities of the local builder. Laminated European Whitewood beams span between the side walls at 8 ft centres, carrying a simple timber roof. White-painted fair-faced brickwork has been used both inside and out, the timber is Columbian pine throughout, and heather brown quarry tiles are used on the floors. Glazing reaches from the floor to the underside of the beams, but above this is a glazed clerestory that runs continuously in the depths of the beams around the house.

Comment. Like the other houses to the west

of Cambridge, White Walls has a straightforwardness which commends itself. The pattern is easily comprehensible; there is a pleasant diversity in the different spaces; and the materials are few and ably handled. Unlike the Meunier or Youngman houses, however, there is a certain blurring of the basic divisions and the planning lacks that special lucidity which distinguishes the other two. The crosswalls are broken too often by full height openings to be entirely convincing as such, nor can they fully acknowledge the desirable orientation of the site to the south and west. Unfortunately, too, the white painted brickwork shows signs of poor weathering and it is to be hoped that it will not suffer the same fate as the walls in the Churchill Graduate Flats. At present it helps to confirm the real virtues of the house, its unpretentious rationality, reminiscent of some post-war Danish houses (see Keelson, page 86).

Appendix A: selected list of modern building of interest near Cambridge

Impington Village College ..	..	1936–9	Walter Gropius & Maxwell Fry
Aero Research Ltd., Duxford	..	1950, 58–60	Ove Arup & Partners
Stable Court, Madingley Hall	..	1951–2	Alec Crook: Sir Edward Maufe, cons
Grain Drier, Chettisham ..	..	1951–2	A. Swift of Ministry of Works
Polak & Schwarz Ltd., Haverhill ..	..	1956–7	Edward D. Mills & Partners
British Welding Research Association offices and laboratories, Abington	..	1957–60	Hughes & Bicknell
Tillotson's Corrugated Cases Ltd., Burwell ..		1958	Ellis & Gardner
Studio House, Hemingford Grey	..	1959	James & Bywaters
Fison's Pest Control Ltd., Harston ..	..	1959–61	Edward D. Mills & Partners
L.C.C. Estate, Haverhill ..	..	1960–	L.C.C. Architect's Department
CIBA (A.R.L.) Ltd. Canteen, Duxford	..	1961	Bryan & Norman Westwood & Partners
Friends' School extensions, Saffron Walden..		1961–2	Kenneth Bayes of D.R.U.
Mr. Adrian's House, Hemingford Abbots	..	1962	Christophe Grillet
Housing Estate, Ely ..	..	1962–3	V. G. Lilley, Isle of Ely county architect
New Village between Lolworth and Dry Drayton ..	..	1965–	Covell, Matthews & Partners
Field Research Station Dept. of Zoology, Madingley ..	..	1963	Hughes & Bicknell
Housing Estate, Houghton ..	..	1963–4	Sir Leslie Martin & Colin Wilson
House at Shelford ..	..	1963–4	Paul Reid

Besides Impington, there are village colleges by successive county architects at Sawston, 1930 (H. H. Dunn); Bottisham, 1937, and Linton, 1938 (S. E. Urwin); Bassingbourn, 1955, Soham, 1958, and Swavesey, 1958 (Wilfrid Wingate); Melbourn, 1959, Comberton, 1960, Cottenham, 1963, and Gamlingay, 1964 (R. H. Crompton). Soham Grammar School has extensive additions of 1957 (Wilfrid Wingate) and 1963 (R. H. Crompton). There are primary schools, new or extended, by private architects at Elsworth, Thriplow and Linton (Lyster Grillet) and at Great Shelford, Linton and Oakington (David Roberts).

Appendix B: prewar examples of the Modern Movement in Cambridge

Finella, Queens' Road (remodelling)	..	1927–9	Raymond McGrath
Corpus, extensions of Old Court ..	..	1930	Graham Dawbarn
White House, Conduit Head Road ..	..	1931	George Checkley
Thurso, Conduit Head Road	..	1932	George Checkley
31 Madingley Road..	..	1931–2	Marshall Sisson
26 Millington Road ..	..	1934–5	Marshall Sisson
Workshop and Mond Laboratory	..	1932–3	H. C. Hughes
Brandon Hill, Conduit Head Road ..	..	1933	H. C. Hughes
19 Wilberforce Road	..	1934	H. C. Hughes
Union Society dining room and kitchen	..	1933–4	Harold Tomlinson
Pinehurst flats, Grange Road	..	1934	T. P. Bennett
King's College Chapel, candlestick ..	..	1934	Benno Elkan, sculptor
Gonville & Caius, St. Michael's Court	..	1934	J. Murray Easton

Zoology Laboratory	1934	J. Murray Easton
Old Schools remodelling	1935	J. Murray Easton
Pitt Press interior	1936–7	J. Murray Easton
Cambridgeshire High School for Girls ..	1937–41	S. E. Urwin
Clinics, Castle Hill	1938	S. E. Urwin
Shawms, Conduit Head Road	1938–9	Justin Blanco White
Anatomy Laboratory	1938–9	J. Murray Easton
2 Sylvester Road	1939	Hughes & Bicknell
Austin Wing, Cavendish Laboratory ..	1939–40	Adams, Holden & Pearson
Peterhouse, Fen Court	1939–40	Hughes & Bicknell
Homerton College Nursery School	1940	Maxwell Fry

Architects' and Artists' Index

Buildings and General Index